TIME STEPS

My Musical Comedy Life

DONNA McKECHNIE

with Greg Lawrence

Simon & Schuster

New York   London   Toronto   Sydney

SIMON & SCHUSTER
Rockefeller Center
1230 Avenue of the Americas
New York, NY 10020

For information about special discounts for bulk purchases,
please contact Simon & Schuster Special Sales at
1-800-456-6798 or business@simonandschuster.com

Book design by Ellen R. Sasahara

Manufactured in the United States of America

1   3   5   7   9   10   8   6   4   2

Library of Congress Cataloging-in-Publication Data
LC Control Number: 2006045809

ISBN-13: 978-0-7432-5520-2
ISBN-10:   0-7432-5520-8

For my sister, Barbara, and my brother, Ron
and
in loving memory of our parents,
Carolyn Ruth McKechnie and Donald Bruce McKechnie

Contents

TIME STEPS

Chapter 1

———— ❦ ————

A MAKE-BELIEVE
CHILDHOOD

"The nominees for best actress in a musical are . . ."

I am sitting in the orchestra section of the Shubert Theatre, on the aisle, seven rows from the front of the stage, next to Michael Bennett, the director of *A Chorus Line* and my dear friend. I hear the words spoken from a podium onstage, and the speaker is Richard Burton. I make a concerted effort to keep breathing and stay in the real world, as I watch the dreamlike scene unfolding before me.

But it's not a dream. Richard Burton is real. The Antoinette Perry Awards are real. And so are the CBS television cameras. It is the spring of 1976, and the awards are being televised live.

I hear a voice cut through the charged atmosphere inside the theater. "And the award goes to . . ."

Did he say my name? Yes, he said my name. "Donna McKechnie." And after my name, time stops. I should get up. I turn to Michael, who grabs my hand and kisses my cheek. I hear the applause accompany my quick, measured steps up the aisle to the stage. *Don't rush,* I tell myself. *Don't fall. Keep breathing.* Despite my efforts, I am no longer in the real world. I feel like I am on a high wire, performing a great balancing act, as I climb the stairs one at a time, meeting the gaze of the most beautiful blue eyes I have ever seen. As Richard Burton presents me with the award, I am still ungrounded, yet manage to be composed as I take the award and turn to the microphone, searching for the first words of my not very well prepared acceptance speech.

Before I begin to speak, my mind is racing with directives from an inner voice that I recognize as my own. *Be here. Be here now. Whatever you do, look out there and take all this in. It is a special moment in your life and it may never happen again.*

I look out into the theater and see so many people I know. I see Michael, beaming. How marvelous to be able to say in front of millions of people, "Thank you, Michael." I look into the wings on the other side of the stage, and I see the glitter of the *Chorus Line* finale costumes, and the smiling faces of the other cast members. I say how happy I am and proud to share this honor with the rest of the company, acknowledging the personal and collaborative experience that brought us all success-fully here tonight. I think of my mother, who is out there in the audi-ence somewhere, and even though I can't see her, I can imagine her happiness. And I think of my father, who died only a few months before this night. I dare not mention his name with the others I thank. I am determined not to allow those feelings to surface, afraid that I may not be able to continue unless I keep them locked inside.

I finish my thank-you speech, and during the applause, I turn and follow Mr. Burton off the stage. When we reach the shadows of the wings, he turns to me and says, "You deserve it."

All this, and a personal moment too!

I was doing so well, but now have to remind myself again that I'm not dreaming. *Remember this moment,* dictates my inner voice.

Don't worry, I say to myself, *I will.*

A *Chorus Line* won nine Tony Awards that night. It was the show of my dreams as well as my dream come true. Or so it seemed at the time. The chorus dancers portrayed in the musical were drawn from some of the personal stories of those of us in the cast. The script was based on our own struggles and dreams, and the stories we told would become the inspiration for the songs. Some of my childhood memories were given to Maggie and to several other characters, while the role that I performed, Cassie, took on aspects of my life in later years. Maggie's lines reveal part of my childhood drama when she says, referring to her parents, "I was born to save their marriage, and when my father came to pick my mother up at the hospital, he said, 'Well, I thought this was going to help. But I guess it's not.'"

My mother told me that story when I was a teenager, I imagine, as a way to share with me how difficult it was for both of them to adjust to certain realities in their young marriage. She then told me, "I said to myself, if my husband won't love me, I have this baby to love, and she will love me."

It was a sad thing to hear, though it made it easier for me to justify those born-to-help feelings that took hold in early childhood. Yet I know my parents had been deeply in love when they first married, because when I was a teenager I found letters my father wrote to my mother during World War II when he served overseas. Army censors had blacked out some of the words that might have given away location and activity, but what survived were beautiful expressions of his love and longing. He wrote how much he missed my mother and his baby, Donna, and how he couldn't wait to be with us. And he went on about all the wonderful things he was going to do for us when he came home. It is such a poignant letter to read now, because it makes me realize how rarely I saw that loving and affectionate part of my father in later years.

I was born in Pontiac, Michigan, on November 16, 1942. My parents were practically still kids when they met and fell in love and married a few months later. When I first heard the story of how they met on a blind date, I remember thinking how romantic it must have been when passion and the pressures of wartime led them to marry. Had it not been for the war, they might have waited rather than rushing into it the way they did. I always preferred to think it was love at first sight. My mother, Carolyn Ruth Johnson, was nineteen. She left Cass Tech in Detroit, where she was studying commercial art, and soon became a war bride when my father, Donald Bruce McKechnie, was drafted into the army and went off to fight in Europe. As a soldier, he would later distinguish himself taking part in the Normandy invasion and the Battle of the Bulge.

While my father was away, my mother and I lived with her parents, Dillard and Gladys Cowling Johnson, who had a home in Huntington Woods, Michigan. My beloved grandmother was my early salvation. When my inexperienced mother was afraid to lift her wailing baby from the crib, my grandmother was the one who picked me up and bathed me. She and my grandfather were from Albion, Illinois, an early English farming settlement that went back to the seventeenth century. Their background was a mix of English and Irish. My mother was their first child, and then a few years later, her brother Francis came along. The Johnsons moved to Detroit to raise their family. I was their first grandchild, and they both doted on me.

My grandfather was a big, kindhearted man, a former schoolteacher who had gone into the insurance business. He took great pleasure in teaching me numbers and the letters of the alphabet, and I swear to God the first word I learned to spell was "show." That was just after my grandmother took me to Detroit's Fisher Theatre to see my first "movie show," *The Snake Pit,* starring Olivia de Havilland. In retrospect an odd choice for a four-year-old child. Well, it terrified me. I sat curled up in my seat, with my hands in front of my face, peering through my fingers only when my grandmother said it was safe for me to watch. I sensed her embarrassment after we got home when she said, "I had no idea it was going to be like that!" But I guess she felt that since she paid for the tickets, we had to sit through it, no matter what.

My grandmother wasn't overly religious, but she was preoccupied at times with behaving in a proper way. For example, she had very definite ideas about hanging the wash out to dry. She would instruct me to make sure that all the underclothes were hung on the rack in the basement, because she believed it was highly improper for underwear to be seen in public. She was raised to be a lady by a very strict mother, even if she did have a few rebellious episodes in her life, like marrying my grandfather partly to get out of the house.

I have a photograph of her that she gave me many years later. It pictured her in her teens, sitting on the fence on the family farm, dressed as a man. It seems that there was a social club in town that didn't allow women, so she "borrowed" her brother's clothes and snuck in and fooled everyone. I loved her for that. That took a lot of spunk in those days, before Marlene Dietrich wore pants.

My grandfather, Dillard, had a very loving nature. He encouraged me when I was very young to recite poems and nursery rhymes for him, and I remember how happily surprised I was when he gave me a dollar bill for one of my performances. I hardly knew what it meant, but his gesture made a lasting impression. These earliest years while my father was away were idyllic and carefree. I didn't see much of my mother, since she was working as a telephone operator during the day to help make ends meet, but I felt safe and comfortable in the home my grandparents provided for us.

I loved my grandparents' quaint brick house with its faux Tudor leaded-glass windows, and morning glory vines climbing up the trellis. The house was surrounded by acres of fields, and in my memory, my grandmother's flowers were constantly in bloom, and her garden in back was always filled with rows and rows of vegetables and berries. There were few homes near us and few children my age for me to play with, so I created a Lilliputian world in the garden bed, making tiny pebble houses for the ants. And I invented a large "family" of imaginary friends. I remember one time I was sitting in the back seat of our car, chattering away, with my grandmother driving and my mother beside her. They heard me, and my grandmother said, "Donna, who are you talking to?" I told her, "My brothers and sisters up in heaven. I have about a hundred of them up there."

In recollecting that time when I lived with my grandparents, I see a little girl holding a picture. My father was gone almost three years, and practically every night while he was away, before I went to sleep, my mother had me kiss his photograph. Sometimes she would read me his letters full of loving promises. Then one morning a telegram arrived and my mother learned that he was coming home that day. I can still remember her excitement when she brought me in from the rain-soaked garden where I had been making mud pies. She bathed me and got me all dressed up to take with her in the car to the train station to meet him. "We're going to see Daddy!" she kept telling me. I was a wisp of a girl in my new white pinafore and little white shoes and socks.

When my father finally appeared at the station, he was wearing his uniform just like in the photograph, but I didn't recognize him. As he embraced my mother, the sudden passion of their reunion frightened me. Who was this stranger? I became hysterical and tried to push him away from her. After we came home, it took me quite a while to warm up to him. I had been living with an eight-by-ten photograph, not this stranger who had moved into our life. I was also possessive of my mother's attention, and now I had to share her with someone I didn't know.

What made the situation even more difficult for us was that he came back from the war suffering from shell shock. He would have flashbacks and terrible nightmares, and when he was awake, he was quiet and distant. My mother later told me that it was months before he seemed to come back to normal. He never talked about the war. I would learn later that my father was by nature a gentle man, much loved by his friends and the people who worked with him. But those early feelings of estrangement stayed with me, even as I tried during my young years to be the picture-perfect daughter to please him.

My father eventually found work as a tool-and-die maker, and my parents moved out of my grandparents' house to begin their life together on their own. I imagine it must have been a trying time for them, getting to know each other after such a long separation, and now saddled with the demands of raising a child, and with my father's job hardly paying enough to support his family. There were times when Gladys and Dillard helped out financially, which created tension between my parents, as my father was a proud man and not one to accept help easily from anyone. But still, I was my father's daughter, and eventually, as daughters will do, I put him on a pedestal.

My father's father, James McKechnie, had a Scottish background and was born in Toronto, Canada. That was where he met his future bride, Edith Poole, whose family had come from Bath, England. They had eleven children, but only eight lived to adulthood: Robert, Dorothy,

Margaret, Donald, Gordon, Merwin, Betty, and William. They settled in Detroit after they started raising a family, and James worked in the car industry. They went to a Presbyterian church, but religion never ruled James McKechnie. He was the true patriarch of the family, and they were all very close and devoted to him. Edith was a loving mother and was worshipped by her family. I grew up hearing stories about their devilish shenanigans and all the fun they had growing up. This was a clan in the true sense of the word.

But the grandfather I knew in my early years was a repressive figure, not so much because of his religious beliefs, but because of his narrow-minded ideas, like anyone who is different is unacceptable. This view also extended to the women who married into the family. When my father's older brother Robert married, his wife, Allene, was able to cope for several years, then finally gave him an ultimatum: "It's either me or your father!" They soon moved to the other side of the country, settling in California.

My father and his seven siblings were all expected to be on call for "the old man," as he was affectionately nicknamed, for whatever he or his family might need. The sons were all expected to work in their father's company, C&M Manufacturing, which supplied parts to the auto industry. James expected complete devotion from his sons, even if they were grown men with families and obligations of their own. Many times my father essentially held down two jobs, with no pay for the extra hours that he put in at his father's shop. And all the while he had to put up with his father's criticisms of the way he and my mother were living their lives. You name it, and "the old man" had a better way of doing it. He was especially critical of my mother when I started my ballet classes. He called them, "a waste of time and money."

It was important to my mother's mother, Gladys, that I would be confirmed in their church, so she saw to it that I went to Lutheran catechism. I didn't like being reprimanded by the pastor for asking too many questions. He expected us to memorize the given questions and the given answers. But I was confirmed anyway, and at least I made my grandmother happy. Gladys wanted to influence my education and upbringing so that I would succeed and marry well. She had little trust

in her daughter's ability. I painfully observed the difficulty she had trying to hide this opinion from my mother. And this was troubling for my
mother, who found it increasingly difficult to cope as her father-in-law
insinuated himself into our lives, demanding more and more of my
father's attention. It was a no-win situation for her.

Yet there was love in my family; it just wasn't openly expressed. I
recall seeing little in the way of physical affection between my parents,
and when I was older, I yearned for the kind of warmth I saw in other
families. I never felt unloved, but I was raised in silence, which felt like
neglect at times. My parents' way of coping was not to discuss unpleasant things. "Don't say anything if you can't say anything nice" was a
mantra handed down from my grandmother Edith. That was how it was
for us in the 1940s and 1950s before the word "dysfunctional" had
been invented. When we were unhappy, and we didn't know why, we
didn't talk about it. There were fights with harsh criticism and accusations, but rarely was an effort made for clarity and mutual understanding. There were so many things that we didn't know how to talk about,
and it always felt to me like there was a lot of tension in the air.

We moved around the Detroit suburbs several times, eventually set-
tling into a small house on Royal in Berkley. It seemed that my poor parents were struggling all the time just to survive. By that time, I shared a
bedroom with my sister, Barbara Ann, who came along five years after
me. She was followed six years later by my brother, Ronald Scott. I had
mixed feelings when my sister was born, and wasn't sure if I wanted her
to live with us. How could there be enough love to go around? I remember the day my mother brought her home from the hospital, and I
looked into the carriage to see what all the fuss was about. Barbara Ann
was an adorable baby; "cute as a button" became her nickname. As a
toddler, she looked up to me as her older sister and followed me
around—too much, I thought.

But my sister did provide a ready audience for me. I'm ashamed to
recall how much I liked the feeling of power she gave me. I remember
one time taking her behind my parents' bedroom door and giving her a
haircut. I left her bangs uneven in front, like one of those spiky hairdos,
but years ahead of its time. I kept after her with the scissors and tried

my best to make her look better, or at least more even, but I just made it shorter, and worse. My mother was furious with me. A slightly exaggerated version of that story was given to the character of Judy in *A Chorus Line* when she says, "I shaved my sister's head."

The age difference and shared bedroom made for sisterly quarrels and mischief. One time when we were visiting Gladys and Dillard, on their farm in Albion, I put my ear to the tracks at a railroad crossing near their home. I told my sister, "If you put your ear on the track, you can hear the train coming." She trusted me enough to do it, and then became frightened and pulled away when she thought she heard the train. She warned me to get off the tracks. I said, "No, I'm going to wait right here until it comes." She cried and cried and begged me to leave the tracks. We each had been given a quarter that day, and she gave me hers so that I would take her back to our grandparents' house. Then my sister tearfully told my father how I had scared her, and without raising his voice, he made me give her back the quarter.

As I try to balance the good and bad memories of my family life, I do take pleasure remembering the joyous times that my parents created for us children, especially when we celebrated Christmas. Our Christmases were always modest, but we were all together, and it seemed the gift-giving ceremony enabled us all to express our love for each other more easily. Even after I no longer believed in Santa Claus, I loved helping my mother with the little ritual of placing cookies and milk on the banister for him. Of course, they would be gone on Christmas morning, and I loved that too.

I remember fondly McKechnie and Johnson family reunions with our many young cousins. These were eagerly awaited annual events. Even then, I knew I was lucky to have so many cousins, and I treasure the relationships I still have with them. In fairness to my father, even though his work kept him away from home much of the time, he did make special efforts on our behalf. There is no question of his affection for his children and the pride he took at times in raising us. He built a swing set for us in our side yard, and one day he brought a horse and sleigh home for a winter ride. Later, he surprised me by giving me a necklace with a mustard seed inside a clear plastic heart. It was especially meaningful because he did it privately. I was so touched by his gesture that I didn't know how to thank him and promptly lost the gift.

But it was the gift of his love that I later felt I was losing, especially as I grew older and I began to get more involved with my dancing. The issue would invariably come down to money, and that clearly reflected my grandfather's influence. My mother took time out of our family life to escort me to classes or to make my first costumes, and I sensed my father resented that. In my childish way, I started to believe that he resented me. I didn't understand why he wasn't happy for me the way my mother was. The pride she took in my achievements seemed only to make matters worse. At times, the atmosphere was terribly stifling, and it affected all of us, but especially my mother. I sensed her sadness, and sometimes it propelled me into improvised skits imitating silent film stars, like Pearl White in *The Perils of Pauline* or Charlie Chaplin doing pratfalls. I loved to make her laugh.

With my mother usually distracted by her sadness and daydreams, and my father working such long hours, I found a sanctuary in my imagination. As Maggie puts it in *A Chorus Line,* repeating my own words, "I did have a fantastic fantasy life. I used to dance around the living room with my arms up like this. My fantasy was that I was an Indian chief. And he'd say to me, 'Maggie, do you wanna dance?' And I'd say, 'Daddy, I would love to dance.'"

I couldn't have been more than four or five years old then, and I would dance to the music I heard on the radio. It was like being pulled into another world, and my mother would see me with my arms reaching up high over my head. Not realizing there was a bare-chested Indian chief wearing an enormous headdress holding me while I danced, she assumed I was trying to be a ballerina. I was a rather anemic and spindly child at this time, having been hospitalized for a time with cellulitis. After my recovery, my mother's concerns about my health reinforced her decision to have me take ballet, and she took me to beginner ballet classes that were given on Saturdays in a grade school, Pattengill Elementary, just down the street from our house.

My first classes were taught by an elderly Italian gentleman, Mr.

Causetta. I remember the classroom with its linoleum floor, the desks pushed against the wall, and the folding chairs in a line that we children used as a barre. Holding on to the chairs, we learned the basic positions and did our pliés and tendus. I was completely enthralled, learning the steps, despite the scratchy 78 rpm records my teacher played. One night when my father was working late, my mother took the initiative to invite Mr. Causetta to come to dinner at our home. I felt embarrassed with her humble offering of a ready-made chicken pot pie, and I was further unsettled after Mr. Causetta finished eating and fell sound asleep at the dinner table. Still, I was grateful to my mother for making this effort for me. I could sense she was trying to guide me to a better place.

When I was six, my mother took me to see the movie *The Red Shoes,* and I was immediately swept away. As the character Sheila in *A Chorus Line* says of the movie's heroine, "I wanted to be that redhead." So did I. I fell in love with the idea of becoming a ballerina, and my life would never be the same again. A short time later, I saw my first *Swan Lake* when the Ballet Russe de Monte Carlo performed at the Masonic Temple in downtown Detroit. The famous Cuban ballerina Alicia Alonso danced the role of the white swan, Odette, and it was my first experience hearing a live orchestra. To sit in the darkness and to see her dance with such power and beauty to such rapturous sounds made me want to cry. With her passionate interpretation, she brought the music dramatically to life.

After that magical experience, I wanted nothing else but to enter that world of dazzling light and make-believe. As I embraced this dream even at such a young age, the ballet classes were my escape, and my mother became my accomplice as she invested in me the love and support that she wasn't getting from my father.

Grandpa McKechnie saw dancing as a frivolous pursuit, and his influence took hold of my father.. His Calvinist sensibility would rear its ugly head from time to time, and I would be admonished for showing too much enthusiasm. I was told, "People will think you have a swelled head." Too much pleasure was equated with sin, and dancing certainly looked pleasurable. On the other hand, Grandma Gladys was proud of my training as long as it was ladylike and in keeping with the pure look of white ballerina tulle. The family was divided, as were my mother and father.

Over time, it seemed to me that my father became jealous of the attention my mother was giving me. I remember hearing them argue at night about how much time she was spending with me, taking me to classes and recitals. She was usually shy and submissive, but she would assert herself when it came to fighting for me, in lieu of being able to speak up for herself. She was never a pushy stage mother. She simply took pleasure in my dancing, and could see how important it was for me. I also suspect she was expressing her own frustrated artistic aspirations.

My mother loved movies, and sometimes she would take me with her to matinees. We were dazzled by the likes of Gene Kelly, Fred Astaire, Ginger Rogers, and Leslie Caron. When my mother was a girl, Jeanette MacDonald was her favorite. At one time she had wanted to be a singer. When I asked her years later why she hadn't pursued a singing career, she would only say, "Oh, that was just not done." It dawned on me what a shame it was that she didn't have a mother like her, who would help her realize her dreams.

My father also had creative leanings. He was something of a dreamer and invented machinery and all kinds of gadgets. He loved building each one by hand, so much so that he never wanted to sell his ideas. He once told me that if the choice had been his, he would have preferred raising orchids for a living. I don't know if he meant that, but his telling me gave me the feeling that he wasn't happy with what he was doing. Looking back, I can see that both my parents possessed abilities and talents that never found expression.

Because of my father's recurrent money problems, paying for my ballet classes was an issue that repeatedly put me in the crossfire between my parents and my grandparents. My mother devised a way to cut the cost of lessons by volunteering to make costumes for the dance recitals. While my father stayed late at work, she would be at the sewing machine all hours, and many times, late into the night.

The ever present tensions at home caused me to avoid the subject of my dancing as much as possible. I tried to hide my excitement about it, especially in the presence of my father. Though he tried to discourage me and often seemed contemptuous, he never quite forbade me from taking classes.

My mother was my only ally. In addition to supporting me with my ballet classes, she took me to auditions for various plays, for which I was unprepared, not yet having studied acting. Nevertheless, at eight, I was cast by local community players in Thornton Wilder's *Our Town,* and my mother took me on the bus at night to rehearsals in downtown Detroit. I played Wally, the seven-year-old boy in the play; it was my first role. The other characters were played by adults, and it made me feel very grown-up. I went through the rehearsals, but I wasn't able to perform in the show because of school. At about this time, my mother enrolled me in a performing arts school called Roth-Berdun Theatrical School, which operated at the downtown Convention Center. At first I took classes on weekends. The school's claim to fame at the time was that the movie star Joan Leslie, a Detroit native, had studied there. Her dancing image graced the front of the school's brochure. I took more advanced ballet classes there, and was also enrolled in an acting class, which was really a class in elocution called "dramatics".

I was soon cast in a school play, *Princess Tenderheart,* in which I played a princess who defies her overprotective father, the king, by refusing to marry the prince chosen for her because she is in love with a humble footman. At the end of the piece, her heart breaks and she dies when her father forces her to marry against her will. My mother, being a gifted seamstress, made the costumes. I wore a red satin cape, a beautiful light blue chiffon dress with sequins, and a tiara, all very feminine and precious. In the play, I had a scene in which I was to throw a tantrum, stamping the floor and screaming, "I won't! I won't! I won't!" During the performance, my mother was offstage making the sound effects of my heart breaking by shaking pieces of broken china in a paper bag. I hadn't quite anticipated the impact of having an audience since we had been rehearsing without one. On opening night before my big scene when I saw all those people sitting out there, I experienced stage fright for the first time. I wasn't sure how to weave this reality into my rehearsed make-believe world on stage. My royal tantrum abruptly stopped as I stared back at the audience. Then I looked desperately to my mother in the wings. She brought me back into the play by miming excitedly, "I won't! I won't! I won't!"

There was an unspoken understanding between us that we were in this together. She made costumes for two other presentations of poetry that I was in, *The Poor Little Match Girl* and *The Moth and the Flame*. Her costumes were always gorgeous, and my chiffon moth wings were tie-dyed before it became a fashion statement. My mother recited the poems and I would dance to the words underscored with recorded music. I remember how beautiful she looked onstage, tall and stat-uesque. But her hands trembled as she read from the page, betraying her fear.

My picture was later spotted on a wall at the school by the producers of a local television variety program, *The Auntie Dee Show,* and I was invited to recite a poem on the air. It was made all the more special when my mother bought me a beautiful white blouse with red piping on the sleeves to go with my red skirt. The show was televised live, and when the director behind the camera made frantic gestures with his hands try-ing to hurry me as I was reciting, I promptly froze. Auntie Dee came over and asked me to continue. I couldn't, and I was mortified. I was then quickly ushered off the set. My mother tried to console me, but I knew I had let her down.

The next day I was distraught going to school, knowing my whole first-grade class had seen me. But my teacher, Miss Ulp, kindly offered me a chance to redeem myself. She said to me in front of the class, "We all watched you yesterday, Donna, and you weren't able to finish your poem. Would you like to recite it for us here?" Overcoming my fears, I went to the front of the room and managed to get through the poem, and the applause of my classmates and my teacher's gentle praise dis-pelled my sense of defeat.

I remember when I was nine going to Thanksgiving dinner at Gladys and Dillard's house where our family usually gathered for holidays. With the family looking on over the dinner table, my father set the tone of our relationship for years to come. I made the mistake of enthusing about my ballet classes and my father suddenly lost his temper, which was shocking because he so rarely did. In a harsh voice, he said, "Don't think this dancing is ever going to amount to anything, Donna! Don't think you will ever achieve anything with this!" I got up from the table in tears, and as I fled, I heard my mother say, "Don, don't spoil her dreams! Don't take them away from her."

From a different vantage point now, I hear my father's voice and the words he spoke as an anguished cry of frustration for the disappointments in his own life, perhaps his own sense of failure. Even then I could see how hard he worked and how much he wanted his father's approval, which he never received. I tried to avoid "the old man" as much as possible. He sometimes tried to be friendly in his rough way, but kids were obviously a nuisance to him. I was meeting all kinds of people in my classes in Detroit, including those from different cultures. My best girlfriends were Lithuanian and Armenian, and my first little boyfriend from dance class was Jerry Goldberg, who performed recitals with me at local YMCAs. My grandfather especially frowned upon Catholics and Jews, and he disparaged me when I spoke up to defend them. Years later when I was pursuing a career in New York, in a letter to one of my aunts, he wrote, "It's a shame about Donna, but I guess there's a black sheep in every family."

At this time, I was taking ballet classes from Pamela Dunworth at the Roth-Berdun school. I adored her. She taught a strict discipline at the barre, and with the combinations in the center, she encouraged us to interpret the music. That direction freed me to bring my imagination and feelings to bear through the steps. It was as if she were showing me a gateway to paradise. She was the first to inspire me with the idea of never letting the movement stop, even when you're standing still, that your energy keeps moving beyond your fingers and toes.

When I was ten, my family moved to Royal Oak, another Detroit suburb. I had followed Pamela to a new studio in Dearborn that her sister-in-law, Loretta, ran with Pam's husband, Jack. It required a longer bus trip, and sometimes my mother allowed me to travel alone. A couple of years later I had to change ballet teachers after a grown man sitting next to me on the bus ride home made some untoward advances and Gladys insisted that my mother find a dance studio closer to home. Pamela suggested I study with Rose Marie Floyd, who owned a dance studio on Main Street in Royal Oak, about ten minutes from my home.

I hated leaving Pamela, and went back to her from time to time, but Rose Marie's studio soon became my home away from home. Rose Marie was a wonderful teacher and offered classical training according to the system developed by the Italian ballet master Enrico Cecchetti. The Cecchetti Council in the Detroit area held annual summer conventions through which I had the opportunity to study with guest teachers, including Muriel Stewart from American Ballet Theatre in New York.

I was twelve or thirteen when my parents let me go to Toronto for three weeks to study with the National Ballet of Canada. It was my first trip away from home and I stayed in a hotel with my dancing-school friend Nancy and her mother. I remember being totally taken with meeting some of the professional dancers from the company. We were invited to take some of the professional classes, and I came back home reveling in the whole experience, feeling more confirmed in my life as a dancer.

In Rose Marie's school, we trained in the Cecchetti curriculum in order to qualify for demanding dance exams that were given to determine our levels of ability. I was proud of my intermediate status, as very few were taking classes at the advanced level. Rose Marie was a resourceful teacher, and she created a company for her young dancers called the Contemporary Civic Ballet. With the South Oakland Symphony, she produced traditional ballets like *Les Sylphides,* as well as ballets that she choreographed for us like *Romanian Rhapsody,* and dances set to many of Leroy Anderson's compositions. I especially liked them because they were character driven.

I found that my dancing improved quickly when I was able to perform with a full orchestra and a more professional setting. We were sometimes invited to perform at the Art Institute in Detroit. Once we danced *Les Sylphides* in a mental institution. I remember at first being frightened when some of the patients in their white gowns walked up to the edge of the stage. Then I was touched to see how they stood there quietly, swaying to the music, transfixed by the ballet.

When I was thirteen, I started teaching ballet classes in my basement, and a year later I produced a recital for my young students. Sometimes my father's critical attitude would soften, and he would surprise me, as when he bought a large used mirror for one wall of the studio, and fashioned a long wooden barre, then mounted them so I could teach my classes. I charged 50 cents a class. Eventually, my class attracted enough local children for me to make as much as $50 a week. I gave my earnings to my parents, and during periods when my father was strapped for cash, my dance money put food on our table. I liked being able to help out.

That I was able to work and earn this income instilled in me a growing sense of independence, but it was hurtful to my father. To have his daughter paying household bills wounded his pride, and we had frequent battles over the dinner table. He vented his anger on me, and I would taunt him by saying things like, "You can't treat me like a child when I'm paying for things." I tried to defend my mother and myself with my own accusations and sarcasm, provoking him even more. Invariably, I would end up in tears and retreat to my bedroom, slamming the door behind me. I sometimes found myself wishing that my parents would break up, thinking it would be better for all of us.

There were bleak winter mornings when I would warm my underwear and socks in front of the oven, then leave for school without breakfast, because my mother was sleeping late. I came to understand later that she stayed in bed many mornings because she was suffering from depression, which was a common but unacknowledged syndrome in those days. Over a short span of time, two women friends of my mother committed suicide and one was institutionalized. It seems horrible that back then women didn't feel they had options. I remember thinking, *I don't want to grow up to be like these women. I don't want to kill myself. I must plan my escape. I'll run away, but I can't do it yet. I'll do it later when I'm taller and I look like an adult.*

In 1956, the local Cecchetti teachers banded together and established a ballet company, the Detroit City Ballet. They invited William Dollar, a well-known dancer and choreographer who had worked with the American Ballet Theatre in its early days, to choreograph a new ballet for the company. Rose Marie submitted some of her dancers as candidates for the new company, and before I knew it, I was a founding member in a troupe of thirteen. I had great respect for Mr. Dollar. He was always very kind, even though he was apparently in pain much of the time and walked with a severe limp. I remember I often saw him taking aspirins washed down with Coca-Cola.

Mr. Dollar recruited an eighteen-year-old dancer from Texas, Paul Sutherland. Paul had only been dancing eighteen months, but already he had the poise and bearing that would one day make him a ballet star. When I was fourteen, Paul became my first partner in a ballet that Mr. Dollar choreographed to the music of Mendelssohn's *Concerto in G*. There was no story per se; it was more like Balanchine: dancing for the sake of dancing, with the geometric patterns of the dancers fulfilling the dynamic of the music. It was a challenge for me to keep my interpretive skills in check in order to blend with the other dancers, as the beauty of the piece depended on us moving in unison. Only two times, once when I danced a pas de deux and once when I led an adagio section, was I able to interpret with my emotions, one of the qualities I would later use to advantage in musical theater.

These experiences with the Detroit City Ballet took hold of me like a religious conversion. I was a strong dancer, but with my long torso, I didn't have the perfect body for ballet. I later found out I was born with an extra vertebra, which gave me a supple back, but one that also was prone to weakness. And my feet weren't really suited for pointe shoes, though I tried to mold them by sitting for hours rolling them over Coke bottles. I did have a lyrical quality and fast footwork; I could do beats and jumps and turns. But I always approached dancing instinctively, as an actress. The music always gave me a story line or an image for me to connect with, and then I could interpret the music and create my own world. Through the choreography, I could make the character come to life, as well as enjoy the athleticism and technical feats of dancing. This was when I started to win some attention. People who saw me dancing at this age would say, "When Donna dances, it's like she's in love."

And I was in love, completely in love with dancing, to the exclusion of everything else. Admittedly, I had started dating and daydreaming about boys, but there was hardly time for that. In an interview for my hometown paper years later, I described myself outside the dance studio as "a nonperson, supersensitive and shy." The only real identity that I had in my life at the time was dancing. It was the only area where I had confidence and a sense of accomplishment. I was finding myself artistically, but beyond the make-believe of the characters I was performing, I had little sense of myself. In high school, I was taking classes after school, rehearsing at night, and getting up to do my homework at five in the morning. I was driven, and I kept myself immersed in activities that allowed me to block out the feelings of rejection I got from my father, and my mother's sadness.

I attended Dondero High School in Royal Oak, and I was a good student—serious, quiet, and well behaved—until school started to interfere with the pursuit of my dreams. Then I began to resent my studies. At some point during my high school years, Gladys offered to pay for my college education. At first I was delighted to hear of her offer, but then she told me that she would only pay for a Lutheran college, because she wanted me to marry a nice Lutheran boy. My interest in college ended at that point, and I felt that my sainted grandmother had betrayed me by trying to exercise that kind of control in my life. I pushed my hurt feelings away with a new resolve to maintain my independence.

Everything changed dramatically for me and my family when we had to move again during my junior year. This time we moved to grandfather McKechnie's home in Troy, on Fifteen Mile Road, which was about that many miles north of Detroit. James retired and moved with his wife, Edith, to Florida. The deal was that we got the house if my father took over his father's shop and assumed its debt. I had no idea at the time how important it was for him to come to the aid of his father, how much he needed "the old man's" love and approval. Nor did I understand the pressure my father was under now that he was running the company.

For me, the move was traumatic, because I had to leave friends behind and go to a new school. For a while I was able to stay with my cousin Marge in Royal Oak in order to continue going to school at Royal Oak Kimball High School, but at fifteen I switched schools and started my senior year at Troy High. Commuting to dance classes and rehearsals became more of a problem, and the cumulative effects of my home life and my hormones were pushing me toward a breaking point. When my rebellion finally came, it would be all the more shocking to those who knew me because up until this time I had always been sweet and lady-like.

In the fall of my senior year, I was encouraged by one of my friends to try out for a winter stock repertoire that was coming to the Cass Theatre in Detroit. Four shows were being produced: *The King and I, Bells Are Ringing, Guys and Dolls,* and *Bittersweet.* The director, David Tihmar, was from New York, as were the stars and most of the dancers. Betty White played Anna in *The King and I.* Peggy Cass starred in *Bells Are Ringing. Bittersweet* boasted Jeanette MacDonald, and Bob Horton had the lead in *Guys and Dolls.* The company needed to hire one female dancer from the Detroit area.

The audition was held at the old Cass Theatre, where I had once visited backstage with my mother and been entranced seeing dressing rooms for the first time. I really wanted to go just to observe the audition, since I had never seen one before. And I felt some apprehension about subjecting myself to such an unfamiliar situation. I certainly hadn't planned on auditioning so I didn't even bring my dance clothes. But after we arrived and I saw all the dancers eagerly warming up, it didn't take much persuasion from Nancy, who was auditioning, to entice me to try out as well. She also was kind enough to lend me a leotard.

It was very exciting to go out there under the stage lights and do on command all that was thrown at me. We were asked to perform combinations from the shows, as well as typical ballet steps: pas de bourrée glissade, jeté across the stage, and so forth. I remember feeling confident and happy as I finished my audition. I was told on the spot that I had been chosen, and though I had little experience, I felt the significance of this moment. I was going to be a professional! I raced home and delivered this piece of good news, and even my father seemed impressed. I soon had my Equity card and my first paying job in the theater.

I was to rehearse each show with the company for two weeks, and then perform each for two weeks. This experience introduced me to a variety of dance styles: the Eastern dances in *The King and I,* a ballet pas de deux in *Bittersweet,* jazz and Latin dancing in *Guys and Dolls,* and a cha-cha in *Bells Are Ringing.* The members of the company welcomed me, and I immediately felt like I fit into their world. Jeanette MacDonald invited me to visit her in her dressing room, and I remember the first time I saw her take off her wig. She had little tufts of red hair. I thought, *Oh, my God, she has no hair! So, that's what an actress looks like.* It gave me a lot of pleasure to take my mother backstage to meet her idol. Of course, I had to prepare her for the possibility of Jeanette without her wig. But Jeanette came through and greeted us with her stage curls. She was lovely and gracious and gave my mother one of the biggest thrills of her life.

At home the tears and ugly confrontations continued over the dinner table. Boys had now entered the picture as an additional source of trouble. Later, I started seeing an older boy who would meet me after rehearsals. Out of respect for his privacy, I'll call him Keith. He was college-age and living at home. My parents disapproved of him from the start, but I was already feeling independent enough to disregard their wishes. After the run of shows finished, I went to a party with Keith at the home of a friend whose parents were away. This was an era before drugs were fashionable, but kids there were drinking beer and carousing. Keith had aspirations to study political science, and he liked to hear himself talk. He was politically opinionated and we had discussions, though he was the type who always had to dominate them.

At some point that night, Keith took me aside to talk and make out, and I followed him into a bedroom. Knowing what he had in mind, I was frightened, but I hid my fear and maintained my outward bravado as if I were acting a role, all the while trying to convince myself that I was ready to take this plunge, that I was a big girl now. This was before there was such a thing as "date rape." He pushed me further into sex than I wanted to go, and I finally said, "No, I can't do this, Keith. I can't!" He then became angry and forced me in no uncertain terms. I wanted to say, "I'm a virgin and I don't want to do this yet," but my fear reduced me to silence and acquiescence. I just waited for it to be over.

It would be years before I was able to tell anyone, and it was not one of the stories that I later shared with the cast of *A Chorus Line*. The ordeal ended with a furious outburst from Keith when he discovered traces of blood. I don't remember how I got out of there that night, but I made it home. Everything then became twisted in my mind. Overcome by guilt, I shut myself off emotionally from what had happened. I thought that because I had let it happen, it had to be my fault. It defied all logic, but because I blamed myself for allowing Keith to have his way with me, I felt I had no choice but to continue the relationship.

The next time I saw him was at his house. Again he pushed me into having sex with him, and this time I left blood all over the bed. I couldn't stop bleeding, and I started crying. I was so terrified that Keith brought in his mother, who hadn't known I was in the house. She was outraged at both of us, but eventually led me into the bathroom and had me sit on towels until the bleeding stopped. Rather than take me to a doctor, she drove me home. I remember feeling so utterly horrid when she told my mother the story. Afterward, even as upset as I imagined my mother was, we never talked about what had happened. She told me to stay away from that boy, but her attitude was *let's not tell anyone.* After all, it was something shameful. As far as I know, she never told my father. I believe that was her way of protecting me. The nightmare was simply buried as if it had never happened, and I continued to see Keith secretly despite the pain and confusion.

A short time later I received a call from the director of the winter stock productions, David Tihmar, who invited me to join a troupe of perform-ers who were going to tour the South, mostly one-night performances in each town. The group was to include a ballet couple, a modern, jazzy couple, a baritone singer, and me. I would fill in with the modern and ballet material. Mr. Tihmar offered me $75 a week, and asked, "Do you think your parents will let you come? It will be four weeks of rehearsal in New York and six weeks on tour."

I said, "I'm sure it will be fine with them." But it wasn't fine, of course, and this time my mother sided with my father. They insisted that I should stay home and finish school. I wasn't thinking of their feelings at all when I screamed, "You can't do this to me! I am not a child! This is my one big chance, and nothing like this will ever happen to me again in my entire life." Leaving the dinner table that night, instead of just going to my room and slamming the door, I went in and started tearing the room apart, sending things crashing to the floor.

My father quickly came into the room followed by my mother, with my brother and sister huddled behind her. I erupted like a little Vesuvius. My mother burst into tears, while my father pleaded with me to stop. In spite of my tearful sobs, my words were hurtful and angry. I felt like a cornered animal who desperately tries to break free. I knew I was crossing a line, and there was no turning back. I had had enough of the brooding, the looks of contempt, my mother's sadness, the stifled tears, and all the needs never met and I was tired of people not expressing themselves. I screamed at them, "No one is going to tell me what to do! No one is going to stop me from doing what I need to do!"

I really did believe it was now or never for me, that my being offered another paying job in the theater meant that my big break had come. Obviously, I couldn't afford to go to New York on my own. Working in Detroit was one thing, but New York was the big time, and I would be living and working in the protection of a professional company. Couldn't they see that?

The next evening, after we had all calmed down, I met with my father in the living room to try to plead my case. I invited Keith for moral support, but I found myself tongue-tied. My father kept asking me, "What do you want?" I didn't know what to say. Finally I stammered, "I just want peace of mind!" I saw the hurt and contempt in his eyes when he said, "Well, everybody wants that, Donna." I felt completely defeated. I also realized what a big mistake it was to have Keith there. I had wanted to talk and come to terms with my father, but with my boyfriend there, I was too inhibited to have any kind of heart-to-heart conversation. I can't say that I was thinking rationally, but soon thereafter, I began to plan my escape, with Keith agreeing to drive me to New York.

My getaway was a scene out of one of those B movies I had seen with my mother. I packed my suitcase in the afternoon, hiding it under my bed in the bedroom that I shared with my sister. That night after she was asleep, I quietly retrieved it and put pillows under the covers to make it look as though I were in bed asleep. With heart pounding, I opened the bedroom window, tossed my suitcase out, and climbed down into our yard. Then I ran across the street and hid in the bushes in a neighbor's yard until Keith picked me up in his car.

We had this farfetched idea that we would be all over the news, so we took the back roads. After driving all night and most of the next day, we stayed in a motel in New Jersey. At the mercy of my boyfriend's increasingly violent temper, I went to sleep that night racked by guilt and fears, but nevertheless determined to go through with my plan. The following day we drove into Manhattan, and I called a dancer I had met in the winter stock shows, with whom I'd arranged to stay. We went to her apartment, a walk-up on 54th Street and Ninth Avenue. As soon as she opened the door, she said, "I'm sorry, Donna, but I had to call your father."

My father suddenly appeared, coming up the stairs behind us. At that moment, I was relieved to see him, because Keith had been physically abusive, and by now I was feeling trapped. Keith was taken off guard at the sight of my father, who said to him quietly, "I want you to get in your car and drive home." Keith left without an argument. I had a scratch under my eye, and my father was concerned and cautious when he asked me, "Did he hurt you?" I denied that he had, fearing that I would only make the situation worse.

I was surprised that night when, instead of reproaching me, my father took me out on the town. It was like we were on a date. He was so friendly and attentive. We visited the Empire State Building and then went out to dinner. It was just my father and I spending time together in a way we never had before. This was now a special occasion, and I was happy to be with him. We didn't talk about what had happened. I had run away from home, and that had to mean something. But the fact that he was there now meant even more to me. Rather than blaming me, he treated me with tenderness. The little girl part of me was grateful that her dad had come to rescue her, though it distressed me to think that he must have borrowed money to pay for the trip. But in my young girl's life, it was the most cherished father-daughter moment. The next day we went to the airport together and took a plane back to Detroit.

But there was to be no lasting reconciliation. After being home for a few days, my father and mother announced, without warning, that they were taking me to juvenile court to have a hearing before a judge. This news came as a devastating blow, and I felt betrayed by both of them. The idea of having me go to court was apparently a scare tactic that someone had suggested to them, thinking that a judge might be able to talk some sense into me. I remember my mother crying in the hearing room and wiping her eyes with a hanky. The judge gave me a harsh lecture and finished by warning me, "Young lady, if you try running away again, we will lock you up in jail."

I don't know where I found my voice, but I suddenly spoke up in measured tones, containing my rage. "Well, you can do that, but I'll find a way to get out, and I'll run away again! And you can lock me up again, and I'll get out again."

The hearing was quickly adjourned, and it was left to my parents to decide what to do with me. Years later, I learned that they had consulted my ballet teacher, Pamela, who encouraged my parents to let me go on the tour. She told them, "Donna will either find a way to survive, or she will come home."

My parents never told me exactly how they arrived at their decision, but they soon relented, and I found myself heading back to New York City to rehearse with the company. My other ballet teacher, Rose Marie Floyd, had misgivings about my quitting high school to pursue an uncertain career, especially at the age of sixteen. Rose Marie later said in an interview, "It floored me when Donna said she was going to drop out of school because so few people know what they want in life at that age. But she did."

Or perhaps I only thought I did. After my big rebellion and all that effort to take my destiny in hand, I was actually scared to death to be on my own. And though I was the one to run away, I felt abandoned by my family.

I moved to New York with little money. The first place I stayed in was a fleabag hotel on West 69th Street between Columbus and Broadway called the Dauphin. Back then, Manhattan's Upper West Side was not the safe, gentrified neighborhood that it is today, and the hotel was a hooker haven. I soon moved down to the Knickerbocker Hotel on 45th

Street, another sleazy place, which was frequented by sailors whenever the fleet was in. Nearby was a nightclub called The Peppermint Lounge, where Joey Dee and the Starliters were inventing the Twist. No one cared about my being underage, and I did have fun there on occasion dancing the night away.

I remember my first rehearsal at Variety Arts rehearsal studio on West 46th Street. I had a 10:00 A.M. call that morning, and not yet knowing my way around the city, I got lost and arrived about ten minutes late. David Tihmar gave me a fierce verbal lashing in front of the company. This was the same director who told me at the Cass Theatre that when an actor enters the stage door, it is like entering a church. His berating me seemed like the most horrible thing that ever happened in my life, but he knew this was my first job away from home and was no doubt trying to teach me a lesson.

We were a diverse group, and I was, by far, the youngest member of the company. Darrell Notara was a Ballet Theatre corps dancer, and his fiancée, Diane, was a budding ballet dancer. Darrell appointed himself my protector on the tour because I was so inexperienced, but he often lost his patience with me. On the road, I roomed with an older ballerina, who didn't like having to room with me because I was so nervous and chatty. Ignoring me for the most part, she wrote letters and kept to herself.

An older dancer, Arnott Mader, took me under his wing and provided emotional support. Arnott was a gorgeous classical dancer, very elegant, though nearing the time when he would have to hang up his ballet shoes. I confessed to him one time that I had run away from home and hadn't finished school. Arnott said, "You shouldn't go to college if you want to be a dancer. You've got to get out there on the stage. The time is now. You can always go back to school later, but a dancer's life is limited, Donna, so you have to do it now." Still plagued with guilt and insecurities, I needed to hear his reassurance that I was doing the right thing, and I took his words to heart.

We traveled in a station wagon, pulling a U-Haul trailer that carried our costumes and sets. We had to take care of washing and ironing our own costumes. I felt awkward at times in the presence of these grown-ups. When we stopped on the road to eat at diners, they would order dinner, I would order a hot fudge sundae, and Darrell would scold me. It was like I had joined another dysfunctional family, but I felt that I truly belonged here and most of the time I was elated with my new life.

I was the jazz baby of the show. I did some modern dances, like "Bringing in the Sheaves," a Martha Graham piece that the baritone David Chaney would sing as we danced. We performed to a reel-to-reel tape recorder and whatever sound system was available. We each danced in a couple of pieces, and then had a finale together. The tour was mostly one-night stands at colleges. Sometimes we played gymnasiums. Usually with very little time to set up, we would arrive, check into the hotel, and then go directly to the school or theater where we were scheduled to perform.

I remember our first stop in North Carolina. After checking into the hotel, I somehow became separated from the rest of the group. I may have wandered off to visit a local graveyard, which was my habit whenever we arrived early and had time for sightseeing. I loved the history that I was able to gather by reading gravestones and memorial plaques, and this was one way I found to continue my education. After returning to the hotel that afternoon, I had the address of the school where we were playing and tried without success to hail a taxi. At first I couldn't figure out why the cabs kept passing me by. Then I saw that some of the taxis were designated *for colored only,* while others were *for white only.*

This was 1959, and the South was still segregated. We were playing at what was then called "a Negro college," one of several we would visit. I was close to tears by the time I finally managed to flag down a "colored cab." I practically threw myself in front of him and begged the cabbie to drive me to the school. I could sense his fear when I was able to tell him where I was going. He reluctantly agreed to take me, but he said I had to lie down on the floor of the cab, so no one would see me. I stayed on the floor for the entire ride while desperately trying to hold my costume up to keep it from getting wrinkled.

For a sixteen-year-old girl from the white suburbs of Detroit, this was a stunning experience. I had seen religious bigotry in Michigan but little racial prejudice, and what little I did see was certainly nothing like this. I couldn't fully appreciate until later how this man was risking his life to get me to that performance. After arriving at the school, I rushed inside to find the dressing room and put on my costume. I was late again, but this time received only a passing reprimand from our stage manager. That night was our first live audience, and we were all delighted by the enthusiastic reception we received, which was repeated at each performance on the rest of the tour.

My success with the show bolstered my confidence. After returning to New York City, I had no intention of going home. My plan was to stay and somehow find a way to make a living as a dancer. I first moved into a dismal little room in a YWCA on 34th Street. The tiny space was such that if I was lying on the bed next to the wall, I could reach out my hand and touch the other wall. It was all that I could afford, but the neighborhood scared me. After some desperate searching, I soon moved into another YWCA, this one at Eighth Avenue and 50th Street. There I made my first gal pals in New York, including Georgia Parrot, who was working as a secretary. Whenever she met someone, she would provide a way to remember her name, "Georgia like the peach, and Parrot like the bird." The accommodations weren't much improved, but it was a relatively safe place for young women like us. My other friend, Susan Lee, who was a singer, coached me to sing my first audition song, "Honey Bun," from South Pacific, because all dancers were expected "to belt it out."

Meanwhile, my parents were waiting. I guess they figured I would run out of money sooner or later and come home. I missed my family, even after all I put them through, but I was determined to show them that I could survive on my own, and that determination enabled me to continue, despite all the loneliness and guilt. I knew that my mother was having a difficult time, and that was especially disturbing for me. I received a letter from my Aunt Dorothy telling me that she was afraid my mother would have to be hospitalized because she was so depressed. It was a great sadness for her that I was gone, and the way I had left home made it even harder on her. I knew how worried she was about me, and I hated myself for causing her such grief.

But I was headstrong, and the discipline of dancing enabled me to fend off the unsettling emotions for years while I gave myself to the music and the mirror. As a dancer, I had learned to perform no matter how I felt, and so it was with my life. I never talked to my parents about the dangers of living alone in the city or about the fears that I had. I would call home with only positive things to report because I wanted to relieve them, and at the same time I needed to keep myself pumped up. The theme of my life for many years to come would be, "I'll show them! I'll succeed." Little did I realize how much success was going to cost me. Nor was I aware that my emotional baggage and unresolved issues with my family were ticking away inside me like a time bomb that would one day have the power to cripple me.

Chapter 2

_____ ❧ _____

How to Succeed
as a Teenage Gypsy

While still newly arrived in Manhattan in early 1960, and trying ever so diligently to give the impression that I was a sophisticated young lady, I was really a seventeen-year-old bundle of insecurities. I didn't yet envision a future for myself in musical theater; Broadway and its gypsies held no special appeal for me. I was proud of my classical background and tended to look down on modern and jazz dance, like so many ballet dancers I knew. Of course, that attitude was a defense mechanism, a way of hiding some of my fear. I presented myself as the aspiring ballerina and always dressed in black, with my hair pulled back in a bun. But beneath the seemingly poised outward image that I cultivated, I was desperate for a chance to prove myself.

I thought I had my first real break when, as soon as the tour was finished, I was given the opportunity to audition for American Ballet Theatre, the international touring company, which was then under the direction of Lucia Chase. Unlike George Balanchine's New York City Ballet, with its abstract modern choreography, ABT offered a more varied dramatic repertory based on traditional classic ballets. Given my body and interpretive approach to dancing, I was more suited for ABT, where dancers were called upon to act as well as to perform the vocabulary of ballet steps and technique. My friend from the Tihmar troupe, Darrell Notara, was then dancing in the ABT corps, and he kindly arranged for me to audition for the coming season.

I was encouraged when Darrell told me, "I think you're good enough to dance with Ballet Theatre, but you have to audition." I took classes at ABT and went through a week of auditions, filled with hope and nervous anticipation. The audition classes consisted of a barre and center work, taught by a ballet master and observed by the directors of the company. The week began with about forty girls who were trying out, and each new day as I walked into the studio, there were fewer dancers. By the last day, only a handful of us remained, and we were joined by several boys from the company. With the formidable artistic director Lucia Chase watching from the side, we did a barre and then a pas de deux on pointe. I hadn't had much experience with partnering, but somehow I made it through the challenge without faltering.

Lucia Chase came up to me and said, "You're a lovely dancer, Donna, but you're still very young. We are going to Russia this year, and I don't believe you are ready yet. I would like you to study with us for a year. We may bring you into the company next year." I thanked her politely and left the studio, devastated to the point of having to hold back tears. Totally under the spell of my own unrealistic expectations, I didn't realize that it was an accomplishment just to be invited to study with the company.

My ever present self-critical voice didn't allow me to interpret the experience in a positive way. To me, it felt like a humiliating rejection. While that self-critical attitude helped me to excel as a dancer, it also distorted my sense of reality, casting me into a tailspin of self-doubt. I felt so hurt, I couldn't go to a ballet class for months, and I didn't attend a ballet for several years. The day after the audition I went to a jazz class. My attitude of "I'll show them!" shifted a bit. I kept up my training with jazz and modern dance classes, in order to find work as a dancer. It didn't take long for me get the idea that I could do this and do it well. I came to love these styles and the freedom of expression they gave me. I actually felt more satisfied emotionally than I had with ballet, yet I kept all of this to myself, as if it were some secret shame. I was able to tap into another kind of energy when I heard the rhythms of jazz, and a different part of my personality emerged when I danced in these more grounded and sensual ways.

I was starting to really worry about not having a paying job. At this point I even made one halfhearted attempt to find work outside the theater. I remember going into a Woolworth's to apply for a job as a clerk. I had no experience, but I assumed they would train me and that I could somehow manage to get by for a while. I started filling out the application, but when I came to the section asking about my education, I immediately felt defeated and gave up on the whole idea. I never had an answer when someone asked where I went to school. I hadn't finished high school, and my lack of formal education would continue to be an embarrassment for years. It seemed to me that my only recourse was to find a job as a dancer. What else could I do? I had to pay the rent.

I next auditioned for that year's Radio City Music Hall Easter show—not to be a tap-dancing Rockette, but to be in the corps de ballet. Apart from a ballet company, that was the only job available for ballet dancers in New York. That corps de ballet job no longer exists, but in those days Radio City was where all the aspiring ballet dancers would go when they came to New York. This audition took place in a studio the size of a football field and was actually a much more demanding tryout than the ABT audition had been. The most excruciating part of the ordeal was crossing the floor doing relevés on one foot in first arabesque and then thirty-two fouettés (a feat like Odile's in *Swan Lake,* turning *en pointe* on one leg, thirty-two times). This was more of an endurance contest than a ballet audition. I don't know how I managed, but I did it. I was soon called in for costume fittings and rehearsals, all of which took place on the premises of Radio City Music Hall, which operated like a factory with its in-house production team turning out show after show. Those of us in the corps were all to be dressed alike in little Dutch girl costumes, with little white hats and flowing tulle skirts.

My initial elation at having the job quickly turned to dismay. We were scheduled to perform a grueling schedule of five shows a day, and the first rehearsal was anything but inspirational. After being given two little baskets of plastic tulips, I was instructed to enter with the other corps girls on the stage riser, and we were then to walk to various places onstage to deliver our tulips. "Pick up your basket. Put your basket down. Turn, walk in formation and pose." That was it? After *that* audition? This wasn't what I had in mind. I thought we were going to *dance*. The aspiring artiste in me was highly offended.

I was running out of money and needed the job, but in the meantime I received a call at the Y from David Tihmar, who was becoming more like a mentor to me and who invited me to do a summer stock season at the Carousel Theatre in Framingham, Massachusetts. I left Radio City on the day of our dress rehearsal, not even realizing that the proper protocol was to give notice. I later received a call from one of the Radio City stage managers who wanted to know what happened to me. "We thought you were hit by a bus!" I really hadn't thought that anyone would miss me. I apologized for my ignorance, though I wasn't about to return to Radio City, not even for the two weeks' pay that was owed me. I was too embarrassed to go back to pick it up.

After my demoralizing experiences with ABT and Radio City, I was more open to the idea of dancing in musicals, and I still had to find a way to survive. The repertory in Framingham included *Silk Stockings* with Genevieve, *Redhead* with Gordon and Sheila MacRae, *South Pacific* with Howard Keel, *Annie Get Your Gun* with Ginger Rogers, and *Carousel* with Inga Swenson and John Raitt, whom I would work with again in just a few years on *A Joyful Noise*. Dancing in the corps and performing small roles for fifteen weeks with some of those great stars gave me much more than a temporary livelihood. To be able to tell a story with music and dance was one thing, but to use my voice and words to express the depths of my feelings through a character was a new and exciting prospect. The role of the daughter Louise in *Carousel* was my first professional acting part, and it inspired in me a new passion and respect for acting. I began my love affair with theater that summer, and I realized during that time that if I were going to have a serious career in musical theater, I eventually was going to have to learn to act as well as sing and dance.

Returning to New York in the fall, I knew that my dancing gave me a certain advantage, at least as far as getting a foothold. There seemed to be more auditions for dancers in those days, and I stood a better chance of getting work in the theater than did most struggling singers or actors who were just starting out. There were also commercials and trade shows that needed dancers. The auditions were often cattle calls, but they enabled me to land some of my first jobs in the city. I was cast in a Welch's Grape Juice commercial with Dan Sorretta, who would later choreograph "Tap Your Troubles Away" for me in *Mack and Mabel*. I also appeared in the first L'eggs stockings commercial, when the new concept of pantyhose was marketed in a plastic egg. For that one, dancer Skipper Damon (who would later appear in the TV show *Soap*) and I did a samba with shopping carts down the aisle of a supermarket. It was also Michael Cimino's first directing job on TV. He would go on to direct some important films.

Those jobs didn't pay much, but whenever I had money, I bought plane tickets to visit my family in Detroit, still on a mission to win approval and support from my parents. I would wear some smashing outfit and try to surprise them, waltzing through the front door, à la Loretta Young, like I was the toast of the town. I remember one of these surprise visits when I arrived home only to find all the doors locked. Unbeknownst to me, my family was away on vacation at the family cottage in East Tawas, and because I couldn't get into the house, I had no choice but to turn around and fly straight back to New York.

My next break came the following year when I was cast in a touring company of *West Side Story* that took me to the tent circuit on Cape Cod. I played one of the Jet girls, and benefited from the tutelage of the show's director, Frank Corsaro. Frank was an acting guru who taught at the Actors Studio, and later had his own school and devoted following. John Mineo was my partner, and he later went on to a long and successful career as a Bob Fosse dancer. Others in that very talented cast included Jay Norman, who had been in the original Broadway production and was later one of my teachers; Lenny Dale who was the choreographer and also my dance teacher; Paula Kelly, a terrific singer-dancer who later played one of Shirley MacLaine's sidekicks in the film of *Sweet*

Charity; Joe Bennett, who became Zach in Los Angeles and on the Broadway tour of *A Chorus Line;* and Julia Migenes, who was to embark on a wonderful operatic career.

As an impressionable teenager hungry to learn, that show was another eye-opener, with its explosive Jerome Robbins choreography and Leonard Bernstein's lush, dynamic score. The challenge to become a "triple threat" as a dancer, actress, and singer was driven home by the way every element and every moment in that show was integrated so seamlessly within the whole. Even as inexperienced as I was, the idea began to take hold of me at this point that musical theater could be a serious art form in its own right, and not just frivolous entertainment.

Life on the road was not without misadventure, and I even had a brief romance. I had been reluctant about dating since my traumatic episode of running away from home with my last boyfriend, but while on tour, I became best pals with Louis Falco, a wonderful modern dancer who played one of the Sharks, and who would later make a name for himself as an innovative choreographer. As if saving myself for future romantic disasters, I never allowed our summer fling to go beyond holding hands and good-night kisses, all very innocent and tender.

When the tour came to an end, a party was thrown at a huge board-ing house on the beach, where most of the company was staying. It was actually located in the middle of a closed-down amusement park. I remember I was wearing pigtails and still had on my stage makeup after the last show. There were electric guitars, bongo drums, and a loud-speaker system, making for the kind of slightly raucous scene that would become more familiar as the decade went on. Unbeknownst to me, some of the people there were smoking pot, and later that night, the neighbors complained that we were "disturbing the peace." The police suddenly arrived with two paddy wagons, and after barging in with guns drawn, they busted all of us, except for a few dancers who managed to escape by leaping out the bathroom windows. The boys in the company were loaded into one paddy wagon, all the while singing a boisterous rendition of "Gee, Officer Krupke," from *West Side Story.*

The guys continued singing even after we were taken to the local jail and locked in our cells. But it soon ceased to be funny. We girls were thrown together in a dismal holding pen that had only a hole in the floor for a toilet, and a plank to sit on. There were no beds, but that was where we stayed the night, all of us mortified and trying our best not to have to use the facilities. It was not at all a pleasant experience. The next morning, one of us was allowed to make a phone call, and the producers of the show soon bailed us out. Even though we were only locked up one night, I have never forgotten the incredible elation I felt when I walked out of that cell after we were freed.

After our release, one of my girlfriends and I were interviewed by a reporter for the local paper. We were asked to give our side of the story, and the two of us went on and on like a pair of Chatty Cathys, thinking we were making our case and exposing this terrible injustice. The next day we saw our pictures splashed on the front page. I was still in pigtails and wearing my false eyelashes, and there was a headline that read, "BONGO-BEATING BEATNIKS ARRESTED AT PARTY!" Later, we had to appear in court, wearing our Sunday best, with boys seated on one side and girls on the other. We were let off with a lecture from the judge, but our little scrape with the law actually made it as a blip on the national news.

Back in Manhattan, I continued my routine of auditioning and taking classes. Even though I felt at home living at the Y with my friends, I still suffered from bouts of loneliness. Thinking a pet might help, I bought a rabbit and kept it in a box hidden under my bed. This little creature was fine company until one day it hopped out of its box and the cleaning lady found it darting around the room. She made a quick exit and went yelping down the hallway. I was reprimanded and given notice to leave the Y. Neither men nor animals were allowed on the premises.

Georgia Parrot and I moved to an apartment in Hell's Kitchen on 54th Street and Ninth Avenue, which we shared with several other roommates over time. One of them was a flight attendant who, we learned later, supplemented her income by picking up guys at the famous Roseland dance hall. Georgia and I next moved to a place on 84th Street and Amsterdam. I was shocked to learn later that this street had the highest murder rate in New York City that year. It was that kind of neighborhood in those days. Nobody I knew was ever killed, but my roommates and I were robbed a couple of times.

Because I was so serious about pursuing my fledgling career, I never really fit the rebel-without-a-cause image, but I do remember being thrown off the beach at Coney Island with another girlfriend that summer because we were wearing bikinis. That sort of daring was unusual for me. I regarded it as the other side of my personality. I spent more time taking classes and auditioning than I did socializing or going to parties, although I was on my way to becoming a jazz aficionado. At the time, counterculture types were labeled "beatniks," and wearing my dance togs on the street before it was fashionable, I fit right in.

My friends and I were often lured down to the coffeehouses and trendy jazz clubs in Greenwich Village, to places like the Village Vanguard and the Bon Soir, where we were thrilled to listen to music and see performers like Thelonious Monk, Bill Evans, and Barbra Streisand. We would go uptown to Birdland to catch others like Nina Simone and Joe Williams. Cy Coleman had a popular trio that played on 52nd Street. On Wednesday nights I went to the Palladium to hear Tito Puente, and to compete in the mambo contests. One of my dance teachers at June Taylor's school (June Taylor made her name choreographing *The Jackie Gleason Show*) was Lenny Dale, and whenever Lenny partnered me in the mambo contests, the two of us reigned. Lenny was famous for his knee slides, and he could bring down the house doing a full roll into a backbend and ending up on the tips of his toes.

Even though I lived on a dime, I always found a way to take advantage of what New York had to offer. I was young and living in bliss, with my future ahead of me. The world was truly my oyster. Later that summer I auditioned for the General Motors Motorama, an annual industrial show that was scheduled to play at a convention center in Los Angeles. This was to be a lavish production, budgeted at over $1 million. It would cost twenty times that today. The show drew the likes of established Broadway producers Cy Feuer and Ernest Martin, who had previously produced *Where's Charley?* (1948), *Guys and Dolls* (1950), *Can-Can* (1953), and *Silk Stockings* (1955). The Motorama troupe would include more than forty dancers and singers. One of the headliners was Cynthia Scott, who had been the lead dancer on the *Your Hit Parade* TV show during the 1950s, and who I loved to watch as a child on our little TV with a magnifying glass.

My audition this time was not a cattle call. An agent named Jack Lenny (who later represented Michael Bennett) had seen me in Framingham and later arranged for me to try out for the producers. The audition took place at the Helen Hayes Theatre. I had seen a couple of shows by then, including *Bye Bye Birdie* with Chita Rivera, my new inspiration, but this was the first time I had ever been on a Broadway stage. Feuer and Martin were there, as was the show's conductor, Peter Matz. My audition piece was a modern ballet number that I had done in *Carousel* the previous summer, when I played the role of Louise. The scene took place on a beach, and I danced with bare feet and bare legs. Shortly before Peter Matz died in 1999, he reminded me of that Motorama audition, saying, "All of a sudden, you walked onstage—this little slip of a girl in a sundress—and you put your music down, and then started dancing to 'If I Loved You.' And we were all totally spellbound."

When I finished my audition, Cy Feuer came barreling down the aisle. Having never seen me before and wondering why, he asked me excitedly, "What have you been doing?" Thinking he meant the number, I quickly replied, "Louise's dance from *Carousel.*" The others sitting in the audience guffawed, amused by my ever so serious, literal answer.

Cy was an exuberant man with freckles and his red hair always in a brush cut. When he was young he had been both a trumpet player and a tough little prizefighter. Cy called me down off the stage and walked me up the aisle to the back of the theater. Then he sat me down to talk, and I remember thinking, *So this is what producers do.* He was the first big-time producer I ever met, and I was impressed by what a gentleman he was. He told me, "I want you to come with us to L.A. to do this Motorama show, and after we come back to New York, I want you to be in the chorus of a new show that we're producing. It's called *How to Succeed in Business Without Really Trying.*"

I was overjoyed just to think that here was someone as important as Cy Feuer who liked me and thought I had talent. And not only did I now have a job that would take me to California for the first time, but I had the security of another job to look forward to when I returned to New York. I knew that I was soon going to be dancing on Broadway, and I was beside myself, filled with excitement and real hope at the prospect of entering that magical world.

The Motorama show turned out to be another great nurturing experience, with choreography by Bob Hamilton, who may be remembered as part of the Hamilton Trio, who performed as regulars back in the 1950s on Max Liebman's TV variety series, *Your Show of Shows*. We performed eight Motorama shows a week, and I was intent on making good, not allowing anything, including men, to distract me. I went so far as to wear a little wedding band, pretending to be married to discourage any would-be Romeos. Some of the male musicians saw through me and were amused by my little act. I had completely forgotten about this subterfuge until I was reminded by some of the same musicians, forty years later, when we were doing *Mack and Mabel* in Los Angeles. We all had a good laugh about it.

Entering the commercial world of musical theater seemed daunting at first, but I was now single-minded in my determination to make the transition and prepare myself to work on Broadway. Rehearsals for *How to Succeed in Business Without Really Trying* started early in August of 1961. With music and lyrics by Frank Loesser, the show was directed by Abe Burrows, who also wrote the book (based on Shepherd Mead's satiric novel). Robert Fletcher designed the set and costumes. The first week of rehearsals was scheduled for the choreographer, Hugh Lambert, who worked with the dancers early, which was the standard practice at the time, in order to get a start on the big production numbers. The rest of the company would come in the following week.

Hugh's choreographic style was highly athletic and energized, with fast footwork that pitched us dancers forward in perpetual plié. If you didn't have strong thighs, you would soon develop them. He first choreographed "The Pirate Dance," which all of us immediately thought was a sensational number. It was a satire of TV choreography that Hugh had originally staged for an industrial show. He then went on to choreograph "Paris Original," but after a few days seemed to get bogged down on what was otherwise a good concept for the number. Without any warning or explanation, we arrived at rehearsal one day and discovered that Bob Fosse had been brought in to replace Hugh. Fosse would choreograph the rest of the show and, at his own request, he was eventually credited with "Musical Staging," out of deference to Hugh, allowing him to retain his credit. We were all surprised by Hugh's sudden departure, but no one in the cast dared to say anything. I remember thinking, *Wow, they really mean business around here!*

Bob's wife, Gwen Verdon, served as his assistant, or dance captain, a role that she loved and had performed earlier in her career when she worked for choreographer Jack Cole. Gwen became my first real mentor and an inspiring role model during the weeks that we rehearsed and went on the road to Philadelphia. I was most impressed by the fact that she was a Broadway star of such stature that she actually had shows written for her—in fact, the musical *Redhead* had been named for her.

Gwen was always more than generous in sharing her knowledge with other performers and offering them opportunities. After we opened on Broadway, Gwen recruited me and Tracy Everitt out of the chorus to appear in a TV talent hunt—the Jim Backus show, *Talent Scouts,* which was set up vaguely along the lines of today's *American Idol*. We were fortunate to have a number created for us by another brilliant choreographer, Paul Draper, who had been an international star as a tap dancer in the 1930s and 1940s, but later had his career destroyed by the McCarthy blacklist. Often compared to Fred Astaire, Paul was famous for blending tap with ballet and classical music, and that was the style of the number that he created for us.

For me, the whole experience of *How to Succeed* was like getting a university education in musical theater. At eighteen, I was the youngest cast member. I made some good friendships in the show with Silver Saunders, who would open the first Improvisation Club with her husband at the time, Bud Friedman, and Elaine Cancilla, who would later marry Jerry Orbach. During rehearsals, my lack of confidence and my inhibitions were replaced by a keen desire to learn everything I could from the masters who were creating this musical. The show itself would eventually win a Pulitzer Prize, with Robert Morse perfectly cast as the window-washer, J. Pierrepont Finch, who backstabs his way hilariously up the corporate ladder at the World Wide Wicket Company.

Bob Fosse was not only a great choreographer, but already had the instincts of an innovative director and acting coach as well. He gave each of us in the chorus an assignment to write a page of personal history that we were to invent for our characters. If we didn't have names in the script, we were to make up names, along with details about where we lived, what we did, and how we related to each other character in the Wicket Company. Each time we made an entrance or exit, Fosse wanted us to know why—where we were coming from and where we were going.

Most importantly for the dancers in the chorus, Bobby encouraged each of us to bring our individuality into everything we did onstage. Even when we danced in unison, he wanted to see individual points of view. By directing us not to be afraid to be unique or different, Fosse opened up a whole world for me. Of course, if he wanted our eyeballs to move in unison in one direction on one count, we did it, but still kept our individual personality alive. It's possible. When he was really pleased with our work, he wouldn't say anything like "Great!" or "Fabulous!" He would simply say, "You did it!" This acknowledgment would mean everything to anyone who worked for him, because his compliments were few and rare.

Charles Nelson Reilly, who played the role of the smirking villain, Bud Frump, later became one of my musical theater teachers, and Frank Loesser was my first voice coach. Frank was a real Damon Runyon type, like one of those guys standing on the street corner in *Guys and Dolls*. Never without a cigar and even as short in stature as he was, he looked tough, but had beautiful soulful eyes. He also had incredible energy and passion and would jump up and down when he got excited. I was later to understudy the roles of Rosemary and Hedy La Rue, played by Michelle Lee and Virginia Martin. I remember after rehearsing one of my numbers, Frank came rushing down the aisle to the stage. He said to me, "Hey, honey, first make the gesture, *then* sing the note!"

Now, when performing in musical theater, if you do it long enough, you come to realize that there are no real rules, but there are some fundamental truths. Frank's point about the gesture coming first is one of them. You physicalize your organic response to the moment, whatever the impulse or stimulus in the scene is, then let the voice follow. The gesture also pulls focus on the stage to let the audience know who is going to sing next.

There were other lessons to be learned from watching the principals performing their numbers, delivering lines, and inventing bits of stage business. Abe Burrows was born with a funny bone, and a very funny one it was. He was a gentle giant who loved to have fun. He was not only a director and writer, but also a lyricist and composer. He would entertain us at parties by sitting at the piano and performing his songs, which I remember were hilarious. I especially loved one of his numbers called "Lopin' Along the Trail," which told the story of a cowboy's life played like the loping of a tired horse.

As a director, Abe had a great sense of timing that was instinctual, like George Abbott, with whom I would work later. Unlike Abbott, I don't remember Abe ever dictating the timing of a scene by saying something like, "Count to three and then say the line." That was the type of note that Abbott would give when an actor was taking too long to find a laugh. Abe was patient, and allowed his actors to find their way.

Early in rehearsals, while we were still in New York, two of the principals had their own way of working that was a challenge for Abe and the rest of the cast. Veteran singer Rudy Vallee played the company boss (J. B. Biggley), but Rudy wasn't really a stage performer, and he had very little voice projection. And Bobby Morse was very restrained during the first few weeks, as if he was struggling to find his role. So the two of them were walking around mumbling, with voices so low we could hardly hear them. No one could really tell what was going on in the show until finally Abe said, "Okay, I gotta hear ya! I gotta hear ya!"

Once we went out of town, on our first preview night, Bobby Morse really let go. He had a grand entrance, lowered from the flies as the window-washer, and from that moment on he electrified the audience and the rest of the company. Rudy rose to the occasion as well, though he needed the help of a body mike, which was probably one of the first times one was used on the Broadway stage. It was such a revelation for me to see those performances come together, fully realized on the road.

Hugh Lambert was a dear man and very encouraging to me when I was learning his choreography; but when Bob Fosse took over, I had the flu, and for his first few days my job was on the line. Fortunately, I recovered in time to prove myself. Bobby and Gwen were all about the work, and they always came in fully prepared. Bob could be brusque and intimidating at times. He had already done shows like *Damn Yankees, The Pajama Game, Bells Are Ringing,* and *Redhead,* and his reputation as a demanding taskmaster preceded him. The stylistic Fosse trademarks, like using the hips and hands in isolation, were already well established. The work he did in *How to Succeed* had terrific humor and style, with a lot of jazzy shuffles and jumps. Gwen was his adorable counterpart, all eagerness and buoyant good humor. She delighted in telling us on occasion how the two of them had invented the choreography the night before by jumping up and down on their bed.

Even though he was no longer choreographing the show, Hugh Lambert came with us to Philadelphia, where we were to open at the Shubert Theatre in September. My closest friend in the chorus was Tracy Everitt, and we adored Hugh and felt sorry for him having been replaced. We would often see the red glow of his cigarette up in the balcony, and knew that he was sitting there alone in the dark, watching rehearsal. Sometimes we would go up and quietly sit down on each side of him. When we were needed onstage we would just get up and leave. Nobody said anything, but I think he appreciated our company.

I was still learning about deportment backstage, and our veteran stage manager, Phil Friedman, contributed a great deal to my education. Despite his big burly appearance, Phil had a sweet nature. I remember one day he came rushing up the stairs to the dressing room, yelling in desperation, "Donna, what have you been doing to your shoes? The wardrobe mistress is complaining! It looks like you've been banging the wall with them!" I was always a strong dancer—no doubt too eager to please and stronger than I needed to be, so my shoes always took a beating. Phil was on my case like a stage father, just trying to educate me. I appreciated his concern, but I never changed my style, and would not allow him to influence my dancing.

When we came back to New York, I worked on the number "A Secretary Is Not a Toy," which was the last number that was put in the show. At Fosse's insistence, the number was changed from a waltz to a marvelous soft-shoe. I was given a line, which was something of a distinction because lines usually went to singers rather than dancers. I was told that when I came down to join the other secretaries in the typing pool, I was to say, "That Mr. Toynbee must think I'm a yo-yo." I told Abe Burrows that I didn't understand the line, and he explained, "You know, he treats you like you're a yo-yo, because you're on his lap, then you're off his lap—you're on, then you're off!" Unfortunately, he soon decided to cut the line because he didn't think I was able to deliver it with enough conviction. With little setbacks like these due to my lack of experience, I was simply paying dues.

Later, I had a crossover, and Frank Loesser gave me a big a cappella line that went something like, "With a mother at home to support!" I was thrilled because not only did I have to cross the stage and come back, but I had a line to sing. I was doing fine with that one until one night they raised the key without telling me, and the unexpected change pushed my voice up into the stratosphere. When I tried to hit the high note on "support," a sound came out that I had never heard before. My voice cracked, and all I could do was sustain it like a yodel. Afterward, I was miffed to realize that simply because I was a dancer rather than a singer, they hadn't prepared me or rehearsed the change to give me a chance to adjust. I knew it was nothing personal—they didn't bother to tell me because I wasn't important enough. As a member of the dancing chorus, I was as expendable as the line in the song, which was promptly cut.

We came back to New York and opened at the 46th Street Theatre on October 14, 1961. The show had been well received in Philadelphia, but the producers didn't yet realize what a hit they had on their hands. Certainly, they were not expecting a musical that would run three years for a total of 1,417 performances. In fact, the producers didn't throw an opening night party until the following year when they knew they had a hit and the show had won seven Tony Awards, including Best Musical. However, there was a party on opening night that was hosted in a Park

Avenue apartment by a socialite friend of Rudy Vallee's. That night is especially memorable for me because my parents attended, and I found myself torn again between my mother and father, their visit turning into an unexpected emotional roller coaster.

I was looking forward to making peace with them now that I had my first Broadway show. It seemed like after all the adversity and conflict of my leaving home, I finally had something to celebrate. I hoped my parents would see that I could make a living in the theater, and that for once they could be proud of their daughter. The opening of the show went fine and had the audience on their feet. I had gotten my parents house seats in the mezzanine, and they did seem happy for me, especially my mother, whose dreams for me seemed to be coming true at last.

But I remember being in a car with them afterward, going to the party, and my father started berating my mother for being so excited by the glamorous scene and the people she was meeting. He criticized her for "fawning." At one point, he lashed out at her, saying, "They're no better than us! They're no more important than we are." It was one of those times when I wanted so much for everything to go right, but somehow it turned ugly, with communication between us breaking down just as it had when I was growing up. In a way, my father was right, but how he expressed himself was unnecessary and hurtful, as if he wanted to spoil my mother's night, as well as mine.

It was painful for me to see him make her cry. Torn between them, and feeling the need to protect my mother, I took my mother's side by saying to my father in an offhanded way, "You need a new suit." It was a ridiculous comment that I immediately regretted. There was nothing wrong with his suit, even though he wasn't wearing anything nearly as elegant as the others at the party. He looked like a blue-collar worker from Middle America, which was exactly what he was. I wasn't being the loving daughter by rubbing it in as I did, and making him feel even more out of place, but at moments such as this, that old father-daughter conflict would surface. There didn't seem to be anything that either of us could do about it. At some point during the run of the show, I went to a psychologist for the first time, and my family gave me plenty to talk about, even if I wasn't yet able to come to terms with my past.

During the next two years that I stayed with the show, I was making the Equity minimum of about $118 a week, which brought some stability into my life and was enough for me to pay for acting, singing, and dance classes, as well as my share of the rent, which was then $70 a month. After we opened, I had some sweet dates with Bobby Feuer, Cy's son. It was a pleasure recently to greet him backstage after one of my shows. He proudly introduced me to his wife and daughter, who is a dancer.

Later in the run of *How to Succeed,* I met Abe Burrows's son, who was just home from college. Jimmy was warm, gentle, and funny, and I liked him a lot. On our first date he took me to Toffenetti's, where we immersed ourselves in conversation and ice cream sodas. I was more relaxed and began to enjoy the experience of dating in a way that I was never able to in high school. However, in the years to come, at different times, I also more or less supported a couple of actor boyfriends I met in class. They were aspiring James Dean types, without the talent to fulfill the image or achieve the success. I gave them money out of my own insecurity, plus the need to feel appreciated and somehow in control. My low self-esteem kept me from being a great judge of character, sometimes, when it came to picking boyfriends.

I had little time for an active social life during the run of *How to Succeed.* I was performing eight shows a week and studying every day. I started taking Charles Nelson Reilly's musical theater class at the Herbert Berghof Studio on Bank Street. I always did a ballet barre, but I also took jazz classes from the legendary teacher Luigi Lewis (with whom I continue to study today) and acting classes from Joshua Shelley, who taught at Variety Arts. Josh had been a member of the Group Theatre during its last years, and had been blacklisted as a young actor during the McCarthy era. Founded in 1931 under the leadership of Robert Lewis, Elia Kazan, Lee Strasberg, Harold Clurman, and Cheryl Crawford, the Group Theatre developed a marvelous ensemble with talents like Stella Adler, Herbert Berghof, Lee J. Cobb, Karl Malden, Clifford Odets, and Irwin Shaw. While much of the work was based on Stanislavski's acting technique, the Group was a hotbed of radical idealism and attempted to dramatize the political, social, and economic issues of the time.

Josh was now teaching acting to make a living after losing the momentum of his acting career. He also made a living at the racetrack. He was part of a group called "the speed boys," because of their surefire handicapping abilities. Like Josh, they had suffered career losses for a time because they took the Fifth Amendment when called into those hideous hearings. Others in this group included Paddy Chayefsky, Stanley Prager, and Alex March. Josh was outspoken on many subjects and at times used his class as a soapbox. He didn't try to hide his anger and bitterness. Though he occasionally lashed out brusquely at his students, he could be very funny. I laughed a lot in his class, and I learned a great deal from him.

Josh, being a Method teacher, emphasized techniques like emotional recall and sense memory, to find the appropriate condition of a character in order to fuel the action in the scene. I learned certain relaxation exercises that enabled me to begin to comprehend "being, without movement or words." These exercises are necessary steps for actors to achieve trust, to be able to experience "being without artifice." Others in Josh's class included Mia Farrow, Michael J. Pollard, the singer Johnny Ray, and Jon Voight, who was my first acting partner in a scene from *All My Sons*.

At the time, Jon was performing in *The Sound of Music* and living in a hotel at 70th Street and Broadway. I was nearby on West End and 85th Street, and we often rehearsed together either at his place or mine. We were both diligent about the work. More than twenty years later, Jon and I reminisced about the early days, and he told me in passing that he had a crush on me at the time, though he was seeing someone else. Even with his charming admission, I didn't have the courage to tell him the feeling had been mutual. I thought Jon was the most divine young man, and I sensed the serious, shy side of him, as I did in myself. After we did our scene, he expressed his displeasure with Josh as a teacher, and told me, "I'm going to study with Sandy Meisner, and that's where you should go, Donna."

Sanford Meisner had been one of the founding members of the Group Theatre, and was now teaching at the Neighborhood Playhouse. I took Jon's advice and went to Meisner for an interview. The meeting was like an impromptu audition that turned into a withering experience. I found myself tongue-tied, unable to speak up for myself when he dismissed me, saying, "You are very young and I don't think this class will be good for you, because you haven't had enough life experience. We deal with a lot of powerful emotions, and I don't think you're old enough." He allowed that I might try again some other time, but it didn't matter because I was crushed, as I had been after my ABT audition. I still didn't know how to deal with rejection.

I continued to study with Josh, and later was brought into a directing course by my friend Paul Blake from the renowned Lee Strasberg at the Actors Studio. I treasured that experience. I had to prepare the "Ice Cream" scene from the Sheldon Harnick–Jerry Bock show, *She Loves Me,* performing the part of Amalia. The scene took place in a bedroom, and I was in my pajamas. I was to write a letter, and the scene built to the point that I started singing, until I was interrupted by the doorbell. I open the door to the last person I want to see (George), having not yet discovered that he is the man I've fallen in love with.

Watching my run-through of the scene with the class, Lee sat rather gloomily until the end. Then, he suddenly became animated and rushed in front of us. He acted the scene out and invented the staging, as he spoke, "You see, it's all about sex, sex is the ball game! When you get up out of bed, you've been tossing and turning all night. You haven't slept. You're disheveled and you don't have your top buttoned. So you show a lot of skin—that's sexy! You titillate the audience! Then you go to the door." He was now acting it out for me. "You open it. You see George. You slam the door in his face, and then you become embarrassed."

Describing how I was to approach that one moment gave me a blueprint for every moment in the scene. I thought his direction was fantastic. He showed me that a musical theater piece, even that one little scene, could be a seamless work of art, as well as being highly entertaining. What Lee taught me was that I had to find the character's intention and make the conflict real for me, which in that scene took the form of the rising sexual tension that had to build before I started singing. When the writing is good, every moment can be explored and fulfilled in that way. I liked the fact that he mentioned pleasing the audience, like an old vaudevillian. This was not the usual approach with his teaching. The Method was the "method," and not the result. I came out of the experience thinking that Strasberg could have been a great director of musicals.

Years later, just after *A Chorus Line* opened on Broadway, I spent a delightful evening having a late supper at Sardi's with Lee and his wife, Anna. They both loved the show, and Strasberg's praise of my interpretation meant everything to me. I didn't want to put him on the spot, so I never asked him, "Do you remember that girl who sang 'Ice Cream' in your directors workshop fifteen years ago?" I wish I had, if only to thank him.

The progress I was making in my classes made me more and more discontented with staying in the chorus. In fact, I was a terrible chorus dancer because I tended to do things my own way and never quite fit into the line. I might hear a different part of the arrangement, like a horn line might stand out to me one night, and then other nights it might be the drums or the violin section. I would interpret the sound emotionally, as in an acting scene, with a point of view. I did the steps that we were given, of course, but I liked to change things so it wouldn't be quite the same every night. I would do an épaulement, with a little head or shoulder thing, and it was often just enough to pull focus, however, that's not why I did it, I just wanted to dance to the music.

A few years later when Michael Bennett was choreographing a big industrial show in New York, Bob Avian, his assistant, would complain about me saying, "That girl is driving me crazy. She's not doing it like everyone else." Michael just said, "It's okay, leave her alone." This would come back to haunt us, but in a creative way, when it became part of Cassie's dilemma in *A Chorus Line*. In terms of the theater's hierarchy, dancers in the chorus were treated as second-class citizens. This disturbing reality in the theater would one day be a motivating force behind Michael's desire to design a show for dancers.

The lack of respect for chorus dancers bothered me a great deal, and I made up my mind at the end of my run in *How to Succeed* that I would never dance in the chorus again. I was also aware of my age, and had in mind specific goals and set time limits for myself. I did a newspaper interview at the time and told the reporter, "I'm very ambitious. . . . I want to be a star. I think I'll like acting, although that is very new to me, and I do love singing. But, of course, dancing is what I really love. My agent says he thinks I could be like Carol Lawrence, who does all three."

I naively assumed that I would continue working and that somehow I would always be on the Broadway stage, performing in a new show, whatever it might be. At this point, I was basically considered one of Bob Fosse's favored dancers, an honor I was slow to grasp, and he soon asked me to be in his next show, *Pleasures and Palaces.* This was a difficult decision for me. Choreographers of Fosse's stature expect loyalty from their dancers. I was terribly flattered that he had phoned me to invite me to work with him again, but I turned him down because of my stubborn determination to go on to larger roles. As it turned out, *Pleasures and Palaces* closed before reaching Broadway.

Bobby later asked me to dance in yet another new show he was directing and choreographing, *Sweet Charity,* which was to be a vehicle for Gwen's return to the stage after a five-year absence. I said no, again. This would be a lasting regret after I saw the show and realized that a Bob Fosse chorus is not a typical chorus. "Big Spender" was a showstopper, as was every dancer who was in it. After I turned down that offer, he wouldn't ask me to work for him again for two decades, when that same show was revived. By then, I would have enough experience behind me to take on the title role. Still, I look back at the road not taken and wonder at what a very different career I might have had if I had been content to remain in the fold as a Bob Fosse dancer.

Chapter 3

---&---

PROMISES, PROMISES

While my experience in the chorus of *How to Succeed* confirmed that my talent held a certain promise, my career had hardly taken off, and at the age of twenty, patience was not one of my virtues. Interviewed by one of my hometown newspapers in Detroit, my mother hinted at my ongoing frustrations: "Donna has been on her own since she was 16, and we couldn't help her financially. It has been hard, and her rise seems much slower to her than it has to us at home."

I made a serious resolution that year, saying to myself, "I'm going to make it by the time I'm twenty-two." Over the next several years, each birthday forced me to a compromise, adding one more year to my deadline for success (a ritual later portrayed in *A Chorus Line*).

My decision to avoid dancing in the chorus might have slowed my progress even more, but at the beginning of 1964, I was fortunate enough to be cast in a national touring company of the hit farce, *A Funny Thing Happened on the Way to the Forum*. As the ingénue lead, Philia, I was to act and sing. In fact, the role called for no dancing at all, which at the time seemed a dream come true. I discovered my soprano voice through voice training and I was as excited as I was nervous to audition for my first singing role. I was to have the opportunity to sing numbers from Stephen Sondheim's wonderful score, and also to have the chance to work for the legendary director George Abbott.

Mr. Abbott, as everyone always called him, and his stage manager, Ruth Mitchell, oversaw the early rehearsals. The book was by Burt Shevelove and Larry Gelbart, and Jack Cole was the original choreographer. The story has often been told how before the original *Forum* opened on Broadway, Jerome Robbins came in as show doctor and saved the production. Robbins did the staging and choreographed the marvelous opening number, "Comedy Tonight." The leads in the touring company included veteran actors Jerry Lester (who was sensational in the Zero Mostel role), Arnold Stang, Erik Rhodes, Edward Everett Horton, and Paul Hartman. Paul and his wife, Grace, had been a famous vaudeville dance team. George Martin staged our production.

Our tour was scheduled for 350 performances and ran most of the year, with lengthy stays in Philadelphia, Boston, Minneapolis, Milwaukee, St. Louis, Chicago, and Detroit. Before hitting the road, we would also give one performance in New York at the Alvin Theatre for the Broadway community. With such a long run, the challenge for me as a performer was to find the humor each night and to make it as fresh and spontaneous as it had been when I auditioned for the part. That audition had been memorable, as it was one of my first singing and acting auditions, and Mr. Abbott and Mr. Sondheim were in the audience. I remember standing in the wings with other actresses, waiting for my name to be called, then walking out onto the empty stage. With the lights glaring, I was unable to see where they were sitting, but I knew, of course, that they could see me. Working with the stage manager, Ruth Mitchell, I was to read a scene between Hero and Philia, in which she reveals her limited education. I hadn't yet learned how to channel my nervous energy into the work. Holding the script, I was shaking and my tremulous hands made it difficult for me to read the scene. I thought my timing was off, but apparently it was the perfect timing for Mr. Abbott, who soon became hysterical with laughter.

I had no idea what was so funny, but I was pleased when I was given the opportunity to sing for him. I had prepared the song, "Baubles, Bangles and Beads," from *Kismet,* and as I began the number, my nerves caused me to sing in a key that was a third too high. The song was high anyway, but I kept going. With my quivering coloratura, I'm sure I sounded like a warbling chipmunk. But Mr. Abbott had another fit of laughter and I got the part, without really knowing what I was doing.

Once we started touring, I started to have trouble being consistent with the role. I didn't have enough experience to know how, night after night, to re-create those same funny moments that I had at the audition. If I was in the right frame of mind and feeling buoyant, in spite of myself, my timing was right. The stage manager would say afterward, "That was great! Perfect, Donna! You got all the right laughs. Do it that way again." I hadn't yet grasped the technique of re-creating moments by playing specific intentions. I would try to remember *how* I said a line instead of *why* the character was saying the line. I would try my scene a hundred different ways, and received direction from a few of the character actors. The audience eventually helped me make my choices with their response—or lack of response. It took me almost the whole year to re-create, eight times a week, the spontaneous success of my audition.

Before the show opened in February at the Shubert Theatre in Boston, my understudy came to me with a heartfelt request. Her family happened to live in Boston, and she asked if I would feign illness on opening night so her parents could have the pleasure of seeing her perform. I was reluctant at first, but she made such a persuasive appeal that I finally gave in to her request. After the opening, I realized my folly at missing the performance when I saw her on the cover of the arts section in my costume and wig. Her parents were socially connected, and she received a great deal of attention in the press, with headlines like "Local Girl Steals Show." I was more than happy to make a "miraculous recovery," and quickly returned to my role. That was a lesson learned, and I never let it happen again.

As we continued to travel, I made it my habit again to further my education in each new city by visiting the local museums and graveyards. The highlight of the tour for me came when we played Detroit for two months that summer and I had the chance to stay at home with my family. This homecoming was a happy one for the most part. Not only was I performing in *Forum*, but I also put together a concert, renting a hall at the Art Institute of Detroit for the occasion. To help me prepare, I hired Michael Rosco, a classical musician, an elegant gray-haired gentleman who was the assistant conductor for the *Forum* orchestra. We rehearsed in the pit each day for several hours before the show. The repertory I chose was varied and included Italian art songs, some Puccini, English operetta pieces, a Noel Coward number from *Bittersweet,* and songs from Rodgers and Hammerstein's *The King and I.*

This was my first public concert, and with my family in the audience I was extremely nervous. But my performance was well received, and I made a reel-to-reel tape recording of the event that I gave to my parents. Later, my mother told me that my father enjoyed listening to the tape. I took this as a great compliment, even though it was my mother who told me. While I was now on better terms with both my parents, our conflicts from the past nevertheless continued to travel with me, unresolved. Only much later, after years of analysis, would I realize how much my choices in life and day-to-day behavior were affected by issues I had buried but never quite managed to quell.

After returning to New York at the end of the year, I was invited to audition for a new NBC television variety show called *Hullabaloo.* The invitation came from David Winters, who was dating one of my roommates and had been one of the original cast members of *West Side Story.* David and another dancer from that cast, Jaime Rogers, had been hired as the choreographers for *Hullabaloo.* The audition was held at Variety Arts, and scores of Broadway dancers tried out.

David and Jaime's audition was like a high-powered jazz class. I was one of four girls and four boys who were chosen for the show's dance ensemble. Although this was a departure from Broadway for me, I was thrilled to be working with David and Jaime. Because they had been involved with *West Side Story,* they were much admired icons and role models for the young dancers of my generation. That same year, I served as David's assistant choreographer on the movie *Billie,* which starred Patty Duke.

Before the days of MTV and music videos, *Hullabaloo* was an innovative showcase for popular music and young talent, as well as more established stars. The idea was to highlight the Top 40 songs, often with us dancing behind the performers. Produced by Gary Smith, the show was shot at the NBC studios on an enormous soundstage in front of a live

My first formal portrait.

In 1916, my maternal grandmother,
Gladys, dressed in her brother's clothes
to sneak into the men's social club.

My mom and dad, after he'd just
returned from the Army.

Mom, my constant support.

Baby ballerina.

By the time I was thirteen, I had already begun finding my personal expression in dance.

Shortly before I ran away to
New York City. I'm about
fifteen.

7

An aspiring dancer
in Central Park,
New York City.

8

9

At a 1970 taping of *Dark Shadows*: I appear as Olivia Corey aka Amanda Harris, and David Selby is Grant Douglas, aka Quentin Collins.

10

On the set of *Hullabaloo*; (from left to right) Roosevelt Grier, me, Michael Bennett, and Barbara Monte.

"Turkey Lurkey Time" from *Promises, Promises*. *Dance Magazine*, October 1971; (from left to right) Baayork Lee, me, and Margo Sappington

12

I played the Rose in the film version of *The Little Prince*, 1974.

13

"Don't pop the head, Cassie."

14

The night my father died, Laurence Olivier was in the audience.

I was honored with a Hirschfeld caricature when I returned to *A Chorus Line* in 1986.

audience. Peter Matz conducted the NBC orchestra, and there was a celebrity host each week. Over the next two years they included Frankie Avalon, Paul Anka, Frank Sinatra, Jr., Trini Lopez, Annette Funicello, Jack Jones, George Hamilton, Johnny Mathis, Michael Landon, and Dean Jones. And there were other musical guests like the Rolling Stones, Herman's Hermits, Chubby Checker, Barbara McNair, Brenda Lee, Lesley Gore, Petula Clark, and the Supremes, who made one of their first TV appearances with us. Before each show aired, we would spend a long, fast-paced week rehearsing with each of the hosts and guest artists. For me, the experience was an exposure to another side of show business, and I worked as hard as I had on any Broadway production.

All of us dancers were trained in Broadway and jazz styles, and we had a great time crossing over to do trendy pop dances like the Jerk and the Monkey. I used to joke, "We brought the Jerk to new heights." The style was sort of *West Side Story* to a different beat, blending 1960s pop and disco with double-turns and jetés. The sets were rather avant-garde for TV at the time. Though rather tame by today's standards, even our costumes were considered cutting-edge. The girls usually wore various combinations of pleated skirts and sweaters with smashing bold colors and white designer boots by Courrèges. Thanks to the power of television, we received national recognition and a steady stream of fan mail. A TV columnist, Jack O'Brian, singled me out week after week, and eventually I had a following of my own. My being a regular on the show seemed to impress my parents and relatives more than anything that I had done previously. But I always had it in mind that I would be returning to Broadway and more serious work sooner or later.

One of my partners on the show was a young dancer from Buffalo, New York, named Michael Bennett, and the two of us hit it off from the first rehearsal. Michael and I were terrific together, and as time went on, we became popular as partners. We seemed to complement each other with our dancing. Michael was a strong jumper, sexy and always dynamic. With my ballet background, I was more lyrical, though able to match his energy and drive. Despite my insecurities, I was aware of my feminine image. I had known as soon as I came to New York and started working that I could turn heads. I was even voted "The Girl That the

Stagehands Would Most Like To . . ." This award was announced by Cy Feuer at our opening night party for *How to Succeed*. Even though it made me blush, I took it as a compliment.

When I performed, I could be the elegant young lady or the sex kitten, even though inside I never felt like the most elegant or sexiest girl alive. Those outward qualities I projected didn't relate to my personality or to who I was in my private life, but I was able to express them in my dancing. Dancing provided a setting for my sexual energy to blossom, but what you see is not always what you get. So far, I was unable to escape from that "look but don't touch" syndrome.

I remember one time asking Michael lightheartedly, "What do you want to be when you grow up?" Without the slightest hesitation, he shot back, "A choreographer." I didn't think much of it then, except to admire him for having such an ambitious goal, as he was obviously aware of the fate of most dancers in this business, especially those without much formal education. Michael later told me, "When I was a kid, I looked in the mirror and realized I was never going to be a star. I was too short and I wasn't handsome enough. I wanted to be tall and blond, everything I wasn't. And since I was never going to do it onstage myself, I made up my mind to choreograph and do it through other people." As long as I knew him, his love affair with the theater and his finding his calling as a choreographer were driven by that self-critical discontent and what he saw as his own limitations as a performer.

During our second season, the dancers were given their own dance number, and we were each given the opportunity to choreograph our own section. Michael created an exciting drum solo for himself. I begged him to help me because I was going to do the last section of the number and didn't know where to begin. That was the first time he choreographed for me, and it was a great success. The piece was highlighted by a complicated series of jeté turns in a circle. I was a strong turner, and the combination showed me off to advantage. He gave me incredible freedom in that regard, choreographing to my strengths. After that first experience, we fell into a kind of mutual appreciation. Because of our creative rapport, Michael Bennett would turn out to be the greatest single influence in my career, for better and for worse.

Although Michael and I didn't socialize very often back then, we had a warm brother-and-sister type of relationship. We discovered that we had a great deal in common. Like me, Michael came from a dysfunctional home where there was tension and conflict rather than nurturing. His background was Italian and Jewish. The family name was DiFiglia, which Michael changed to the name of his school, Bennett High, when he started performing. As a boy, he was put in the position of having to take care of his younger brother Frank while defending his mother from his abusive father. Like me, Michael always yearned for his father's love, and dancing was a kind of imaginary refuge for him as it had been for me. He arranged his marbles like formations on a stage. At seventeen, Michael dropped out of school and was cast in a European tour of *West Side Story* which was where he met Bob Avian, who would be his lifelong friend and associate. After the tour, Michael moved to New York and danced in the chorus of several Broadway shows, including *Here's Love, Bajour,* and *Once Upon a Mattress.* Michael had also gained experience choreographing for summer stock. He was guided by agent Jack Lenny, a shrewd, but kindly father figure, who also became my agent after seeing me in *Carousel* in summer stock.

During the two seasons that we worked together on *Hullabaloo,* I had only a vague idea of Michael's sexual orientation. I just thought there were people with big sexual appetites and then there were people like me. I really was still clueless as far as what it meant to be gay. And he had girlfriends as well as boyfriends, which made it even more confusing for me. I visited Michael one time just after he and one of his boyfriends, Larry Fuller, moved into an apartment together. Larry was a dancer, and he and Michael had a spacious one-bedroom place on West End Avenue. I was under the impression that the two of them were just roommates. I remember Michael was painting their bedroom that day, and I pitched in to help him. There was an enormous brass bed in the room, and at one point, I said to Michael, "This is really nice, but where is Larry going to sleep?" Michael looked at me, taken aback. Then he said, "Oh, I'm going to put him in the corner over there in a single bed."

Years later he reminded me of my visit that day and admitted that he had been so enamored of me at the time that he couldn't bring himself to explain the situation or talk about his relationship with Larry. Michael had tried to hide his gay lifestyle because he wanted to live up to my expectations of him as a heterosexual man. Looking back on the two of us, I can see there was already a serious conflict built into our relationship, long before our collaboration in the theater started and we became more personally entangled.

While still working on *Hullabaloo,* I became romantically involved with a manager of recording artists and a promoter in the recording industry named Al Schwartz. Al was a charming, charismatic character who at one time worked with Sam Cooke, Damita Jo, Timi Yuro, and later, Stevie Nicks. My relationship with Al began with a certain resistance on my part and against my better judgment. He was much older than I was, and I thought he was a little too flashy with his expensive, shiny Italian suits. Hanging around the set, he had asked me out a number of times and I had rejected all his invitations. He made me nervous, but I liked the attention he gave me as well as his assertiveness. At a certain point, I relented and said, "Okay, if I go out with you one time, will you leave me alone?" We went to a Chinese restaurant in the Theater District, and I enjoyed his company because he showed me a more vulnerable side by talking about his family and upbringing. I decided there was more to Al than just the glossy exterior, and we soon started dating regularly.

Al moved in glamorous circles, and his world fascinated me. It was a special thrill to go to the famous Jilly's on 52nd Street, and to meet Jilly, who was his friend, and to be introduced to Frank Sinatra, with all his bodyguards. Moving in those circles, Al, a Brooklyn native, exuded the kind of savvy, sophisticated confidence that I lacked. He could be a real mensch too. He knew how to take care of business, and he was never afraid to speak up to people. I loved his sense of humor, and we had great times socializing and double-dating with friends. Longing for a sense of security and stability in my life, I soon moved into Al's apartment on East 64th Street. I did feel I loved him, and he seemed to love me.

While we were together, we moved several times, though I didn't initially understand why. Al had a knack for finding grand, luxurious apartments. I was unaware that he was living well beyond his means, with his Jaguar sports car and upscale lifestyle. He had a taste for expensive toys. I thought it was a little strange that he had a set of fancy Dunhill golf clubs even though he didn't play golf, but that was the kind of character he was. He appeared to be successful in the record industry, though I wondered about his business sense because he joked about having turned down Barbra Streisand as a client. Al had an office in the Brill Building that he went to during the week, but when I began finding Yonkers Racetrack tickets in his pockets, I realized that he was spending a lot of time out of the office, betting on horses.

Al made excuses, and I didn't realize at first how serious his gambling problem was. I was in such a state of ignorance-is-bliss that I agreed when he suggested that we get married. Gladys didn't approve of Al, and at first I chalked it up as a generational thing. Al and I had visited my grandmother in Illinois one time early in our relationship, and I remembered how awful and rejected I felt when she pleaded with me not to rush into marriage with this man. I thought it was because she didn't approve of Al being Jewish. She would later tell her neighbors that Schwartz was a "German name." Even though my parents were more fair-minded, I didn't tell them about my engagement or invite them to the wedding. In April of 1966, I went ahead with the marriage, essentially as an act of rebellion, fearful of more rejection, and because I didn't want them to feel they had to pay for anything. I told my mother and father only later because "I didn't want it to be a big deal." However, they thoughtfully sent out wedding announcements for us, as it seemed the proper thing to do.

Our wedding was a rushed, no-frills affair that involved nothing more than a visit to City Hall on a day when Al had to get back to his office. One of Al's friends, Joe Weinstein, was there with a carnation in his lapel, and we waited with several other couples, sitting on folding chairs in a bleak outer office. Al was impatient, and I was in a total daze, detached from it all and feeling like a coward. I had acquiesced and was just going through the motions. I remember thinking *I can still get out of this if I just get up and walk out.* The judge wanted to leave for lunch and tried to get us to come back later. Al managed to prevail upon him, and he performed a whirlwind ceremony with his coat over his arm. It was

"I do, I do," and then everyone left. Al and Joe went to their offices, and I suddenly found myself standing alone at the elevator. The deed was done. That afternoon I went home to our apartment and set about washing the kitchen floor. I remember being on my knees and asking myself, "What just happened? What am I doing here?"

After *Hullabaloo* went off the air at the end of August, I continued taking classes and also performed in some industrials. In fact, I was sort of the industrial queen of New York at that point because I could sing a high C and tap-dance at the same time. I was bringing in money and giving all my paychecks to Al. He teased me, saying, "Honey, one of the reasons I love you is because you never ask about money." As time went on, I was *afraid* to ask. He lavished me with beautiful gifts—a pearl necklace and a fox coat. He had also given me a lovely gold bracelet; then one day I noticed it was missing. Later I discovered that he had taken it to a pawn shop. Al was his own worst enemy, but he was never mean, and he possessed enough charm most of the time to be able to keep the affection of those friends whose loans he would never pay back.

One time when we were living in a penthouse on the Upper East Side, I came home after doing some grocery shopping and found a man with a cigar and a notepad rummaging in our living room. I said politely, "Excuse me, can I help you?" He said, "I'm the marshal. The rent hasn't been paid in six months and I'm here to take inventory." I rushed into our second bedroom that was Al's home office, and in a panic I asked him what was going on. "Who is that man in our living room who is going to take our furniture?" He said, "Don't bother me now, Donna. Can't you see I'm on the phone!" Still, I stayed with him, unable to fathom what he was doing with the money. I became an enabler, a co-dependent before I knew there was such a thing. In desperation, I told him, "I'll help you, Al. Just don't hide things from me."

A short time later I had an audition downtown and found myself running late. Al came to the rescue by offering to drive me. I waited in the lobby for him to bring the car up from the garage. After a few minutes, I started getting nervous, so I thought I would walk outside to meet him at the curb when he pulled up. As I walked out the lobby door, I came face to face with Al. "Where's the car?" I asked.

"They took it."

"Someone stole it?" I shrieked.

"No," he said, "they took it. They took it back!"

I added another word to my vocabulary: "Repossessed."

We soon moved into another fabulous, though smaller, apartment in the Chalfont on West 72nd Street. I continued living with the deluded hope that things would somehow work out for us. In the summer of 1966, I was cast in a new musical, *A Joyful Noise,* which was scheduled for a long tryout run out of town on the tent circuit. One of the show's producers, Edward Padula, wrote the book and was later also credited as director, though there would be more to the story by the time *A Joyful Noise* opened on Broadway. Ed had hired Michael Bennett to choreograph, and this would be Michael's first Broadway-bound show as a choreographer. The star was John Raitt, and in the show he played a wandering Tennessee balladeer named Shade Motley. I played a preacher's daughter, Jenny Lee, who, against her father's wishes, fell in love with the yodeling singer.

My role in *A Joyful Noise* was another one that involved no dancing, and this time I really felt like I was missing out. I remember going to rehearsals and watching Michael choreograph numbers for his chorus, which included Tommy Tune, Baayork Lee, and Scott Pearson, all three of whom would later be identified as Michael Bennett dancers and protégés. Michael was involved with Leland Palmer, his dance assistant, who was also in the chorus. She would later portray the Gwen Verdon character in Bob Fosse's film *All that Jazz.* I knew I was not being reasonable, but their relationship really annoyed me at times. I was also having a very difficult time taking charge of my role while the show was going through constant rewrites. I was very accommodating, to the point of accommodating myself right out of my own choices as an actress.

Although we received good notices out of town (Michael's dances would later win him his first Tony nomination), the book never quite came together and it was clear that the show was in trouble. A Hollywood director-producer, Dore Schary, was brought in to take over the direction. He had a mighty career as a studio head running MGM for a while until he was fired. It can happen to anyone, even the mightiest.

This fact did not console me when my contract for Broadway was not picked up. Al told me after our last performance on the road, since he was now acting as my manager. There were no cries of anguish or rage on my part. It was a solemn and inwardly devastating moment. I took it so well. I remembered reading on my first-grade report card: "Donna takes disappointments well." No, she didn't, in reality, and this was a terrible blow. My life in the theater seemed like it was over. Who would ever hire me again after being fired from my first important role? I later took little solace in the fact that the show's Broadway run lasted only twelve performances.

I felt like I only had my husband to turn to for support. But our marriage was deteriorating and my going to therapy wasn't solving Al's problems. He would do things that made me realize how desperate he was, like opening my mail and stealing a birthday check that my Grandmother Gladys sent me. When Grandfather Dillard died that year, we didn't even have enough money for me to fly to Illinois to be there for my grandmother. I felt trapped with him, but I blamed myself rather than Al.

The final rude awakening came one day when my mother called to ask me when Al was going to honor his word and pay back a loan he had taken, unbeknownst to me, from my father. I was shocked to learn that Al had the audacity to appeal to my father to help him financially. Al had actually conned my father, though of course, he didn't think of it that way. When I confronted him, he acted remorseful, and insisted, "Oh, I'll make good on that loan." But my parents had to refinance their mortgage, and my father never recovered financially. It was more guilt for me to bear, and at that point I knew that I had to break away from Al.

I had no job and nothing to fall back on, so in desperation I went to Jaime Rogers, who happened to be choreographing a new George Abbott show, The Education of H*Y*M*A*N K*A*P*L*A*N. I begged Jaime for a job. I told him, "I'll do anything! I'll get coffee for you. I need a job to get out of my marriage." (That "begging moment" found its way into Cassie's appeal to Zach in A Chorus Line.) Thanks to Jaime and Mr. Abbott, a role was eventually created for me. Benjamin Zavin wrote the script, based on a series of *New Yorker* stories written by Leo Rosten. Oscar Brand and Paul Nassau contributed the score. The cast included Tom Bosley, Barbara Minkus, and Hal Linden in the leads. I was to be the only Irish immigrant in a comic story about Jewish immigration, and I was given a song and dance at the end of the first act called, "Ain't It a Pretty Night?," along with David Gold and Dick Latessa of *Hairspray* fame.

At the age of eighty, Mr. Abbott was as brilliant and powerful as ever, with his tall, patrician good looks. He made me feel like I had been taken back into the fold. During rehearsals, he would beckon to me when he gave the company a break. Then a rehearsal pianist would play a waltz, and Mr. Abbott and I would dance around the studio. He had a passion for ballroom dancing and was known to be a frequent patron of the Roseland dance hall, going there with whomever his latest paramour happened to be. Dancing was simply Mr. Abbott's way of relaxing, and each time he waltzed with me, I was in heaven.

I remember that on opening night, the company assembled onstage with Mr. Abbott before the curtain went up. We had requested a special meeting, and we presented him with a long necklace of "love beads," in keeping with the hippie fashion trend of the time. He was very pleased, and placed them around his neck with a jaunty air and beaming grin. We all had great expectations that night. But the show opened on April 4, 1968, the same night that Martin Luther King was assassinated. News of the tragedy arrived during the first act, but Mr. Abbott wouldn't let anyone tell us what had happened. Mayor John Lindsay was in the audience, and he had to leave the theater. After the intermission, we played the second act to a much smaller and less enthusiastic audience. The show closed by the end of the month, but for me it had been a lifesaver, enabling me to regain my independence once again.

My little comeback continued when I was cast in a revival tour of another George Abbott hit, the Irving Berlin musical *Call Me Madam*. The revival featured Ethel Merman as the Washington-hostess-turned-lady-ambassador, Sally Adams, a role that Merman triumphantly created in the original 1950 production. She had a clause in her contract that specified that Russell Nype, who had won a Tony playing her new secretary in the original production, would also serve as her personal driver on the tour. Russell didn't mind in the least. He was a kind, affable man, and he knew that Miss Merman required special care. I was to play Princess Maria, an ingénue part normally performed by a singer-actress. Our choreographer Buff Shurr was delighted because I was also a dancer, meaning that he could give my character two production numbers.

I remember how excited I was the first day Miss Merman joined us for a run-through. We were going to open the tour in August at the St. Louis Municipal Opera, an enormous open-air pavilion that seated twelve thousand. Merman walked in with Russell, and they sat at the director's table. I was dancing my newly acquired routine in "The Occarina," rising to performance level because I knew she was there. After I finished to applause from the other company members, I heard her booming voice cut through for everyone to hear, "Who did she fuck to get two dance numbers!" There was a stunned silence, then nervous laughter from the cast. I didn't say a word. I'll never know whether she was just trying to be funny, or really meant to give me a warning. Maybe it was a little of both.

After that incident, Merman was standoffish toward me, never even offering a hello when going from dressing room to stage door. I would watch her performances from the wings whenever I could, captivated by her incredible stage presence. Her way of working was so precise, with attention paid to every detail and every gesture, and she expected the same from others. I worked hard to be consistent and to meet her expectations. This was a sweltering summer, and of course there was no air-conditioning outdoors. Despite the heat, I thought the show was playing well, until one day the stage manager, John Wessel, came to my dressing room and said, "I have a note from Miss Merman for you."

I said, "Oh sure, what is it?"

Hesitating, he said, "Remember, it's not from me, it's from Miss Merman."

I said, "Please, anything!"

He told me, "All right. She said to please stop sweating so much. It disturbs her concentration onstage."

I searched for a twinkle in his eye or some sign that he was joking, but there was none. I tried to be agreeable and said, "Okay, I'll see what I can do."

There was little I *could* do. We tried having towels waiting for me in the wings when I came offstage, but I don't think I stopped sweating until we left Missouri.

We were in Ohio when I gave my two weeks' notice. I was leaving the tour because I had been cast in another Broadway musical, *Promises, Promises,* which was scheduled to start rehearsing at the end of the summer. During my last performance of *Call Me Madam,* while I was onstage doing a scene with Merman, her eyes crossed and she suddenly made a strange little clucking sound while I was speaking. I hesitated, thinking something had to be wrong. I had never seen anything like it; the way she changed her deportment was frightening. I continued the scene until she did it again! I was frantic when I came offstage. But then the stage manager informed me that it was an old vaudeville tradition. When a company member leaves a show, on the last night, the other actors drop their professional discipline to pay homage by trying to break up their departing friend—sometimes, by turning upstage and smiling with blacked-out teeth, or by crossing their eyes. That was good to know, since I thought she was having a stroke!

Afterward, I was touched by Miss Merman's homage, and even more so later when I found out that the last person who played my role was her daughter, Ethel Jr., who had committed suicide earlier that year. It occurred to me how difficult it must have been for Merman to have to look at me wearing the same costume her daughter had worn. She was still in mourning, and I suspected that was why she had agreed to the tour in the first place, as touring was not something Miss Merman ordinarily did. Being onstage must have been her way of coping and keeping her sanity in the face of emotional adversity, as it was for many of us.

My agent, Jack Lenny, was the one who arranged for me to audition for *Promises, Promises,* which was a David Merrick production. There were three smaller roles for secretaries who shared two songs. My part initially didn't involve any dancing, which pleased Jack, who felt my priority now should be singing and acting roles if I was going to make a mark. David Merrick was seldom directly involved with the day-to-day running of the show, but he had a hatchet man named Jack Schlissel who did most of the dirty work. As Merrick's general manager, Schlissel had a reputation for abusing people with his negotiating manner and imperious style. He was pleasant enough with me at first, though he later found a way to make my life miserable even in my rather lowly position in the show.

Merrick brought together an extraordinary team of collaborators for *Promises, Promises*. The director, Robert Moore, having been an actor himself, was an actor's director, always very giving and encouraging. Bob had recently done the off-Broadway hit *The Boys in the Band*. Coincidentally, the choreographer on *Promises, Promises* was Michael Bennett.

The script was written by Neil Simon and was based on Billy Wilder's Oscar-winning movie *The Apartment*. In the musical, Jerry Orbach took on the film's Jack Lemmon role as the bachelor, Chuck Baxter, who lends his apartment to company executives for their extramarital affairs. Jerry was proving to be a consummate musical star, having previously distinguished himself in *Threepenny Opera* and *The Fantasticks*. Jill O'Hara played the heroine and love interest, Fran Kubelik, who had been portrayed by Shirley MacLaine in the movie. Jill brought a wonderfully soulful quality to her part. Her character attempted suicide when her adulterous lover, J. D. Sheldrake, refused to leave his wife for her. This plot line was unusually dark and dramatic for a musical comedy, another aspect of the show that would set it apart. The villainous Sheldrake character had been played by Fred MacMurray in the movie, and was now to be performed onstage by Edward Winter. I was cast as Vivien Della Hoya, a hot-blooded, sexy, and slightly tipsy secretary. I had a few scenes and shared two songs with two other secretaries, Adrianne Angel and Barbara Lang. Another actress, Millie Slavin, who played Miss Olsen, became a fast and lifelong friend.

The innovative score for *Promises, Promises* was composed by Burt Bacharach, who was then at the height of his fame as a pop songwriter. Hal David wrote the lyrics, and neither he nor Bacharach had ever worked on Broadway before. They brought in arrangers from the recording industry, as well as the high-powered music producer-engineer Phil

Ramone. The show marked a transition from the traditional Broadway sound to one that was pop-oriented. This was the first time the orchestra pit was covered, and a high-tech amplification system, like that found in a recording studio, could be used to modulate the sound. There was great anticipation to see what Bacharach and David would do on Broadway, and their score, along with Neil Simon's storytelling, promised to be a departure from traditional Broadway musical fare. Robin Wagner designed the brilliant set.

We started rehearsals in the Ansonia, an Upper West Side landmark building with a great space. On the first day, I spotted a handsome young actor in a black turtleneck and jeans. His name was Ken Howard, and he was fresh out of Yale Drama School. He looked like Adonis to me. I remember he was sitting at the lunch table, and somehow I summoned the courage to ask him if I might sit with him. Being so forward was out of character for me. While it might not have been a big deal for most people, for me it was monumental. I was usually reticent and inhibited with men socially, but there was something about Ken that put me enough at ease that I could take the risk of introducing myself.

I remember saying to myself, *Don't be afraid this time. Just go over and say hello.* After I sat down, he was charming and seemed riveted by everything I said. Ken later admitted to me how scared and insecure he was at the time. I was immediately drawn to this sensitivity, plus he made me feel good about myself. It was a sweet, innocent time, and the beginning of a romance that enabled me to put my marriage behind me.

By the time we left New York for our out-of-town runs in New Haven and Boston, there was great enthusiasm and the atmosphere of the company was charged with excitement. But we soon discovered that with an audience the show was running about a half-hour too long, and there were scenes that we knew were going to be cut. We had rehearsed a song called "Tick Tock Goes the Clock" that was very interesting, but had a weird rhythm and a melody that didn't seem to build into a full-blown production number. This was one of the two numbers I shared with two other secretaries. Each of us had a stanza, and then we were joined by the dancing chorus. That number was cut in Boston, and the other number I shared, "Turkey Lurkey Time," wasn't working and was also in danger of being cut. This was a song-and-dance number that took place at the company Christmas party, and was to provide a back-drop for a dramatic scene with Jerry Orbach. The office party was to underscore the moment that his character discovered that J. D. Shel-drake had been having an affair with Fran Kubelik.

In Kevin Kelly's biography of Michael Bennett, Neil Simon recalled Michael's contribution with the "Turkey Lurkey" number: "The show was working great out of town, but we were having some problems at the end of the first act. There was a lot of discussion about what needed to be done, the usual give-and-take among the creative people, and here was Michael looking like this kid on a college football team sitting on the bench and pleading with his eyes for the coach to let him in the game. He looked like he was saying 'Gimme-a-chance-gimme-a-chance-gimme-a-chance!' When we agreed to give him a chance, his eyes went wide and he went to work like a shot. And the 'Turkey Lurkey' num-ber he came up with didn't just solve the problem we were having, it was a sensation. He was just an awful quick intuitive study, and he was fearless."

Michael always had definite ideas and the courage of his convictions about what he wanted to accomplish. His role model was Jerome Rob-bins, whom he idolized. The idea of bringing story-driven realism into musical theater wasn't new, but Michael wanted to take it to new heights. The first way he staged the number called for the three of us secretaries at the office Christmas party to push our desks together. Then the boys helped us up on chairs to mount the desks where we were to perform our party entertainment. This was all very realistic, as it might have happened at a real office party. It was charming and delight-ful in rehearsal. But in Boston, we got up on the desks, and we were wearing these over-the-top Donald Brooks costumes with all these feath-ers and elaborate papier-mâché turkey heads for hats. Made to look silly, the costumes actually required a dozen seamstresses to construct, and were beyond anything that real office secretaries could put together. They seemed inconsistent with this realistic style, and illogical.

Realism was used on our choreography as well. On opening night, we suddenly found ourselves stuck on the desktops with no place to go, and looking like we just improvised our steps, like in real life. The scene didn't work that way. It made us look amateurish. It's painful to be aware of the audience trying to like you, but they just can't. In rethinking the piece, Michael said, "Okay, I tried realism, now let me get back to musical comedy. If my Aunt Belle can't understand it, what good is it?" He also explained to me, "The audience told me what the number needed."

This was the first-act finale and he knew it had to be strong enough to bring the audience back after the intermission. Knowing my strength as a dancer, Michael centered me in the number dancing next to Margo Sappington and Baayork Lee, and perhaps saved me from being fired again. The other two secretary parts were cut, and one was eliminated from the show altogether.

Working with his assistant, Bob Avian, and the musical director, Harold Wheeler, Michael rechoreographed the number overnight, using the mirror in his hotel room. The next day we rehearsed the revised version in the hotel conference room. Instead of putting the desks together, we pulled them apart and created a dance floor. The mood was celebratory with us drinking and partying, and Michael played that to the hilt with the choreography. He knew that the more we danced beyond endurance, the better the release of dramatic tension would be for the audience, especially after the last scene that left Jerry Orbach sitting heartbroken on the side of the stage. We also enjoyed the takeoff on *Hullabaloo*, as Michael had several dancers get up on the desks to take advantage of levels and to mirror what we were doing on the floor.

Michael encouraged my individuality and wanted me to be my own character. He always appreciated the fact that my approach to any dance started with my specific choices as an actress. With "Turkey Lurkey Time," he knew how to use me to make the number build to an exciting climax, in such a way that Neil Simon later told Michael that I was his "secret weapon." The dancing was incredibly athletic, one of those times where you come off the stage and want to go directly into an oxygen tent. Still, it was one of the most exciting and satisfying pieces musically and physically that I've ever done. And it was a brilliant stroke of luck for me, simply because I happened to be a dancer, and the number stopped the show from the first night it went in. I would have been happy with my part in the show without "Turkey Lurkey Time," but then it became something more than I had ever imagined. The impact was amazing, and it became something of a shared triumph for Michael and me that further cemented the bond between us.

Not everyone had such a positive experience with the tryouts, reminding me of the old joke that if Hitler were still alive, the best punishment for him would be to put him in a musical that's having trouble out of town. Burt Bacharach had such a difficult time that he vowed never to do another Broadway show (and he didn't). Much of the time that we were in New Haven, he was in the hospital with pneumonia—which didn't stop David Merrick from badgering him and Hal David for a new song. Merrick apparently didn't believe that Bacharach was really sick, and later we heard that Hal David, who is one of the kindest people I have ever met, had been locked in his hotel room until he produced the lyrics for the second-act number, "I'll Never Fall in Love Again." After Bacharach came out of the hospital, he finished the song in a few hours, and Jill O'Hara then had a poignant number that she performed sitting on a bed, accompanying herself on acoustic guitar.

Promises, Promises opened in New York at the Shubert Theatre on December 1, 1968. The opening was marked by some scary offstage drama because this was the first Broadway show to incorporate computerization of the backstage set machinery. The stagehand union was upset because the computerized sets reduced the number of union members needed to run the show. The apartment set was quite elaborate and could actually move forward, then across the stage. It could also move on the diagonal from the upstage corners to downstage center.

During one preview, the machines broke down and the set jolted forward, knocking out one of the dancers, Graciela Daniele. It was a dangerous incident; she could have been killed. David Merrick suspected sabotage. On opening night, he arrived splendidly dressed and in high spirits. But before the opening curtain, he took a fire axe in hand and stationed himself in the basement, right by the controls with an "over my dead body" attitude, to make sure that nothing went awry. Fortunately, nothing did go wrong, though those of us in the cast were more nervous than we would have been if it had been just another opening night.

After the show, there was a glitzy gala party at El Morocco that I attended with Ken Howard. The event attracted celebrities like Carol Channing, Ethel Merman, Ben Gazzara, and George Segal, all of whom had seen the show that night. David Merrick later remarked, "We don't allow celebrities in for opening night. . . . Celebrities come to be seen, and it's my show I want to be seen, not them." Apparently, he made some exceptions, master showman that he was. While the party was still in progress, the first reviews were announced on the late night TV news, and we were jubilant when we heard that we had a sure hit, what *Variety* would later describe as "a great big fat smash hit."

In the *New York Times,* Clive Barnes called it "the kind of show where you feel more in the mood to send in a congratulatory telegram than write a review." He went on to extol the virtues of the creative team and the leads in the cast. His review also credited me for "leading the number at the end of the first act with the power and drive of a steam hammer in heat." In the early edition of the newspaper, I was misidentified as "Margo Sappington," but Robert Moore went out of his way to intervene on my behalf.

Bob's longtime companion, George Rondo, told me that when Bob heard about the mistake in the review, he immediately left the El Morocco party to find a phone booth. Then he called and prevailed upon the *Times* to replace Margo's name with mine in the later editions. Being an actor himself, he had real empathy for actors. And as a director, he was simply taking care of one of his actors. I was moved by his effort on my behalf that night, realizing there weren't many first-time Broadway directors who would have left a glamorous opening night party to right such a wrong. I shouldn't have been surprised, because his decency and humanity always prevailed in his work.

The "steam hammer" image was not what I had ever imagined my first Broadway notice would be, but I was delighted to have been singled out, especially for my dancing. I told *Dance Magazine,* "*Promises* was a turning point for me. For the past five or six years, I tried to give up dancing for singing-acting parts. But then in *Promises* I realized I really loved dancing. It made me realize that you can sing and act without having to throw dancing away. It's too much a part of me."

With the Broadway run of *Promises, Promises* underway and selling out every night, Ken and I were already something of an item in the gossip columns. We had been dating steadily, and decided that we wanted to live together. Ken soon found an adorable apartment for us on West 69th Street for which we paid $175 a month. The place was a little run-down, but we were near Central Park, and the living room had a marble fireplace and high ceilings. We furnished it from the Salvation Army and even brought in a chair we found on the street.

Ken and I had relatively small roles in *Promises, Promises,* and we weren't getting rich, but we were very much in love with life, with the theater, and with each other. With my own life and career seemingly on a secure course for the first time, it occurred to me that I might soon have other promises to fulfill. I was beginning to have a sense of entitlement, almost coming to believe that I deserved my good fortune, and though it wouldn't last, at least for a little while, my luck continued.

Chapter 4

COMPANY

Promises, Promises was destined to play 1,281 performances and lasted more than three years on Broadway, but neither Ken nor I stayed with the show for the entire run. Early in 1969, Ken was cast as Thomas Jefferson in *1776*, another hit musical. During that summer, he landed a lead role opposite Liza Minnelli in the Otto Preminger film *Tell Me That You Love Me, Junie Moon*. This was a special time for both of us. It seemed that Ken and I were perfect for each other, and I appreciated his generosity in sharing his success with me.

Thanks to Ken's involvement in the movie, I was offered an interview with Mr. Preminger for a small role. I was excited to meet him, but having heard the rumors about his tempestuous personality, I was also a little anxious at the prospect. On the day of my interview, I went with Ken to Mr. Preminger's Manhattan office, which was elegant and impressive. I was even more impressed with the great director himself. He greeted me with a warm smile, and couldn't have been more charming, with his jovial spirit and old-world manners. He put me at ease immediately, saying, "Thank you for coming, Donna. It's so nice to meet you." There was to be no talk of work or scripts, so the interview wasn't like an audition at all, but more of a friendly get-together.

Leaving the office, I wasn't wondering if I got the part, but thinking that I could understand how Otto Preminger swept Gypsy Rose Lee off her feet. Later, I received a message to contact his office. I called and spoke to his son, Erik, who informed me that I had the part. I didn't yet have a script, but he described my character as "a young woman running along a beach." Then he added, "There will me some nudity. How do you feel about that?"

I was immediately uncomfortable with the idea, and without hesitation said, "Oh, I'm sorry. I couldn't possibly." I really wasn't interested in selling myself that way. I hung up the phone, feeling bad about losing the opportunity to be in a major film. However, a few days later, Erik called and offered me another role, one that was a much better part for me because it involved more acting. This turn of events was a welcome surprise, and also a lesson for a girl who usually had great difficulty saying no.

In the movie, Junie Moon (played by Liza Minnelli) was a young woman whose face was horribly disfigured from burns inflicted by a psycho boyfriend. I was to portray a young married woman whose disabled husband was in the same hospital as Junie Moon. My husband had lost his legs, and I had a very dramatic scene in which I was to tell him that I loved him but was leaving him because I didn't think I was strong enough to cope with his disability. The very sweet fellow they hired to play my husband was not an actor by profession, but fit the part realistically in that he was disabled in the same way as the character. This by itself was a powerful element for me to deal with, in that I felt concerned about his feelings when I had to say some of the scripted lines about my inability to accept him.

Acting was tough enough but this was beyond acting. I never felt comfortable being "uncomfortable" in the scene. The story line was heavy-handed, with my character suddenly becoming terrified by the sight of Junie Moon's grotesque face, and then instinctively turning back to her husband for protection. At that moment, she realizes how much she loves him and depends on him. The scene would end with their passionate kiss.

Even with that bit of melodrama, and a little too much reality, the role was a worthy challenge and an opportunity for me to prove myself as an actress. The scene was filmed in New York. Although Liza and I were not onscreen together and no lines were exchanged between our characters, she was considerate in helping me get a realistic reaction. On the set, she stood next to the camera, so when I turned to her, I could react to Junie Moon rather than the exit sign over the door. I admired Liza for being so caring, as well as so determined to succeed. I knew that she fought hard to get that film, and when she was working, she always gave one hundred percent.

I thought that I had done well with my scene and never considered the possibility that I might end up on the cutting room floor. After Ken later finished filming his part in Los Angeles, he returned to New York with the bad news that I had been axed and wasn't going to appear in the movie after all. Naturally, I was disappointed, but Ken had even more shattering news for me. He had decided to end our relationship. I don't think I ever really understood the reasons for his decision. He tried to explain to me that Otto Preminger had advised him that he could have a great movie career if he got rid of his girlfriend. Whether or not Ken's story was true—and I had my doubts—his point was that a young actor shouldn't be attached. This idea may have reflected the old Hollywood mentality when studios like MGM tried to control the personal lives of the young stars they had under contract. In any case, the breakup with Ken sent me reeling into another emotional tailspin. Even months after he moved out, I would find myself bursting into tears with no provocation. I found a therapist, Gerald Sabbath, who was helpful, and I would continue to see him for the next few years. I had no idea yet how much this feeling of rejection triggered my childhood sense of abandonment.

This time I felt like I had lost the love of my life, and once again, work was my only refuge. I was still performing in *Promises, Promises,* and in August I auditioned for another television show, *Dark Shadows,* an offbeat ABC soap opera that featured vampires and supernatural gothic characters. The series would later go into syndication and win a devoted cult following.

Dark Shadows was the brainchild of producer Dan Curtis, who auditioned me in his office at ABC. I was happy to be sent up for an acting role, and my growing confidence as an actress gave me the freedom to stretch myself and take more emotional risks. I read an outlandish scene in which I had to tearfully confess to my lover, the show's dashing playboy, Quentin Collins (played by David Selby), that I was not a real person, but rather a painting come to life. Ordinarily, a cold reading of that kind of material at an audition could prove to be a challenge, but not for someone whose feelings were so close to the surface as mine were at the time. Mr. Curtis fed me lines from the script, and the tears flowed.

Happily, I was soon hired for the job, and it reconfirmed my belief in the acting profession. Where else could you use your neuroses and negative feelings in such a healthy, positive way—and get paid for it? The show had two story lines that played out in different time periods. One was set in 1897, and the other took place in modern times. Initially, I was to appear in the period scenes and I was only scheduled to work for a week. However, my character, Amanda Harris, quickly caught on. David Selby had a huge following among teenage girls, and now they had someone they could identify with as his romantic partner. They wrote enough fan mail for the show's producers to bring me back and keep a good thing going.

I stayed on that season and into the following year, appearing in twenty-four episodes. Basically, each show played out the same kind of drama that I read in my audition. My character was always desperate, fearful that she was about to be found out. She kept trying to confess the truth about herself to her lover without losing him, so there was always the drama of her romantic dilemma for me to work with. At one point, a modern-day character, Olivia Corey, was written for me, but she was really Amanda, in keeping with the supernatural story line.

Between *Dark Shadows* and *Promises,* I settled into an exhausting routine that gave me little time to brood about losing Ken. I would get up early in the morning and read through the "sides," my scenes in the TV script, familiarizing myself with my lines without memorizing them. Later in the morning, I would go into the ABC studios and we would have a reading, with the cast sitting around a table. Then we would quickly block our scenes and head to wardrobe for our wigs and costumes. That part of the routine was often an ordeal due to the elaborate period costumes. The wigs alone must have weighed twenty pounds because of the number of hairpieces they required, all of which had to be coiffed and pinned into place. Finally, we would tape our scenes, which was accomplished at a breakneck pace, with the cameramen, crew, and cast rushing from set to set. I quickly learned that this television show was all about holding on to your wig and hitting your mark without tripping. At the end of my day shooting the soap, I would hurry home, take a quick catnap, grab something to eat, and then head to the theater for *Promises, Promises.*

I left *Dark Shadows* temporarily in the fall of 1969 when I was asked to join the London production of *Promises, Promises,* which was scheduled to open at the Prince of Wales's Theatre in October. I was to open the show, play for four weeks, and then return to the Broadway production. Having never traveled to Europe, I was delighted with the prospect, and thrilled by the idea of performing in London's West End. Since only travel expenses would be paid, my agent asked for a $25 raise in my weekly salary. He had to wrangle with the company manager, Jack Schlissel, who finally relented. Only later did I learn that Michael Bennett had paid the difference out of his own pocket. Michael apparently thought that it would be in his best interest to have me open in London to show off his choreography.

It was to be my responsibility to find a place to live in London, but after arriving at Heathrow Airport, I still didn't know where I was going to stay. I had no London address to offer customs, so an official pulled me aside. When he questioned me, I felt tears welling up and wondered what I could possibly do in this predicament. It was late at night, and the only number I had to call was the theater. I was under the impression that someone would be at Heathrow to pick me up and help me find a place to stay. But apparently Jack Schlissel had decided to have the last laugh at my expense. No one came to meet me, and I was stranded at the airport. I imagined myself being deported and sent back to New York.

As I stood there in despair, the music producer and sound designer for the show, Phil Ramone, came walking through customs. I had no idea we had been on the same plane, but he was in London to help open the show as well. He saw me, and when I frantically told him of my plight, he kindly offered to help the damsel in distress. He told me that he had an apartment on Kings Road, and invited me to sleep on his couch until something better could be worked out the following day. He said he had one stop to make before heading to his place, and asked me if I would mind. "Of course not!" I told him.

With that, my nightmare turned into a magical dream. I was whisked away in his limousine and taken to the penthouse of film composer John Barry, who was hosting a party for a group of British stars, including Diana Rigg. John was dating actress Ingrid Boulting at the time. Ingrid's father, John Boulting, and his twin brother, Roy, were prominent British filmmakers of that era. Next day at the theater, I was complaining to the stage manager, Charlie Blackwell, about my not having a place to stay. A young stagehand overheard me, and coincidentally, he was Ingrid Boulting's brother, Fitzroy. He invited me to stay in the family town house on Kings Road, as there was plenty of room with just his sister living there. Fitzroy generously enhanced my experience and education by becoming my London guide, as my run of luck continued.

The leads in *Promises* for the London production were played by Tony Roberts, Betty Buckley, and James Congdon. We were among the American minority in the company that also included Ronn Carroll and Jack Kruschen. I was so excited to be in England. My love of history, or rather an unconscious desire to know where I came from, and why I was the way I was, was stimulated by being in the country of my forebears.

My dresser was a middle-aged widow named Lucille, who prided herself on her profession. She served me tea in my dressing room before the show, with little homemade treats—a style to which I was not accustomed at this point of my career. She had been a Red Cross nurse during the Second World War. I was curious and wanted to know more about her experiences. I think it meant a great deal to her that I wanted more than a cup of tea and a zip-up before I went onstage.

When I first arrived for rehearsals, I felt like I was getting the cold shoulder from the rest of the dancers. One day, early on, I was pulled into the boys' dressing room and they told me that Michael's assistant, who had come over earlier to train them, was hard on them. They surmised that one of her tactics to induce fear was to tell them how difficult I was going to be if they didn't do what she demanded. Apparently, she told them, "If you think I'm tough, just wait until Donna gets here! She's a real bitch!" After a few days, the dancers started seeing that I wasn't such an ogre after all, and the atmosphere became friendlier. In fact, I developed some close and long-lasting relationships to this day from that company, including Alix Kirsta, Albin Pahernik, and Ralph Wilton, our English stage manager.

I had no idea why Michael's assistant held that kind of grudge against me. We had worked together in the New York production of *Promises, Promises,* and I never had a clue that she didn't like me. My feelings were hurt by the London episode, but I never confronted her. I just kept working with a positive goal in sight. I knew that she would be gone after we opened anyway.

Our opening night was a smashing triumph, and "Turkey Lurkey Time" stopped the show—literally. Tony Roberts and I were recently at a dinner party and we reminisced about that night. He reminded me that the applause went on so long that he couldn't continue the rest of the scene that would cue the curtain down on the first act. He made three attempts and each time the applause would build up again, until finally I had to go out onstage and, with the conductor's assistance, repeat the tag of the number with the rest of the dancers. That had never happened to me before and never happened again during the run of that show. This was the first time a London audience had been exposed to the slick sophistication of this popular music, combined with such highly energetic and innovative choreography. It was all very American and they loved it. I started my own love affair with England that year and I knew, even then, that it would be one of the best times of my life.

After four weeks of performances, I left London with a comforting sense of "job well done." I seemed to be right on course when I was soon cast in another Broadway musical that was being produced and directed by Harold Prince. The show was called *Company,* and I was pleasantly surprised when I met with Hal at his office and learned that I was being cast without having to audition. That was a first for me.

Apparently, Hal had seen me in *The Education of H*Y*M*A*N K*A*P*L*A*N* and had been impressed with my work. "I said, 'Who is that girl?'" He also may have been using me as a kind of lure, because he wanted Michael Bennett to choreograph the show, which Michael later agreed to do, after initially having reservations about the script and working with nondancers.

With rehearsals for *Company* scheduled to begin in January of 1970, I gave my notice on *Dark Shadows,* which prompted the writers to kill off my Amanda character in dramatic fashion. For my last appearance on the show, the script called for me to cross a bridge with David Selby and die under an avalanche. During the run-through in the studio, I was told to place a plastic bag over my head, because the avalanche would be made of peat moss as well as Styrofoam rocks, some of them the size of boulders. Our bridge was actually only a couple of feet off the ground, and there were stagehands stationed above us to deliver the avalanche.

For the run-through, we wore rehearsal clothes, and I did my part as directed, reaching out for David's hand and screaming as I was caught under the falling debris. The scene went well and I survived the avalanche without too much difficulty. For the taping, I had to wear my wig and heavy period costume. I wasn't warned that the stagehands would be dumping about ten times more peat moss and Styrofoam on me than they had earlier, and this time I had no plastic bag to protect my face. I remember hearing my cue, then looking up and screaming as this tremendous load of peat moss and fake rocks came down and knocked me to the floor. It was suddenly in my mouth, in my eyes, and in my ears. As I lifted my head, the lights went out, and everyone hurried off to another set to tape the next scene, leaving me there, under the avalanche. Though it seems funny now, I thought it was such an ungracious way to say goodbye.

I was relieved to be off the TV show and heading back to Broadway. At the time, I was still recoiling from a recent meeting I had with a certain producer who wielded some power in the film industry. This man had contacted my agent and invited me to his office. I took all morning to dress, primping to look my very best, and left my apartment excited and eager to make a good impression. I remember the meeting began with him telling me how much he liked me. He described himself as a fan, but then he went on to say, "I just had to meet you because I couldn't figure out why you never made it." It was jarring to realize that I was twenty-six years old, and this guy had me figured as a promising performer who never made it. Even though I knew better, I let his remark pull me back into a race against time where my career was concerned. There were times like this when I would tell myself, half-kidding, "Oh God, I've just got to get out of this business, but I don't know how to type."

With *Company*, I hoped that I might finally make a more decisive mark. I was going to be part of a distinguished ensemble, including Elaine Stritch, Dean Jones, Barbara Barrie, Merle Louise, John Cunningham, Beth Howland, Charles Kimbrough, George Coe, Teri Ralston, Charles Braswell, Alice Cannon, Audrey Johnson, Steve Elmore, Pam Myers, Susan Browning, Marti Stevens, and Larry Kert. I was given a role that would allow me to act, sing, and dance.

Under Hal Prince's direction and with a score from Stephen Sondheim, *Company* promised to be a cutting-edge production. It was the first adult-themed musical of its kind. George Furth's book evolved out of a series of one-act plays, so the show was composed of revue-like vignettes on the subject of love and marriage. Sondheim later said *Company* was about "the total possibility and impossibility of relationships on the isle of Manhattan." I always thought of the show as being impressionistic, with its songs seemingly coming out of nowhere to comment on the action and characters, like flashbacks and overlays in a film.

I played the role of Kathy, a girlfriend of the central bachelor figure, Robert. Initially played by Dean Jones, he was replaced by Larry Kert early in the run. The show revolved around Robert, who was about to be given a surprise thirty-fifth birthday party by his friends, five neurotic couples who repeatedly encourage him to take the plunge into marriage. *Company* was truly a New York show and very modern at the time, with its *Sex and the City* concept. The fantastic chrome and plexiglass set design by Boris Aronson underscored the urban theme with a towering elevator and scaffolding that connected the various levels and apartments.

With this show, there was a lot on the line for everybody, and the electrically charged atmosphere was both exciting and nerve-racking. On our breaks, I would usually see Beth Howland standing in a corner with her nose practically touching the wall, relentlessly going over her song "Getting Married Today," with its complicated lyrics sung at break-neck speed. Barbara Barrie and Charles Kimbrough would be in another room on a mat, practicing their karate scene until they were black-and-blue. We were all together in this show, and I thought that was great.

We first went on the road to Boston, and after our opening night, Hal advised the entire cast, "You know everything you need to know about these characters. Now think of it as an upside-down cake and play for comedy." Of course, he meant that we had been playing it too seriously. As always, there were adjustments that had to be made once we had an audience.

Elaine Stritch gave an upside-down performance on opening night in Boston, but not quite in the same way Hal was talking about. Elaine played Joanne and left her indelible mark with a performance that is now legendary.

On opening night in Boston, I finished my dance and climbed up to one of the stage platforms with the other women, who were sitting facing the back wall, wearing prop hats. We were to be part of the look and background while Elaine sang her big number, "The Ladies Who Lunch." During the previews, I had enjoyed watching her performance reflected on the plexiglass box in front of me, even though I was still sweating buckets from the dance. On our first night, with the critics in the house, she began as usual, but halfway through the number, she stopped singing. The conductor, Hal Hastings, started throwing her lyrics as the orchestra continued to play, but still no sound from Elaine, only Hal repeating the lyrics.

I tried to make out what was happening onstage. I thought I saw her hands covering her face, then sliding down, with her fingers going into her mouth. Was she having some kind of breakdown? She then made a valiant effort to end the number and get on with the show, but the incident left us all with an unsettled feeling.

After the curtain came down, I ran to her dressing room. "Are you okay?" I asked. "What the hell happened out there?"

She looked at me in surprise, and then said with mild alarm, "I forgot my lyrics!"

"Oh, is that all," I said. "I thought you were having a nervous breakdown! What were you doing with your hands in your mouth?"

"I was trying to find the words!" she yelled as she acted it out for me. I laughed and thought, *She is such an original.*

I asked her, "Has that ever happened to you before?" Elaine sighed and told me it happened to her in London, opening Noel Coward's *Sail Away.* "I was so nervous, but I was fine the next night."

After leaving the theater I walked over to the Tiki Hut, our local watering hole, where everyone met after the show. As I walked in, I saw Hal Prince and Ruth Mitchell (who was given associate producer credit on this show) along with Steve Sondheim with his head in his hands. "Hi Ruth," I said cheerfully, wanting to share my relief. "I just saw Elaine and she's fine."

"You saw her?" she asked incredulously.

I had everyone's attention as I told her, "Yes, I just came from her dressing room. Didn't you go back?"

"What did she say?" Ruth asked with a little more intensity. I could tell she was concerned and *really* wanted to know.

Feeling a little on the spot, I acted out Elaine's dilemma with my hands while saying, "She forgot her lyrics and she was trying to find her words! Isn't that funny?" I laughed, though nobody at the table thought it was funny. I continued, "But it's okay, Ruth. Elaine said it only happens to her on opening nights!"

The ending of the show evolved on the road and fell into place when Robert's final number, "Being Alive," was added. Sondheim wrote it to replace the song "Happily Ever After," because Hal thought the latter was too bitter, with Robert rejecting marriage in favor of bachelorhood. Earlier, Sondheim had written "Happily Ever After" to replace "Marry Me a Little," which was an ambivalent affirmation of marriage. I thought the first two songs were wonderful, but "Being Alive" was perfect for that moment in the show.

"Being Alive" had a lyrical melody that was slow and insistent. It was more of a hopeful, plaintive song that gave Robert more vulnerability in his yearning for intimacy. His desire to love and be loved despite his fears was represented musically with a dramatic number that supported the passionate expression of the character. This was a very human expression that everyone could relate to, and it made the audience want to root for him. He became a kind of heroic figure for all of us.

It was fascinating for me to see how Hal made his choices as a director. He was never afraid to try something to see if it could work, or to see it not work, then try something else. At one point, the show ended with Bobby sitting on a park bench next to a girl the audience had never seen before. That scene created the impression that he might be able to do it differently this time. It also brought home the point that he wasn't gay and he wasn't going to be a loner for the rest of his life. Then one day the park bench and the girl were gone. Hal happily reported to us the way he discovered the perfect ending was to not have a perfect ending. He later said, "It occurred to me that we can't presume to give people the answer to personal happiness."

There were other changes that were made out of town, and I suddenly found myself in danger of having my scenes cut. The evolution of the dance number "Tick Tock," and the changes that it went through musically and choreographically, determined my fate with the show. In rehearsals, "Tick Tock" had started out as a kind of rock ballet. The number was a solo dance for me and was intended to comment on Robert's inability to commit to a relationship. The dance took place while Robert was having a one-night stand with a stewardess, played marvelously by Susan Browning.

Coming off the pop music score of *Promises, Promises,* Michael as choreographer had wanted to go further in that groundbreaking direction. His intention as always was to come up with something that was artistically daring. Early in rehearsals, he told me, "I have an idea for this number. You know when you're in bed with someone, and you're making love but you're not really into it. You hear the clock ticking and you're more aware of that sound than you are of the person you're with. So you really feel alone. Do you know what I mean?"

I said, "Um, no, I really don't." At that point, I wasn't aware of the kind of isolation and loneliness that he was talking about. I hardly gave myself a chance to in those days. I did think his observation was revealing, drawing from his own experience and the difficulty he had in making connections with people he cared about. I could relate to that. As we began to work on the number, he asked me to start with that tick-tock rhythm as I was coming up the elevator, with my hands resting on my breasts. I was going to be wearing only a slip, and moving to the clock's rhythm, with tiny isolations of my fingers and shoulders. That was a beginning, and it was exciting and titillating. But then he had another idea and suggested to me, "I'm thinking about a new take on this number, a different concept for it. I think I'd like you to be nude or half-nude, maybe under a see-through chiffon fabric."

My old feelings about nudity came up like a slap in the face. I remember stammering, "Gee, Michael, I don't know. Let's talk about this. I could do it that way, but I think you would lose all the mystery." Sensing my discomfort, he set his idea aside and I kept my costume on.

The concept of that piece was still in question when we went on the road. Fortunately, I had another number, "You Could Drive a Person Crazy," which was more secure and polished. It was a hilarious takeoff on the Andrews Sisters that I performed as part of a trio with Pamela Myers and Susan Browning, who played two of Robert's other girlfriends. I have fond memories of the three of us going over that song for hours and hours in a rehearsal room with Bob Avian, probably driving him crazy. We were trying so hard to find the right level of volume that would keep the energy high at such a fast tempo. If we slowed the tempo, it wasn't as funny. If we kept the tempo up, it was difficult to hear the words. One day we were rehearsing onstage, just marking it, singing softly but in the fast tempo. Stephen Sondheim came running down the aisle and said, "That's it!"

Shortly after we opened in Boston, Hal Prince came over to me and said he wanted to talk, escorting me into the lobby of the Shubert Theatre. He put his arm around me as we walked, and it was obvious that this was going to be the kiss of death. He told me, "Donna, there are two numbers that we have to cut temporarily to find the right balance in the show. 'Tick Tock' and 'Another Hundred People' aren't working where they are. Perhaps we'll find another place or another way to do your number. We have to try something else."

Hal was a true gentleman of the theater, and I appreciated how considerate he was by telling me beforehand. That doesn't always happen. He wanted me to understand his point of view, that those two songs were somehow not supporting the show as a whole. Of course, I knew that it was the show as a whole that was important. But still, the cut meant that my part in the show would be further diminished, as another one of my scenes had already been trimmed during rehearsals. I couldn't help but feel that my job was on the line.

It was hard for me to hear what he was really saying because I went into shock. He never said it was out for good, but that's what I heard. Hal also took Pam Myers aside and told her that her song, "Another Hundred People," was being cut. That was a shock too, because it was a great number that she sang so brilliantly. After breaking the bad news to each of us privately, Hal went back into the theater. With the rest of the cast waiting in the orchestra seats, he announced the cuts to everyone. I don't know what possessed me or how I found the nerve, but I decided that I had to fight to keep my number. I reacted in a life-or-death way, as if I were on the brink of losing my job. I found Hal backstage at the half-hour before curtain and cornered him, blurting out, "Look, Hal, I really think this number can work, and the show needs this dance!"

As I went on to defend my position, I felt like a desperate lawyer struggling to make a case. Michael and Steve soon came up to us and listened to my pleas. I looked to Michael, thinking that he would be an ally and come to my aid to try to protect his choreography. But he was under the weather with a cold, and most likely had other pressures to deal with. So I had to plead my case alone, explaining why that dance could be a more powerful moment in the show, a connection to deeper feelings that weren't being expressed in the other numbers or in the action specified in the script. Hal listened to me patiently, and then he asked me, "But how do we make it work?"

I knew the number wasn't working. It felt repetitive musically, which made it seem one-dimensional. As an actress I was having trouble find-ing a point of departure and emotional point of view. The number felt static to me. After thinking about it, I said, "Okay, this is how we can do it. You don't do a rock or disco thing. You bring in the string section and make it reflect a deeper feeling."

I thought the dance had to express the need for a relationship and intimacy in order to support the central theme of the show. Of course, my suggestion to change the music infringed on Stephen Sondheim's territory, and I was so bold as to suggest that he try reprising some of the more lyrical melodies that came earlier in the score. Stephen said, "I don't want reprises in this show." I tried to explain to him that it didn't have to be a lyrical reprise, but possibly a musical reprise.

At this point, Hal intervened, telling me, "Just go to your dressing room, Donna. It's fifteen," meaning that we now had only fifteen min-utes until curtain.

I looked at Hal and in the heat of the moment said, "I'm not leaving this stage until you tell me you'll fix it!"

He could have fired me on the spot, but instead he said, "Okay, we'll fix it. Just get dressed and do the show."

I knew by the way he made the statement that he meant what he said, and in the end, both Pam's number and mine would stay in the show. Hal, Stephen, and Michael were all intense collaborators, com-pletely devoted to the work, and ironically, it was their commitment and my admiration for them that inspired me to make my stand to keep my number, even if my distorted perceptions almost tripped me up.

Hal kept his word to me and soon brought in David Shire to change the musical arrangement of "Tick Tock." At the time, David was on his honeymoon, and his bride was not at all pleased when her husband spent a very long day and night with us in the theater revising the piece. Both the music and choreography were changed dramatically, and with the alterations and orchestration by Jonathan Tunick, the number immediately became a huge success, stopping the show during the first New York preview.

Once again, Michael's choreography enabled me to distinguish myself. I had always had that dream of dancing alone onstage to create an emotional experience and to make a personal statement through the character. Building relentlessly to a climax, the dance was charged with longing as well as eroticism, and I took special satisfaction when the *New York Times* critic Walter Kerr later wrote, "Nudemongers take note: Sex is more accurately and more excitingly summoned up in Miss Mc-Kechnie's limber metaphors than it would have been in any amount of bared-shoulder bedplay by the principals. Dandy."

Company opened at the Alvin on April 26, 1970, and ran 705 per-formances, winning six Tony Awards in 1971, including Best Musical. The success of the show landed me on the cover of *Dance Magazine,* and I remember being amazed by the effusive praise that I received from Michael, who was interviewed for the article. He showered me with compliments that he would never have given to me directly. "Donna's the most beautiful dancer I've ever seen . . . She's an expressive lyric actress. I've seen people be cute or sexy, but Donna has it all. She learns incredibly fast, has amazing objectivity and works almost as a collabora-tor." Michael went on to make a somewhat self-serving reference to fel-low choreographers Jerome Robbins and Bob Fosse and their Broadway muses, saying, "Jerry had Chita, Bob had Gwen, and I can't tell you how happy I am that Donna is mine."

To some extent, I took his comments with a heady grain of salt, knowing him well enough to realize that he could exaggerate when it was convenient or to his advantage. Nevertheless, with *Company,* the bond between Michael and me was solidified through dancing, espe-cially with "Tick Tock" bringing down the house each night. I started being able to feel that I had a real hold on something. I was in a hit show, working with people I liked and respected, even if I was always being so hard on myself. Nothing was ever really good enough. At home after the show, I would go over that night's performance step by step before I could sleep, always trying to figure how it could be better the next time.

That kind of perfectionism is fine in theory, and most dancers wouldn't find that at all strange, but I couldn't leave myself alone. It was as if I wouldn't let myself enjoy the success I had worked so hard to achieve. I remember I was always asking Michael for notes, to help me improve my performance. Finally, one night he said, "Okay, I have a note. You're working too hard!"

It was becoming more difficult for me to hide from myself. My low self-esteem kept rising up, trying to have the last word, "You're not good enough!" I spent a great deal of energy trying to live up to the expectations of that voice. I was also aware of the idealized image that Michael had of me, and how it related to his own self-image. I told *Dance Magazine,* "Of my whole career—whatever I've done—Michael has been the most influential person. I've picked up most of his style. Someone once asked Michael, 'Who do you dance like?' And he said, 'A male Donna McKechnie.'"

My friend Jim Burrows came back into my life when he saw *Company* and I was encouraged by his high praise. "If you do nothing else in your career, it will have been worth it, you've reached a pinnacle." This meant everything to me since my identity was so dependent on my ambition, and not who I was as a person. It was still difficult for me to see the value of me without career success. Jim and I soon started having a more serious relationship. He was a good friend and I felt comfortable with him. We shared our dreams and talked about what we wanted to accomplish in our careers.

Jim showed me his favorite places in the Village, and we also spent some time in one of his favorite bars on the Upper West Side—which was, I feel certain, the inspiration for one of his most successful TV shows, *Cheers.* The regulars were friends with assorted backgrounds and professions. Their common denominator was their camaraderie and good humor. Everyone had a nickname in that place. I was especially pleased when Jim initiated me into the club by dubbing me "Timestep."

Jim had worked as a stage manager for his father, Abe Burrows, whenever his father directed a show. At the time, he was stage manager for *40 Carats,* with Julie Harris. He was then offered a director's job for a theater in San Diego. Knowing how much he wanted this opportunity and knowing how devoted he was to his father, I felt privileged when he wanted me in the room with him while he made the call to tell his father that he was going to take the job in San Diego. Later, I appreciated how that brave step to independence paved the way for all of his future success.

After taking part in a highly successful West Coast production of *Company* at the Ahmanson Theatre in Los Angeles with George Chakiris in the lead, my next project was a Broadway revival of *On the Town*. The original 1944 production had been directed by George Abbott and choreographed by Jerome Robbins, with the sensational score from Leonard Bernstein and lyricists Betty Comden and Adolph Green. The leads in the 1971 revival initially included Kurt Peterson, Jess Richards, Phyllis Newman, Bill Gerber, and Bernadette Peters. I was cast as Ivy Smith, Miss Turnstiles, a role that seemed an ideal stepping-stone, offering me the chance to prove that I really was a genuine "triple threat" with my acting, singing, and dancing. Sono Osato was the original Ivy Smith. I was to have three big numbers—two complete ballets and a song and dance.

I thought this quintessential musical comedy about World War II sailors on shore leave would be a terrific vehicle for its entire cast and creative team. The show was being directed and choreographed by Ron Field, a Tony Award winner for his work on *Cabaret* and *Applause*. Although he wasn't credited, he also had a hand in producing *On the Town*, thus stretching himself to the limit. Ron had given Michael Bennett a break in 1962 by making him assistant choreographer on *Nowhere to Go but Up*, and the two had been great friends ever since. Knowing about my relationship with Michael, Ron called him as a courtesy to get his blessing to cast me in the show. "I asked him if I could steal his favorite girl," Ron later told *Dance Magazine*. "Michael . . . said he hated to lose her but he wanted her to do it. . . . It was impossible to think of anyone doing the part today other than Donna."

I went into rehearsals thinking that at this point in my career this role had everything I ever wanted. I had a great deal of respect for Ron's work, and by the time we went on the road, I found myself happily immersed in a new romance with Kurt Peterson, who was performing the role of Gabey. I fell in love with Kurt's voice first. It had a full, rich natural sound, and he reminded me of Gordon MacRae. Kurt had made his mark as Tony in the Lincoln Center production of *West Side Story*.

He left Stephen Sondheim's *Follies,* playing young Ben, to play Gabey in *On the Town*.

Despite the high hopes we all had for the show, we received less than favorable reviews. Historically, shows go on the road to work out the kinks and solve problems with the help of the audience and the out-of-town critics. That's when the real work begins, usually. That's why we were all taken aback when we arrived at the theater soon after we opened to find that Kurt and Bill Gerber were given their notice and replaced by Ron Husmann and Remak Ramsey.

Kurt, who has gone on to much success as a performer and producer, reminisced with me recently. "I was truly hurt by being let go, but especially by the fact that it was handled so poorly. I found out during intermission at a matinee when I returned a call from my agent. It made it even worse that day to hear my replacement in the background, rehearsing my numbers from the orchestra pit. Some very good things came out of that experience, however. I returned to a successful run in *Follies* while collecting an extra salary from *On the Town,* and most importantly, I met you."

I thought Kurt and Ron were both terrific in their parts as were Bill and Remak. The whole cast was struggling then. To be singled out that way seemed unfair to me, but everybody knew that sudden cast changes were inevitable when a show is being put together on the road. It always takes a toll on a company when you lose a "family" member that way, and it's something that we all had to work through. Meanwhile, I had my own problems on the road. My second-act ballet wasn't working, and Ron had yet to take the time to fix it. This was a gargantuan, daunting piece that Ron had left until the end of rehearsals to choreograph. It was staged in the style of a farcical cartoon, but it had never quite come together and didn't measure up to that incredible Bernstein score.

The setup for the ballet involved a dream that Gabey, the idealistic sailor, was having. I appeared wearing a gorgeous white dress, as in a beautiful dream. I was to dance across the back of the stage on a ramp and Gabey would try to catch me. His dream quickly turned into a nightmare when, thinking he had finally caught me, the object of his romantic love turned out to be the obese singing teacher, Madame Dilly, who came out in the same dress to replace me. Then I reappeared in a cutout cartoon car, with feathers flying and dancers pulling the car across the stage. I remember posing to that glorious music and being frustrated by the staging. Ron's idea was that my character was unattainable, and as a concept it was probably workable, but I wasn't really dancing, and therefore the moment was not living up to everyone's expectations.

During one of our rehearsals, Bernadette Peters had an intense discussion with Ron about the staging of one of her numbers, "I Can Cook Too." Bernadette was marvelous in the role of the pushy cab driver, Hildy. Her agitated discourse with Ron continued in the dressing room next to mine. Listening to them, I realized that Ron wasn't communicating well with the cast, a special problem for me since I needed his help on my number. As he left her dressing room and went into the hall, I stuck my head out the door and called after him, saying, "Ron, I know you're gonna fix my number, right?"

He looked back at me as if to say, "Oh, God, another one." Before taking off, Ron promised he would fix the ballet, but he never did. That was a great disappointment for me and for the audience.

Although the musical as a whole had its charms, Jerome Robbins would undoubtedly have been disappointed in this revival. And while most of the critics were favorable, there was also an element of being damned by faint praise when the show opened at the Imperial Theatre on October 31, 1971. Writing in the *New York Times,* Clive Barnes noted in passing, "Donna McKechnie made a sweet and talented Ivy Smith." The reviews of the show as a whole were similarly lacking in superlatives, and one pointed out that I didn't have a showstopper as I had in *Company.* There were money problems as well, and shortly after the opening, Ron called a meeting in the basement of the theater with the cast, musicians, and stagehands. We were all asked to take a paycut to keep the show going for a few more weeks. We all agreed, which was unheard of, since stagehands and musicians must always get paid. That was a moment, that terrific spirit of camaraderie behind the scenes, but *On the Town* lasted only two months before closing on January 1, 1972.

That same month I returned to *Company* when Hal Prince was planning a production in London with most of us from the original cast. Only Pam Myers and Susan Browning stayed behind. Theater history was made because this was really the first time that an American cast was sent to London to open an American show in the West End.

We opened to rave reviews at Her Majesty's Theatre. The British critics had few reservations about the show and treated it as a serious statement about contemporary culture and values. The review in London's *Daily Telegraph* was typical, concluding, "*Company,* like *West Side Story,* illustrates the American conviction that the musical can say something relevant about modern living, and do it with irresistible gaiety and exuberance."

There was a funny moment during a technical rehearsal when we were running late and everyone was totally exhausted. The story was later repeated by Stephen Sondheim's biographer, Meryle Secrest. Larry Kert was a wonderfully funny man and terrific actor who was gratefully reviving his career with the show after his glory days as the original Tony in *West Side Story.* In the wee hours that night, he suddenly became exasperated and walked to the front of the stage. Looking out at the orchestra, he said, "Who do I have to screw to get out of this show?" His line took everybody by surprise, especially in that stuffy British atmosphere. After a tense moment of silence, Stephen Sondheim's voice came from the back of the theater, "Same person you screwed to get in!"

The show's enormous success in London bolstered my spirits after my disappointing experience with *On the Town.* After the opening, Michael asked me if I had ever been to Paris, and when I told him that I hadn't, he declared proudly, "Well, I'm going to be the one who shows you Paris for the first time." We flew over on my next day off and checked into L' hotel on the Left Bank, staying in separate rooms, of course. One night we had cocktails in the lounge with Mike Nichols, who was also staying in the hotel. It was all so glamorous; the architecture, the sense of history, walks along the Seine on cobbled streets. There was lunch at La Brasserie, dinner at Maxim's, and singing and dancing at Chez Castel and in the streets afterward.

Our Paris visit was magical, and it was the first time I remember feeling sorry that Michael and I couldn't be together in a different way. I liked when he asked me who I was dating or who I found attractive. I confided in him to a point, always trying to be entertaining as I engaged him by talking about the other men in my life. But then I would pull back and remind myself, "This man can only be your friend!" This was brought further home to me when back in New York he fixed me up with his psychiatrist, socially not professionally.

In May I returned to *Company* yet again for a three-week run at the National Theatre in Washington, D.C. With this touring company, the part of Robert was played by Gary Crawford, a Canadian actor who had understudied Larry in New York and also played the love interest in *The Education of H*Y*M*A*N K*A*P*L*A*N.* Julie Wilson played Joanne, and the production was well received. The mixture of accomplishment and promise in my career was summarized in the most flattering way by Tom Shales writing in the *Washington Post.* "Donna McKechnie is by all odds the stand-out in the group with her almost apocalyptic second act dance solo 'Tick Tock.' Miss McKechnie is the electrifying dancer whose 'Turkey Lurkey' lit up *Promises, Promises,* and whose physical elocution was the saving grace for the *On the Town* revival last winter. It's too bad she can't appear in every Broadway musical there is."

Of course, I dearly wished the same for myself, but there was nothing on Broadway for me at the time. I was still living in a pressure cooker, feeling like I might never work again. Despite my misgivings, I decided to try my luck in Hollywood, and so made the move to the West Coast. I had a hard time going to agents and producers, hearing them pick me apart. Still, I played the game as well as I could, and did manage to land roles in a few television pilots. But more often, I would go to an audition and find myself up against some movie star who was being considered for the same role. When that happened, I felt defeated before I even read for the part.

At one point, I was cast in a Dick Van Dyke TV variety special called *I'm a Fan,* produced by Roy Somlyo. I was ecstatic when they flew everybody back to New York to rehearse. Bob Hergot was the choreographer and Carolyn Leigh wrote a song for me called "Basketball." At the time, I was represented by the William Morris Agency, and I knew I was in trouble when the director, Clarke Jones, took me aside during our filming in Los Angeles and told me, "You should think about getting a new agent. When I called William Morris and told them I wanted you for this show, they tried to talk me out of it."

I was flabbergasted and said, "What do you mean?"

He explained, "They tried to push another one of their clients on me, somebody who could get more money. So the agency would get a bigger commission."

I would later discover that changing agents wouldn't improve the situation. After six months in L.A., I was seriously depressed. I had a momentary lift when I visited my friend Jimmy Burrows in San Diego and saw how well he was doing and how talented he was as a director. Feeling safe with him, I broke down and told him how unhappy I was. He allowed me to fall apart in his apartment for a couple of days. Jimmy tried to be a friend, but I couldn't tell him what was wrong, and finally there was nothing he could do.

I went back to Los Angeles and stayed in an apartment building on Hollywood Boulevard called St. James Terrace. This was low rent in every sense of the word. Aside from the difficulty with finding work my routine was debilitating. I wasn't accustomed to sitting and waiting for the telephone to ring, with my days organized around going to the gym. The orange shag rug literally made me feel sick if I looked at it too long. Meanwhile, I heard the same story again and again from agents and casting directors: "You're so wonderful, Donna—you act, you sing, you dance. But I just don't know what to do with you."

By the time my thirtieth birthday came in November, I had the feeling that somehow life had passed me by. I was in a real crisis. I couldn't seem to draw any hope or reassurance from past success, since I didn't really have a high opinion of myself. Having so much time on my hands seemed to break down my defenses. This might have been a healthy thing, but to me it felt dangerous. I felt abandoned and alone. I had no money, no job, and as far as I could tell, no future. I looked around my dingy apartment and asked myself, "What happened? How did I become a failure?" Little did I know that one day soon my dismal experience would be played out on the Broadway stage, and against all odds, it would give me the role I had always wanted.

Chapter 5

—— ❧ ——

A CHORUS LINE

By the end of 1972, I was so desperate to escape from Los Angeles that I was willing to overcome my pride and turn to my family for help. I knew my father was not well off financially, and I had never asked him for anything before, but I was at such a loss that I had no choice but to call him. As far as I was concerned, this had to be the ultimate admission of failure, especially since my mantra for all these years away from home had been, "I'll show them." Hearing his voice on the phone, I was on the verge of tears. I told him that I was stranded emotionally and financially, and that I needed to get back to New York. He didn't press me with questions. He said, "Don't worry, Donna. I'll wire you the money."

He promised to send me $500, and I was stunned by his offer, realizing that his willingness to help was a sure sign of his love. This wasn't something that he would say to me directly, but at that moment he couldn't have communicated his feelings any more clearly with words. What had seemed like the worst day of my life turned around completely. I was the grateful prodigal daughter as I traveled back across the country. Fortunately, I still had my apartment on the Upper West Side and would soon be able to move back in. With my humbling nightmare behind me, I was anxious to start over.

My return to Broadway came unexpectedly with a call from Kurt

Peterson, who was producing a gala in honor of Stephen Sondheim. The evening would be entitled *Sondheim: A Musical Tribute*. Kurt asked me to choreograph the show, and I was flattered that he trusted me to take on such a challenge. I was also going to perform in two numbers, "Buddy's Blues" from *Follies* and "You Could Drive a Person Crazy" from *Company*.

The production was being directed by Sondheim's longtime friend and collaborator, Burt Shevelove. Steve trusted Burt, and rightly so, to pull off a very ambitious evening. Burt was a funny, fabulous character who had very definite ideas about what he wanted for the show in terms of the look and style. An enormous organizational effort was devoted to creating that one-time-only performance, which was to be recorded live for a two-record set. There were months of preproduction meetings, during which numbers were assigned to more than thirty extraordinary performers, including Angela Lansbury, Chita Rivera, Nancy Walker, Glynis Johns, Hermione Gingold, Alexis Smith, Alice Playten, Larry Kert, Jack Cassidy, Larry Blyden, Len Cariou, John McMartin, Teri Ralston, Tony Stevens, and Harvey Evans.

The experience as choreographer eventually enabled me to discover that I knew more than I thought I did, even though I had never created dances before on such a grand scale and with such an awesome array of talent. I was nervous about the work and made sure that I was prepared in advance for our short run of rehearsals. Working with Angela Lansbury quickly taught me that my preparation was not always going to be appreciated. Angela had flown in from London where she was rehearsing the part of Mama Rose in the West End production of *Gypsy*. For the gala, she was doing the number "A Parade in Town" from *Anyone Can Whistle*.

I had worked out exactly what I wanted her to do, and in our first rehearsal, I showed her the staging. She watched me go through all the moves with the fancy footwork and she said graciously, "Oh, that's lovely, but I don't think I want to move that much. I'll just stand here." I soon came to realize that she knew exactly how she wanted to perform the number, and to perform it in a way that was perfect for her. She stood and sang the song center stage, sometimes moving a little here, sometimes a little there, while Tony and Harvey were dancing around her. She made me look like a genius. Like most new choreographers, I had over-choreographed the piece, but thanks to her I was saved at the end of the day and I learned a great lesson from a great star.

I had a fantastic time working with Chita Rivera and Pam Myers on a little concert version of "America." They were going to perform the song with one dance break, and I wanted to play up the humor and have the number build to a comic payoff for the audience. Though I was a bit intimidated by Chita at first (after all, she was one of my idols!), she was a joy to work with. I thought she might tell me what she was going to do with the number, but like many dancers, she wanted to be told exactly what to do. I showed her what I had prepared and she loved it, and fortunately, so did the audience. I had even more fun working with her and Larry Blyden in "Buddy's Blues" from *Follies*. Larry was a charming and talented actor who was married to one of my favorite dancers of all time, Carol Haney.

The gala took place at the Shubert Theatre on the night of March 11, 1973. In addition to the Broadway stars who performed, there were also stage appearances by Leonard Bernstein, Hal Prince, Anthony Perkins, Jule Styne, Sheldon Harnick, and Burt Shevelove. The performances cul-minated with the ladies seated on little gold opera chairs—Angela Lans-bury, Hermione Gingold, Nancy Walker, Alexis Smith, Glynis Johns, and Dorothy Collins—each getting up in turn and walking to the mike at center stage to sing the songs some of them had made famous. In Nancy Walker's case, there was a perfect combination of artist and song when she performed "I'm Still Here." Near the end, the ladies were joined by Sondheim himself, who sang "Anyone Can Whistle," with everyone gathered around the piano. It was a beautiful ending to a beautiful evening.

Stephen appeared to be overwhelmed by the ovation from the sold-out audience. After the show, there was a lavish supper party at Pub The-atrical, and the reviews were all highly favorable. I was deeply moved when Steve went out of his way to express his thanks to me by giving me two extravagant gifts to mark the occasion, a beautiful Tiffany ring and an exquisite antique dance ornament from Bali.

My life, at least as defined in my mind by my career, appeared to be on the upswing again. At the end of March, I teamed up with Gwen Verdon, Helen Gallagher, and Paula Kelly to perform the opening number for the Tony Awards, an exhilarating piece entitled "It's Broadway." At about the same time, I was also preparing to play the Rose in the movie *The Little Prince,* which was being directed by Stanley Donen, who had directed *Singin' in the Rain.*

Stanley had seen me in the London production of *Company* and later invited me to his office to read for the part. Alan Jay Lerner adapted the script from Antoine de Saint-Exupéry's classic tale, and Frederick Loewe composed the score. Bob Fosse was to appear in the movie, choreographing himself in the role of the Snake. Michael Bennett had also been invited to participate, but he was busy with other projects after coming off *Seesaw,* which opened in March, with my ex-boyfriend Ken Howard playing one of the leads. The fact that Ken was working for Michael reminded me what a small world the theater is, and one that is not without its bittersweet ironies. I remember attending the opening with Michael, and feeling awkward seeing Ken with a new girlfriend, actress Louise Sorel, whom he would marry later that year.

The Little Prince was filmed in London. Stanley was staging the movie, but he needed a choreographer. With Michael not available, I prevailed upon him to hire Ronn Forella, a teacher with whom I had been studying in New York. Intense and sometimes temperamental, Ronn had never choreographed either a Broadway show or a movie. In spite of his rough edges, I thought he had real potential and I wanted to help him. I also figured that we could work well together since we had similar styles and training. After holding out ungracefully for more money, he finally joined us in London, and we stayed at the Savoy.

Elaine Stritch was also living at the Savoy, having stayed in London after the run of *Company.* Spending time with her and catching up was the highlight of my trip. Meanwhile, Stanley was agreeable about letting me choose the music for my dance, and encouraged me to use something that was already recorded. The idea was that after the filming was completed, a different arrangement would be written, using the recording as a guide for the musical dynamics. I decided on a modern piece with intricate jazz chords from the rock group Chicago, and we soon went to work at Elstree Studios.

I was thrown at first by Stanley's direction, as he wanted the number to be seductive, a hot dance with bumps and grinds. I admired Stanley and his work, but I was reluctant to go that way with it because I was performing the scene with the Little Prince, played by an adorable, seven-year-old English boy, Steven Warner. I tried to compromise with a more playful approach, which was sexy but not too hard-edged, as if I were a child in a woman's body. My efforts really didn't matter in the end. I found myself frustrated by the whole process of making this film. I wasn't helped along the way when the director and choreographer had "creative differences." Stanley would stomp his feet in frustration, and eventually he barred Ronn from the lot. The atmosphere on the set was tense and uncomfortable.

I felt like I was working in a bubble, an experience so different from that of performing in front of a theater audience. In the film, I was going to be superimposed, so I was shot against a black velvet backdrop on a set surrounded by an army of technicians. The Little Prince hadn't quite learned his lines, so the script girl kept bellowing, "I love you, Rose." It didn't really matter who said them anyway. I never knew when the camera was going to cut away, or if the music would be coming in underneath the scene.

When I saw the movie months later, I was mortified. My scene had been cut to ribbons and the music was changed completely. The song I sang, "Be Happy," was in my soprano voice, but my voice in the scene was dubbed by someone with a very low, sultry English accent. It occurred to me that he never had any intention to use my speaking voice.

Returning to New York after the filming, I had no idea how disappointed I would be when the movie was finally released. It's not that I had any great aspirations for a film career, but I had hoped that it might be good for me by giving me that important recognition value. In the summer of 1973, I went out of town again to perform in a show at the Wayside Theatre in Middletown, Virginia, located in the Blue Ridge Mountains. I was scheduled to perform the title role in *Irma La Douce,* the farce about the Parisian hooker with a heart of gold. The show had been a hit in London under Peter Brook's direction, and later came to New York thanks to David Merrick.

The Wayside was a charming jewel box of a theater, but it was so tiny that the actors couldn't even run behind the stage. We had to go out a door that led behind the theater, and whenever it was raining, one of the stagehands would hold an umbrella over me. I had great fun rehearsing the show even though we had very little rehearsal time. In an interview with David Richards of the *Washington Star-News* I enthused: "I've never operated this way before in my life. Here I am with the score in my hand, improvising some dance steps with the fellows. I'll say something like, 'What if I do a big kick here?' and then I'll jump on their shoulders and they aren't even half expecting it. . . . We've got so little time to put it together, there's this enormous thrust into the material. It's driving us all berserk and I love it."

I hadn't anticipated the problem beforehand, but the size of the theater ultimately worked against me. I wasn't able to sail as I had on the Broadway stage. I may have also over-glamourized my Irma, perhaps trying to compensate for a leading man who was too young for me, talented as he was. There were some marvelous character actors in the cast, and even though the director, Davey Marlin Jones, was clever with his staging, in the end it wasn't the fully realized experience for me that it might have been.

Back in New York in the fall and winter of that year, I started spending more social time with Michael. He called at one point out of nowhere and said, "Donna, I just want to take a walk with you through Central Park." It was a beautiful day, and we walked and chatted. He wanted to know if I was dating anyone and I recounted my most recent debacle on the dating scene. I entertained him with my story, and I thought how different it was to be with Michael this way. It felt very personal and I liked that, even though it did make me a little nervous to be with him in a way that was unrelated to work.

That day elevated our friendship to a new level in my mind. He would call like that to keep tabs on me, and we sometimes met for dinner to commiserate about the state of the theater, and our lives. He had been frustrated by his two most recent outings on Broadway, *Seesaw* and George Furth's collection of one-act plays, *Twigs*. With those shows, Michael had been trying to emulate Jerome Robbins, as a director of both musicals and straight plays. Despite his earlier successes, Michael still considered himself to be in a pre-takeoff position with his career, and he was aware that people expected great things from him. Full of angst and ambition, he confided in me, and it made me feel special that he trusted me in that way. Michael also believed in my talent. He would say titillating things like, "I've got to get a show for you, Donna." Whenever he said that, I always encouraged him, saying lightheartedly, "Yeah, great! Please, hurry!"

I had reached a certain age and wanted to be a leading lady, so I was enchanted that Michael was thinking of me like that. But at the same time, I knew that he had to get his own show before he could do anything for me. My big complaint was that people didn't know how to categorize me as a performer, and therefore I wasn't getting parts. I continued to hear the line, "What do I do with a soprano who can dance like you?" And as always, my identity as an actress seemed to get lost in the shuffle. Michael's major complaint was that he didn't have the control in the theater that he needed to realize the very specific aspirations that he had to become a director-choreographer.

I remember at one point having dinner with Michael and Bob Avian. I told them about an article that I had read that described incredible real estate deals in New Zealand, and went on to suggest that we might consider moving there to start our own theater company. It seemed like a lark at first, but for a while Michael seemed to take the idea seriously. First and foremost, however, was his all-consuming dream to create what he called "the perfect musical," one in which all of the elements of storytelling, music, dance, and design supported each other. This idea really was a serious quest on his part, and it took a number of forms. One of his ideas was to do a show about dancers, and he was exploring several concepts along that line.

One day Michael showed me a picture that he said inspired him. The image called to mind a Vargas girl. She was wearing a slip and sitting on a chair in front of a makeup table. The style was very 1920s and he said that she reminded him of me. That inspiration led him to the idea of doing a backstage murder mystery, and he soon commissioned a script from Leonard Gershe, who had written *Butterflies Are Free*. The musical was called *Pin Ups,* and the story involved a chorus girl who was murdered. But when the script was finished, Michael was already pursuing another project and decided to pass on it. Leonard then gave him back his $5,000 fee and Michael was astonished by the gesture, telling me that he couldn't believe anyone would ever do such a thing.

One night I had dinner with Michael at his place on West 55th Street. It was just the two of us and his cook, Bernice. At a certain point, Michael said, "You know, I want to do this new show about dancers, but I especially want to do it for you." There I was with no money and no job again, and he was telling me that he was going to have a part written for me. Of course, I was elated by the prospect, and he went on to describe the concept of a show with a set reminiscent of the one in Jerome Robbins's famous ballet "Afternoon of a Faun." Michael intended to have the musical open with dancers entering the empty studio and warming up. He loved the idea of all that clean space, and using the entire stage as a set. As in the Robbins ballet, Michael wanted the audience to understand who the characters were without any dialogue, but simply by seeing how they related to each other through their attitude and physical behavior. While he didn't yet have a full plot worked out, he knew that he wanted to do a show in which dancers would tell the story—their story.

Coincidentally, on New Year's Day of 1974, Michael met with two friends, Michon Peacock and Tony Stevens, who also had in mind the idea that a show should be done about dancers. Michon and Tony were zealous in their desire to draw attention to the plight of chorus dancers. I had worked with Tony in *On the Town,* and he had more recently choreographed a show in which Michon had performed, entitled *Rachael Lily Rosenbloom and Don't You Ever Forget It.*

Michon had also danced for Michael in *Seesaw,* and during that show, a ritual had developed. Each night a number of dancers in the cast would have class and then sit around and talk after the show about the plight of dancers. After Michael met with Michon and Tony, and under his guidance, they decided to invite a group of dancers to participate in exactly that kind of rap session. This was intended to be a freewheeling exploration, an opportunity for dancers to express themselves, to air their grievances and learn about what they had in common.

The first session was scheduled to take place a couple of weeks later at the Nickolaus Exercise Studio on Third Avenue at 28th Street. Michael asked me to go with him that night, and I remember he was nervous and held my hand as we went into the building. Because some of the dancers were in shows, the meeting was held late, and at around midnight, we were the last to arrive. Twenty-four dancers showed up, and many of them, like me, had worked for Michael before. There was a class given by Wayne Cilento, who had danced in *Seesaw,* and then we all sat on the floor in another room with wall-to-wall carpet, a jug of wine and one of those old reel-to-reel tape recorders.

Michael started by telling us, "I don't know what this is going to be— a musical, a book, a movie, a play—but we're going to talk about dancing and what it means to be a dancer. What I want each of you to do is tell me your name, where you were born, and why you wanted to become a dancer." The tape recorder was turned on, and one at a time, progressing around the circle, each person was to tell his or her story. Michael initially offered some of his own personal history to set the tone and to draw people into the process. He had already spent a number of years in analysis, and to some extent his methods reflected that background.

Michael already must have had the idea of using the audition as a conceit for the show, because the session actually became a kind of audition under his direction, and those opening questions that he asked us were eventually used as the starting point in *A Chorus Line.* Michael later said, "I wanted to know why they had started dancing. In a sense I wanted to know why I had started—and hadn't I lost something along the way." Part of what he lost was the camaraderie of being in the chorus. As a thirty-year-old director and choreographer, he missed those carefree days of being in the chorus with friends, and he missed dancing; he missed that happier and more innocent time when his dreams and bright future lay ahead of him. I believe this show was a way for him to reclaim that part of his life.

As we told our stories, a number of common threads quickly emerged: how we all loved dancing as children and eventually arrived at the point where we had nothing else on our minds, and how we all came to feel like we wouldn't have lives unless we pursued our dreams of dancing. Despite our diverse backgrounds, personalities, and sexual persuasions, we discovered that we had all found acceptance in the theater, and that was ultimately how we had managed to survive.

There may also have been an element of competition that night as to who could tell the most horrific story about growing up. People would say things like, "Oh, you think that's bad. We were so poor that I had to eat coffee grounds for breakfast," as in that very funny "who-had-the-worst-childhood" scene in Murray Schisgal's play *Luv*. But the typical reaction for many of us was "Oh, that happened to you too?" The strategy of developing a musical from this kind of raw material was very much a product of the mid-1970s confessionals and the so-called "me" generation. Talking about his own experiences, Michael was extremely forthcoming and candid. I admired his courage, though there were some things he had to say that I didn't necessarily want to hear.

As I recall, Michael described his Italian background and stifling family situation growing up in Buffalo, his early dance training, and sexual experiences as a teenager. He told us he lost his virginity with his first dance teacher, a woman who had taken advantage of his youth and inexperience. Then he had an affair with another dance teacher, who was a man. That pattern was to continue throughout his life, but it sounded to me like his problems had less to do with being straight or gay than with his being unable to trust anyone, male or female, on an intimate level. I felt sorry for him when I learned how complicated it had been for him. While Michael often said things purely for effect or shock value, most of what he confided that night rang true, and afterward, I felt closer to him.

That first session was emotional for all of us, and went on until noon the next day. Initially, Michael seemed to want to discourage me from taking my turn and talking about myself. It was as if he didn't want to alter the impression that he already had of me, or else it didn't matter what I said because I already had the part. I really don't know. I thought perhaps he didn't want me to leave the little pedestal he seemed to put me on, just as I did with him. I finally insisted on talking because I was so excited after hearing the others. The sun was up, and it was amazing that any of us were still awake. Like the others, I went through a kind of catharsis as I described my family history and the conflicts with my parents that caused me to run away from home as a teenager.

There were parts of my story that Michael had never heard before, and the connection between us certainly strengthened that night, though neither of us talked about it at the time. It was also exhilarating for me to feel the common bond with the rest of the dancers, even though I had worked hard not to be in the chorus after *How to Succeed*. There were times when I was out of work that I thought maybe I was wrong in making that decision, but I knew that I wouldn't be happy just dancing in a line. That just wasn't me.

It was my goal to find my true voice, to find a way to express myself creatively in a unique and personal way, and therefore it was fascinating to hear how some of these gypsies would go from show to show, knowing each other, with their lives interconnected in that way. Some dancers depended on dancing as a regular job in order to live and raise a family, while others saw dancing in the chorus as a stepping-stone to a more expansive career in show business. Some were happy to dance on Broadway and get paid for it while going to school to prepare for a second non–show business career.

They had a history with each other, through good times and bad, friendship and rivalry. Sometimes it can get very sticky in a chorus dressing room. "Chorus Mentality" is an unattractive label I've heard over the years that refers to the bitchiness and pettiness backstage that becomes a survival tool in that highly competitive arena. Dancers historically work the hardest, longest hours, are usually paid the least, and are rarely called upon to share their creative ideas about what a show needs. They are often made to feel expendable. And like an abused child in a family, some learn to give it out just like they take it.

That shared reality was one of the reasons Michael wanted to pay tribute to them. He felt they deserved better. The chorus line was where he started and learned so much about theater, where his dreams were set in motion. Even though I felt that Michael and I were on the same page as far as developing what could be a breakthrough role for me, there were times when I thought that few others realized that.

While I was always there to hold his hand and offer my support, our friendship put me in an awkward position with some of the others. I soon felt the need to pull away and isolate myself for my own protection and also for the sake of the work. It was quite a different experience from working with the cast of *Company,* where everyone knew the part they were to play, and to make the show work we had to get along with each other. Ironically, in *A Chorus Line,* my isolation from the group suited my character, Cassie, as she was supposed to be an outsider, a featured performer who had fallen on hard times and was returning to beg for a job in the chorus. In retrospect, I sometimes wonder if I didn't unconsciously set myself apart in order to fulfill the role.

The next session took place a few weeks later, with most of the same dancers, though a few had dropped out and been replaced by newcomers. The process of taping and transcribing our memories continued, with scripted characters eventually emerging as composites. Michael encouraged an aspiring writer in the group, Nicholas Dante, to take the lead in putting a script together. Later, Michael brought in James Kirkwood to help with the writing, and for the next year or so, the book for *A Chorus Line* was in a constant state of revision. Much of Nick's own personal story went into the character of Paul, almost verbatim as he told it that night. Like the rest of us, Michael was moved by Nick's affecting tale about finding his identity and self-respect in the early 1960s by way of performing in a drag queen revue.

The first hurdle in launching the project was winning support from Joseph Papp at the prestigious New York Shakespeare Festival. Joe didn't like commercial theater, but he had a high regard for Michael. At that point, Michael had more than twenty hours of tapes, which included the group sessions as well as interviews with other dancers that had been conducted privately. After listening to some of the tapes, Joe offered his support for a workshop production to be staged downtown at the Newman Theater, one of six houses that were part of the Public Theater. The evolution of the workshop progressed in fits and starts during the next year, as many of us, including Michael, were distracted, working on other projects.

For the most part, our individual stories as dancers were mixed and rearranged in the script, with the events from one person's life often given over to another in order to suit the drama. While the character of Cassie absorbed some of my experiences, like my disastrous time in L.A., she was the most fictionalized of all the characters. Unlike Cassie, I never did a toilet paper commercial and never appeared as a singing Band-Aid and never felt I couldn't act. When the show was promoted as based on the true stories of dancers, it was hard to convince people that it was only partly true, especially when the audience was so affected by it.

Cassie also took on some of Michael's experience in the way that she had a personal history with the fictional director, Zach. Of course, Michael and I had never been involved that way. In the contentious squabbling scene between Cassie and Zach, Michael was drawing from his breakup years earlier with dancer Scott Pearson, one of the loves of Michael's life. There were to be so many layers to Cassie. In her relationship to Zach, she also reflected what I had told Michael about my breakup with Ken, and how we had never had a "last conversation" or a sense of closure.

Later, there would be contentious arguments over who among us said what, who did or didn't do what, who wrote which sections of the script, who contributed the most to the process, and who was paid what. But the reality was that Michael was the driving force that kept the project on track. He was the one who elicited our contributions and managed to put them on the stage. Numbers like "Hello Twelve, Hello Thirteen, Hello Love" were ultimately the outcome of Michael directing Marvin Hamlisch and Ed Kleban to compose songs using the dancers' own words. And after all, what were the chances that a show could succeed with no stars, that a show could be a hit opening as it did on a bare stage with only a rehearsal piano? Michael made it happen, but there was a price to be paid by all of us.

What began as wonderfully idealistic was destined to become something that none of us could have foreseen, even Michael. This was a unique experience. On the one hand, the production needed Michael's vision, talent, energy, and clout to be a commercial success; on the other hand, his manipulative approach was bound to leave behind wounded feelings and bruised egos among his collaborators and the entire cast.

Looking back, I can see that Michael used two instinctive strategies over and over. One was divide and conquer, as he continually played us against each other in order to stay in control. The other was seduce and abandon, as he would favor, charm, entice, or befriend whomever he needed to make something happen. People often fell in love with Michael because he could make them feel so special simply by devoting his attention to them. But sooner or later, he would cut them loose, or commit some outright betrayal. Over time, most of them would return and get back on track. "They always come back," he would say. But there would be those who could never forgive him completely.

Of course, our fate in the show as dancers wasn't all Michael's doing. There were always conflicts for us to work through with each other, as well as enjoying our shared success. Each day in rehearsals we were called upon to delve into our personal lives and reveal our inner feelings while our parts were being written. Most dancers aren't used to expressing themselves this way. By the very nature of the discipline, dancers tend to be in denial about their feelings much of the time.

As a dancer, you must do your daily ballet barre regardless of how you feel. In a sense, a dancer will physically repress and resist these emotions, pushing them down into the body and literally into the muscles as he or she exercises. These undesired emotions don't just evaporate, but will more than likely find a place to settle inwardly. I believe in the organic and natural order of things, that feelings were meant to be expressed outwardly, appropriately, and fully, not trapped inside the body. Initially, for me, that process of stifling my feelings in this way reached a kind of personal culmination over the next two years of work on *A Chorus Line.*

In April, I appeared in a revue called *Music, Music,* Alan Jay Lerner's tribute to the Broadway musical that played at the City Center. Tony

Stevens did an excellent job choreographing the show, and I had a few little patter numbers, which I enjoyed, singing a duet with Larry Kert, but nothing that showed me off to any real advantage. After we opened, Clive Barnes wrote a scathing review in the *New York Times,* suggesting that I shouldn't even have been on the stage. I kept the notice for almost a year, and then felt I had to bring it to Michael's attention. After all, Clive Barnes was the most important critic in New York, and if he were prejudiced against me, then I was a liability and it was only fair that Michael should know.

I finally went to him in tears, having blown up the review in my mind to the point where I was certain that I would be the cause of *A Chorus Line* failing. Michael listened to my fearful tale and then said, "I'm going to get him on the phone right now, and when I signal you, pick up the extension." He actually phoned Clive Barnes at home and quickly signaled me. He said, "I've got a young lady in my show who is very upset about what you wrote about her. She told me that you hated her and she's very worried." During their conversation I heard Mr. Barnes say, "Oh no, I really like Donna, but I just didn't think she was up to par in that show."

As I listened, I found myself agreeing with him. Then I thought, *Oh my God, I've been carrying that review around with me for the last year. How insane!* I walked back into Michael's living room and saw a smile on his face, and I thought, *Is anyone smarter or better than him?* I gave him a grateful hug and left his apartment with an enormous sense of relief, knowing that I could return to work the next day and not worry, at least not about Clive Barnes. On the ride down in the elevator I felt a tug at my heart and I remember thinking how I could love a man like that—someone who could be fearless in the face of adversity, a man of action who could protect me and take care of me.

During our break from the workshop that July, I went off to the Williamstown Theatre Festival in Massachusetts to play the role of Lucy Brown in *The Threepenny Opera.* This was a special experience for me, with Peter Hunt directing a sensational cast that included Raul Julia as Macheath, JoBeth Williams as Polly, Virginia Vestoff as Jenny, and Austin Pendleton in the role of Filch. I was grateful to be in such company and again taken seriously as an actress. One of my fondest memories of that production was my first entrance, when I came out and flew into a temper tantrum, slamming Raul with my pocketbook. Sounding like a young Ricky Ricardo, Raul would yell at me, "Lucy! Lucy!" For me, that set a carefree tone for the rest of the show each night.

The happy experience that summer enabled me to get away from the relentless psychic digging in our *Chorus Line* workshop. At the end of the run, Peter Hunt, who had also directed *1776* on Broadway, flew me and Michael to East Hampton in his Piper Cub for a one-night revue that was to benefit the John Drew Theatre. In a two-hour session with the pianist just before the show, Michael and I prepared Gershwin's "I Won't Dance." Each of us took turns singing a stanza, and then we did a sweeping dance chorus together, à la Ginger and Fred. This was a special delight for both of us because this was the first time we had performed together since our *Hullabaloo* days, and the first time we had ever done a song-and-dance number together.

That occasion was also a beautiful respite for both of us, a break from the rigors of the workshop. We were singing and dancing together, and it was a bit of heaven for me. It seemed to me like Michael was having fun too. He could be sweet and when he was, he was irresistible. I now had a new dilemma to deal with because of this growing feeling of love for Michael. I wasn't sure what to do about it. Was he going to define a new category for me, a man I loved but could never marry?

Meanwhile, the work on *A Chorus Line* continued, although many of the people involved were frustrated at how slowly it seemed to be moving. Those who stayed did so out of loyalty to Michael and the expectation that he would deliver. A couple of people in the cast eventually left because they didn't like the idea of doing an off-Broadway show. Another dancer left to do an industrial show because he needed the money, since we weren't getting a proper salary yet, and there wasn't any real guarantee that we would in the future.

Our first workshop didn't have any songs and ran for more than four hours. We called it "The Towering Inferno," reminiscent of the movie where people jumped to their death with great flair. Every monologue recalled a troubled or traumatic childhood, with each one trying to top the last. Around the half circle on the stage, we would go, one after the other, all of us sitting there listening until it was our turn. There was a kind of built-in lack of surprise. The show was really boring after the second monologue, and then became really depressing as you just waited for it to be over. We improvised a great deal, since we were still experimenting with the material and exploring our characters. Ed Kleban wrote lyrics based on the taped sessions and the scenes that we were acting out. Marvin Hamlisch, who by this time had won three Academy Awards, came in to compose the music.

The first song that was written was "At the Ballet." It was played for the cast at the beginning of the second workshop. Marvin was onstage at the piano with Ed standing next to him, and they performed the song for all of us sitting in the orchestra seats in the Newman Theater. It was so moving to hear my early childhood story so beautifully expressed in that song, sung by Maggie's character. I think everyone was affected and in awe. It was thrilling to feel the first emotional heartbeat of our show in that song. From that moment on, I knew that I was involved in something remarkable, and for my money, it was already an artistic success.

Ed and Marvin moved us to tears with each new song, while the collaboration between Marvin and Michael had its ups and downs. Marvin would feel discouraged at times and Michael would needle him saying, "What do you want, Marvin, to win more awards, or do you want to make art?" Michael would sometimes scream in Marvin's face, "This is what I want! Ya got it?" Several times Michael told me that Marvin had walked out on the production, and he was going to have to woo him back by wining and dining him. That was another part of the process because they both eventually made amends and produced brilliant work together.

Michael had more than one way of getting what he wanted, and he sometimes went to extremes with the dancers, though there is no question that he had great affection for all of us. We were all handpicked by him. We worked in this insular way for weeks and months, growing, I thought at the time, like hothouse tomatoes.

As the workshop progressed, there was a crucial scene that required a definite spontaneity and realism from the performers, and not all of the dancers had enough training in acting to be able to pull it off effectively. Near the end of the audition, which is the premise of the show, Cassie makes her appeal to Zach that she should be hired, and then he runs all the dancers through a routine. The fates of all those seventeen dancers trying out hang in the balance, and there comes a moment when Paul, played by Sammy Williams, wrenches his knee and falls on a turn. His accident was supposed to elicit a deep reaction from the rest of the dancers, but Michael was frustrated with what he saw us doing in rehearsal and decided to intervene.

Michael took over and started dancing Paul's part in the routine. He was totally concentrated on the movement, and his energy as a dancer was still as intense and focused as it had been back in our days on *Hullabaloo*. But at a certain point, his knee buckled and he fell hard to the floor. We all saw him clutching his knee and writhing in pain. A few of us quickly ran to him to try to help. Some people just stood transfixed in surprise and shock as his assistant Bob ran out, to call an ambulance. After a few minutes of anguished confusion, Michael looked up at us and said, "Do you all remember what you just did?" As the realization hit us that he was just acting, he added, "That's what I want you to do! Exactly what you just did."

There were sighs of relief mixed with laughter, while some of us were on the brink of tears. Others felt violated by his tactic, which was like a dirty practical joke that he had played on those who cared about him. Baayork Lee, who played Connie Wong, was also serving as dance captain. She screamed in anger at Michael, but he insisted, "I want you to remember everything that you felt!" He was trying to create an immediate emotional memory for each of us, to be able to personalize the scene and re-create it night after night in a spontaneous way. This was Michael's calculated take on the more abrasive methods of his idol, Jerome Robbins, who had a reputation for doing whatever he thought was necessary to make a show work.

In fact, after that rehearsal, the scene with Paul worked every time, and for Michael, the end no doubt justified the means. I understood what he was doing, but at the same time, a part of me resented his having to resort to that kind of deception. As an actress trying to prove myself, I didn't like the idea of a director manipulating the feelings of actors to get a desired effect. But since some of the cast were not trained in acting techniques, it may have been the best choice to Michael's way of thinking. I also think he got a big charge out of doing it. On another level, what the incident stirred up in me was a sense of how much Michael meant to me, which was something I never told him. I suddenly knew just how deeply it would affect me if anything were to actually happen to him.

Michael's attention was drawn to wherever there was trouble in the show. If a dancer was working well, he or she was ignored. Fortunately, most of the time, I was left alone. He later told me, "I had other things to worry about. I wasn't concerned about you." There was only one time when I felt he mistreated me. We hadn't seen him for a few days, as he had been going through a difficult time with Joe Papp. Apparently, Joe had decided at the last minute that he wanted to have the show go into the Vivian Beaumont Theater at Lincoln Center instead of the Newman. Michael insisted on the Newman because it offered a more appropriate, intimate space with its proscenium and 299 seats. He threatened to break with Joe Papp and the Shakespeare Festival by going to Bernard Jacobs and the Shubert Organization. Michael won that round, but when he came back to work, he was in a foul black mood.

I remember him sitting in the audience at the Newman that day. We were to begin working on my solo that afternoon and I was excited to finally get to it. He had me go onstage with the drummer, Bobby Thomas, who was always there to set the rhythm and start the dances. We hadn't had any real discussion yet of what I was going to do. But Michael said to me, "Okay, go." With an impatient tone, he added, "Do something."

With my heart racing, I tried to improvise, but there was no specific starting point or basic idea with which to work. I had to ask myself, What is this about? Where was the collaboration that I had become accustomed to? I tried a few combinations and looked at Michael's reaction reflected in the mirror. He just sat there glowering, and finally I shut down completely. Then he said, "Okay, we'll do this later."

Michael wasn't verbally abusive, but it was like he was saying, "I'm tired of doing everything myself, and I'm tired of working on this number. Why don't you choreograph it?" That was a Michael I had never experienced before, and the situation was embarrassing for everyone who was there. Bob Avian told me that he later scolded Michael, but it was one of those nights when all I could do was go home and cry myself to sleep. That was just one situation, however, after years of being treated so well.

Fortunately, most of the time the work did go very well, and Michael tried in rehearsals to make the part special for me, sometimes overdoing it to the point where I would say to him, "You're killing me with kindness, Michael." That was the case with my first entrance. After the other dancers had done their first combination and were standing on the line, he had me running in late, like a starlet, a young Betty Bacall, in my fox coat and silk pants, suddenly interrupting the audition. I was waving a ten-dollar bill and asking excitedly, "Does anybody have change for a ten? I have a taxi waiting out there."

That was Michael's attempt to give me a star's entrance, besides giving the character stature, making Cassie different from the others. He soon realized that making her different from the others wasn't appealing to the audience. It sent the wrong message after seeing all the hard work the dancers went through just to stand on the line together. I felt the "flop sweat" immediately when I made my entrance that way in the first preview. The scene was cut for the next show.

In much the same way, my second-act number, "Inside the Music," suffered from being overly ambitious in the wrong direction. Beautiful as it was, the song was too operatic and rangy to lead into the dance. It was overkill, in the sense that I was to hit a sustained high C and then somehow make a transition into the choreography. It felt awkward and silly. Michael gave himself the freedom to make mistakes like that, and once he saw the error, he pushed for a complete revision.

Ed and Marvin came up with a new song, "The Music and the Mirror," which was a powerful evocation of a dancer's reality and dreams. I had been interviewed by Ed Kleban, and he wrote lyrics that reflected what I told him about my relationship to music and dancing. I had never verbalized my feelings about my desire to dance and the protective fantasy life that dancing gave me, allowing me to live in the music. I felt my efforts to explain this to Ed were clumsy, but hoped that I had given him something to work with. I had to hold back tears the first time I heard his lyrics. He captured me and my feelings perfectly in the most simple, beautiful, and poetic way. At the same time, there was a lesson in those lyrics that I had yet to fully appreciate and take to heart, because, like Michael, I made no separation between my life and the work:

Give me somebody to dance with
Give me a place to fit in.
Help me return to the world of the living,
By showing me how to begin.
Play me the music,
Give me the chance to come through.
All I ever needed
Was the music and the mirror,
And the chance to dance
For you.

The song was perfectly appropriate for the character, and the challenge was then to come up with equally appropriate choreography. The first approach that Michael tried with the rewritten number was overdone. Again, I thought he was killing me with kindness. He wanted the number to stop the show in a big way, and at first he thought that meant more production values to help build the number to an exciting finish. At a certain point, he had the male dancers join me. First they came out disguised in black jumpsuits, moving on counts behind five full-length mirrors, which they rolled out to center stage. The inspiration for elevating the dance with multiple mirrors came from a Lalique art deco statue of a dancer that I had given Michael. He had it displayed in a mirrored corner of his living room. Onstage I danced a slow section in front of the mirrors. Then, on counts again, and much to their chagrin, they moved the mirrors back offstage, as if they were stagehands rather than dancers.

When they came back onstage in costume and joined me, I came across like Ann-Margret and her boys, and it didn't suit the character or the drama, though it might have been a big hit in Las Vegas. By the end we were all facing the audience and reaching out, as if to Zach. The piece was exciting, but it stood out inappropriately and detracted from the show as a whole.

But that was how the number was done during the first preview, which took place at the Newman on April 15, 1975. While well received, we knew there was still a great deal of work to be done. After our second preview, Michael phoned me late at night, and Bob was on the line as well. Referring to my performance in "The Music and the Mirror," Michael said, "So why aren't you dancing?" Taken aback, I asked him what he meant, and he said, "You're not dancing. It's like you're marking."

"Well, give me a little time," I said, and then tried to explain. "We're still just learning the piece. And we have all these numbers across the front of the stage to keep our formations. I'm trying not to hit Wayne, who's dancing on six; then I'm on seven, and Rick Mason is on eight. I'm just trying to hit my number and keep my place."

He said, "Is that why you're not dancing?"

"Yeah!" I told him. "But it'll come together."

Later that night, unbeknownst to me, Michael or Bob called each of the male dancers and gave each of them the bad news that they were out of the number. When I came in to work the next day, no one bothered to tell me that they had been cut. But it wasn't long before I could sense the resentment in the silent treatment I was getting from the guys. Whatever Michael told the others, he undoubtedly didn't discourage them from thinking it was my idea to cut them. I got the feeling that he didn't explain the reason for the change to their satisfaction, or if he did, they chose to think otherwise.

I was conflicted about the way Michael handled the situation, but I was also relieved that I would be given a chance to be alone in the number. This was a chance to prove myself as a dramatic solo artist, and it felt like the right choice for the character that I was beginning to inhabit. I decided the best thing for me to do was to forge ahead and keep my feelings in check.

After the dancers were cut, of course, the number had to be revised again. I remember at one point walking outside one of the dressing rooms and overhearing a couple of the girls talking about me. One of them said, "I don't know why she's even getting a number. She can't dance anymore."

I felt the stab in my back as they wondered aloud why Michael was working so hard on my number when several others that weren't working had already been cut. After that incident, I did my best to stay insulated from the negative energy, from all the tempers, frustrations, and fears. It is ironic that from the outside, the chorus line is such a picture of unity, while on the inside there can be such fierce competition and rivalries. I confided to only a few friends in the show: Trish Garland, with whom I shared a dressing room, Baayork Lee, and Kay Cole. We were pals in the theater but rarely socialized together.

I had a boyfriend at the time, Harvey, who owned a hair salon on 72nd Street called Harvey's Bazaar. I had gone in one day for a haircut and he was very cute and flirty with me. I immediately liked him, especially because he wasn't in show business, and he liked me, I think, because I was in show business. I started dating him just before I started the workshop, and soon I sublet my apartment and moved into his. Harvey was easygoing and relaxed. Being with him gave me a sense of normalcy. While we were together and I was rehearsing downtown, I was usually too exhausted to cook, and he would make me salads for dinner each night and snacks for the next day.

I was starting to feel a balance in my life for the first time in a long while and it made me feel positive about the future. I had no money to speak of, only enough to survive, but I was genuinely happy. For the most part, I took solace in my spartan, solitary routine. I would take the subway downtown to the theater each day, reading and meditating during the ride, all the while anticipating the work ahead.

As the previews continued, "The Music and the Mirror" was turned into a solo for me. I went to Michael's apartment one night along with Bob Avian, drummer Bobby Thomas, and Marvin Hamlisch, who was at the piano and writing while we talked. They allowed me to break down what I thought should happen musically following the dramatic line of

Cassie's experience. This was a collaborative situation that I had never experienced before with a composer of Marvin's stature. I was excited by the uniqueness of such a creative opportunity and I tried to take advantage of the chance to express my ideas.

I thought a changing tempo could reflect Cassie's emotional rollercoaster ride from the moment she connected with her anger in facing Zach at the audition. At that point, I suggested going into a slow 4/4, which feels sexy, showing another kind of determination after a driving rhythm, then building again toward a climax. We didn't have strings, but we had brass, and Marvin suggested a trumpet solo over the rhythm. I thought that was fantastic. In my mind there was an emotional dynamic between those two levels in the music, a really exquisite ambivalence with Cassie's sexuality emerging from the rhythm of the drums and her yearning reflected in the plaintive trumpet line.

By the end of the solo, the dance perfectly reflected the idea of the lyrics, and the audience was able to see Cassie's transformation, ideally realizing that she had resolved something in her feelings that she had never dealt with before. Part of the reason the number ultimately worked so well was that Michael pushed me almost beyond endurance, adding a fourth turn at the end, when I was exhausted, so the audience would see my sweat and strain when I had to reach for it like it was life-or-death. He wanted everyone to be asking themselves, "Will she make it?" And I found myself asking the same question, night after night. But that was Michael at his best, when he was inspired and pushing for that kind of raw excitement that was suited for the character, and ultimately culminated in the success of the whole story.

That was one of the ways that Cassie's struggle became universal, a metaphor that not only dancers could identify with. I was dancing and singing about this rarefied existence of a dancer: "God, I'm a dancer." But the image resonated in so many ways: "God, I'm a teacher . . . I'm a doctor . . . I'm a person." People from all walks of life connected with her, especially her desire for a second chance. Before the show opened, however, Michael was concerned about how the character would land and he had misgivings about the ending of the show.

Originally, Cassie was not among those who were cast at the end of the audition. After making her plea for Zach to hire her, she was brusquely rejected. That was Michael's original take on the cutthroat reality of show business. But he was ultimately forced to compromise his artistic intentions with that very dark ending. Michael had worked with Neil Simon the year before on *God's Favorite*. After Neil and his wife, Marsha Mason, saw *A Chorus Line* during previews, they insisted that Michael had to offer at least some glimmer of hope to the audience. Marsha apparently went so far as to call the show a "downer." As an actress analyzing the story line, Marsha helped me to realize that if Cassie were to lose out that way, then Zach would also lose, proving that he was unable to face the demons called up by his encounter with her.

Sensing the audience disappointment, Michael relented, allowing Cassie her triumph at the audition, and at the same time holding open the uncertain future possibilities with Zach. I loved that bittersweet resolution. It said their lives would go on, and that they had learned something, whether they were together or not. I was proud of Michael for having the courage to show that kind of compassion and to give Cassie her second chance. He later told the *Times*, "The show says you can't go back in life," but he added, "Anybody should have the right to begin again."

As it evolved through the creative process, that perspective was the kind of thrill for me that offset the tensions and ultimately made the work worthwhile. I remember one beautiful sunny afternoon when Pam Blair, who played Val, and I took a walk on 8th Street in the Village during our lunch break. We were window-shopping and chatting, and our spirits were carefree. At that point, with so many weeks of dancing behind me, I was feeling especially strong and light and agile on my feet. There came a moment as we were walking back to the Public Theater when I thought to myself, *I'm finally doing exactly what I've always wanted to do. I have friends and I have a place to go every day to work—to dance, act, sing, and create. I've never been happier in my life.*

There were a total of forty-one previews, and they were extremely successful as a work in progress. We drew a repeat audience as many people returned just to see how Michael would fix the show. There was an immediate recognition that something special was happening, and each night the level of excitement seemed to surpass that of the night before. With the opening night approaching, my nerves were on edge, and Michael hit me with another surprise. I was already anxious, knowing that my parents would be coming, and feeling like my life and career were once again literally on the line. After one of our last rehearsals, I was on the stage and Michael took me aside. He was so agitated that he was shaking. He said, "Ken is back in town, and he's trying to get in touch with you. He wants to see you, and he called me."

Shocked by this piece of news, I said, "Why is he calling you, Michael? Why doesn't he call me?"

"He called me to get your number," Michael explained. "But I told him that I didn't want him to see you now. Of course, you can see him if you want, but I told him not to call you until after you open."

I was flabbergasted that Michael was trying to take charge of my personal life that way. Of course, he knew all about my history with Ken, and he was afraid that my performance would somehow be affected by an untimely reunion. I said, "I appreciate your concern, Michael, but Ken can call me if he wants to. He doesn't have to wait."

There had been subtle indications before that Michael harbored certain feelings about me, not so much romantic as proprietary. My romance with Harvey had recently cooled, but Michael had been aware that we were together. One night as I was about to leave rehearsal, Michael said, pointedly, "Say hello to Harvey for me." He sounded almost jealous, and I thought it was an odd thing for him to say, because he barely knew Harvey. I wrote off his comment at the time as a little jab coming from Michael's basic loneliness. He had very few real friends, and he didn't like being left behind at the end of the day.

Looking back, I can see that I felt a similar ambivalence toward Michael. His relationships with men never bothered me, but when I would hear that he was involved with a woman, I sometimes found myself suppressing a kind of jealousy. I dismissed those feelings as inappropriate, because I knew that I could never be more than his friend. After all, we had known each other for years, and our relationship was clearly defined by our collaborations, wasn't it?

As it turned out, Ken apparently took Michael's advice and didn't call me before the opening of *A Chorus Line*. That night of nights at the New-man, May 21, 1975, was one of those magical performances when everything gels and months of effort pay off for everyone in spectacular fashion. All our sacrifices proved to have been worth it, and for a while at least, all the slights and excesses were forgiven. Clive Barnes raved in the *Times* under the headline, "A Tremendous 'Chorus Line' Arrives." While describing the reception as "shattering," he also singled me out as "wonderfully right," and there was no doubt in my mind whom I had to thank for that. Michael had given me the gift of a lifetime, and through his work with all of us, he had given the audience a remarkable experience.

My own feelings of accomplishment were tempered later that week when my parents came to New York to see the show, and afterward we went out for dinner. I was still flying high with all of the excitement, and they were speechless. I didn't yet realize how this show would touch people, or how overwhelming it could be. My mother and father were so quiet, I finally said, "Well, what did you think?" I had been aware that parts of their own story had been used in the script, for example, the line about me being the daughter who came into the world to save their marriage. I had told my mother, "You know, you're in the show," but I hadn't really prepared her, and only later would she tell me that she had been touched that something so painful had been used in a creative way.

That night she and my father would only say that they enjoyed the show and thought it was good. In fact, they were so moved they could hardly talk about it. I don't know what I expected. In my fantasy, I wanted them to embrace me, to forgive me, to tell me that it was all worth it and that they loved me. But they didn't, and I fell back into my old behavior and acted like everything was fine. I didn't speak about my feelings. Again, out of fear and guilt and not wanting to embarrass them or make them uncomfortable by forcing the issue, I allowed them to put me back into my childhood—trying to please them but not getting the validation I wanted so desperately.

By the time we finished dinner, I was deflated. To this day I wished I had opened up to them, and talked to them in a way that wasn't part of my defensive act, sending out the message that I didn't need anybody.

They were probably afraid to say anything to me. In that way, they gave me the power that I unconsciously demanded, and I regret it. I could open up to them now. I would be able to tell them that I loved them and that I was sorry that I caused them so much grief and had so much trouble communicating my feelings. I would tell them how happy I was that they came to see me in the most important role of my life. I would say these things and keep saying them even if we all broke down and cried, but I couldn't do that at the time, and it's a shame, because I never saw my father again.

Not long after the opening, I heard from Ken and agreed to see him, though I was very cautious. There was so much happening at once, with *A Chorus Line* generating enormous publicity, and now definitely on its way to Broadway. Ken's marriage had ended, and he was in town doing a show, *Little Black Sheep,* which had a short run at Lincoln Center. I met him for dinner, without having great expectations, though I hoped that now that we were more mature we might relate on a new level, that we might at least be kind to each other. I was surprised when Ken suggested that he wanted more than that. But then I began to think that we had such an unhappy ending in the past, and maybe we could have this second chance to make it right. After seeing him again that night, I realized that I still cared enough to want to find out if that love we had shared could somehow be rekindled.

As the Newman run continued, I found myself spending more time with Ken. We were more or less living together again, though I hadn't formally moved in with him and I still had Millie Slavin's sublet on West End Avenue. He had recently moved into an apartment in an art deco building at Riverside Drive and 86th Street, and his mother was helping him decorate the place. We tried to pick up where we left off years before, and on some level, I was operating on an unspoken assumption that eventually we would marry. Doing eight performances a week, I was pretty crazed and exhausted most of the time, and I wasn't always thrilled with the arrangement.

After we had been together a few months, Ken decided that he had to see an ex-girlfriend who was visiting from Los Angeles. When he told me about her, I went off at him and said, "What do you mean you have to see her?" Then he became angry, because I was jealous and didn't want to understand that she deserved to hear his explanation as to why he left her. After he went ahead and met with her, there was an ongoing issue of trust for me. Still, never one to give up or easily let go, I kept hoping that we could find a way to have things work between us.

Meanwhile, *A Chorus Line* was scheduled to open on Broadway at the Shubert, and previews started that summer. But the official opening had to be postponed because of a musicians' strike that began in September. The delay threatened to destroy the momentum of the show, and all of us were living in a kind of limbo as we waited and the strike dragged on. During this period, my friend Marti Stevens gave me a fantastic gift, a week of my own in her beautiful home in Pacific Palisades in Los Angeles. It was very private with the yard and pool overlooking a golf course. I was able to relax somewhat, but I knew that Michael was going crazy because he called every day.

The show finally had its grand opening on October 19, and it did not disappoint in the larger Broadway house. In fact, the show's renewed impact was so singularly resounding that I found myself featured on the cover of *Newsweek* in early December. By then *Chorus Line* fever had taken hold of our little group. The pace was frenetic day in and day out and Michael was already negotiating to set up national and international touring companies.

That period was a painful blur for me. I wasn't able to appreciate the attention, in particular the *Newsweek* cover, because on November 11, 1975, my father died. Two weeks later I was rushing to the theater for rehearsal. I ran past the magazine stall in the street and caught a glimpse of what I thought was my foot on the cover of a partially covered magazine. I went back and pulled it free of the clothespin holding it up on top of the stand. "Hey, lady put that back," said the seller. "Take one from the pile."

"That's me," I said, holding up the magazine now and taking in the whole picture. I quickly paid for it, put it in my bag, and started for the theater, my excitement dampened with the realization that my father would never see this.

My mother was the one who called and told me that he had suffered a fatal heart attack, and that night I went on with my performance. Gwen Verdon once told me that she had performed on the night her mother died, and I thought at the time, *How could she do that?* But that was exactly what I did. I remember Laurence Olivier was in the audience that night. I did my best to fend off the feelings, but the entire time I could feel my legs quaking uncontrollably. I was unable to process the grief at that point, or even later, when my mother came to New York to be with me. She was very fragile, and like me, just trying to cope. This was a time when I had to turn to Ken, and regardless of the difficulties that we had been having with our relationship, his loving support as a friend was steadfast.

November 16, my birthday, I fortified myself for the gala party I was to attend with Ken. Marti Stevens was always a good and very generous friend, but this night she outdid herself. She told us she wanted to take us to see a special friend before the party who wanted to wish me a happy birthday. We went to the Pierre Hotel, up in the elevator and through the hallway, and stopped in front of a door. Marti had invited me to dinner once with John Gielgud, who was a good friend of hers. Needless to say, I was enthralled, so I'm now assuming that's who will open the door, and I'm preparing myself. Well, I hear the voice before he opens the door and it's not Gielgud. That voice! As I recognize the voice of Laurence Olivier, I fall back onto the wall in disbelief. He opens the door and invites us in.

I don't think I've ever received a better birthday present. We had drinks and chatted and he told me how much he enjoyed the show. He was filming *Marathon Man* at the time and couldn't go with us to the party. He was so thoughtful and kind, justifying all the years I'd been madly in love with him. And for a short time my sadness faded into the background.

At a certain point, Ken had an artist create a neon sign in his dining room. It took up one entire wall with the image of me in the same pose that was on the cover of *Newsweek*. More than just a conversation piece, this extravagant creation was an amazing sight, even setting aside the fact that it was me at the center. One night when Ken was away, Michael visited me at the apartment. Walking into the dining room and seeing me on the wall for the first time, he suddenly threw himself onto his knees under the "shrine" and lifted his arms in mock adulation. We laughed and made light of his antics. I teased him, saying, "Oh, Michael, very funny. You're just jealous."

In fact, he had already made some snide remarks and his tone made it clear that Michael wasn't pleased about my being with Ken. Later that night Michael went so far as to suggest that I shouldn't marry Ken because he didn't like the way Ken had been talking about me. This was an unsettling revelation, but when I asked Michael what exactly Ken had said, he wouldn't tell me.

Early in 1976, I was so run-down and sick that I finally had to take some time off from the show. Ironically, my absence led to my getting a pay raise, which was offered as an enticement for me to return to work. At that time, the top ticket price was only $15 and I was making about $600 a week. There was already a backlash about the way Michael had structured the financial arrangements with the cast. We were divided into three groups, each of which was to receive a different percentage of any profits: those of us who contributed to the taped sessions and were later cast in the show; those who only contributed to the taped sessions; and those who had not been involved in the sessions but were in the cast.

Everyone participated in the profits to some extent, but the percentage for each group was minuscule, like a fraction of one percent. Some dancers who had contributed their intimate stories to the script later felt ripped off when they saw how much money the show was making for Michael and the producers. Early on, Baayork had suggested that he give the dancers proceeds from the merchandise concession associated with the show. Her proposal was that we would buy the concession for a few thousand dollars, but Michael balked at that plan. My own sense was that he wasn't so much motivated by greed as by the need to control us. I always thought the idea that we might be independent frightened him, and as crazy as it may sound, in some irrational or even paranoid way, he feared that we might leave him.

Shortly before the Tony Award nominations were announced in March, Michael took me to dinner at Joe Allen's. He told me, "I know

I'm risking a lot with you and the Tonys, but I'm fighting to have you put in the Best Actress in a Musical category." He went on to explain that there was a rule stating that in order to be nominated in that category, a performer had to meet certain credit qualifications. Because *A Chorus Line* was an ensemble piece, we didn't have credits above the title. There were actually six of us who had larger roles, but we didn't quite meet the standards set by the rules committee. Michael was also trying to get Robert LuPone and Sammy Williams nominated in the Best Actor category. He was worried, though, that they might cancel each other out and lose the category, and likewise Priscilla Lopez and Carole Bishop, who would both be nominated in the Featured Actress in a Musical category.

I wasn't even aware then of the political machinations that were going on behind the scenes. *A Chorus Line* was in a fierce competition that year with Bob Fosse's hit *Chicago,* and Michael was determined to win as many awards as possible for his show. All of this went over my head. I told him, "Whatever you want, Michael." I hadn't really thought about the Tonys. I was still reckoning with my sorrow over my father's death, and I was mostly just relieved that *A Chorus Line* was open and running. With all the pressure, excitement, and hard work, it was all I could do to keep up with the show and the parade of celebrities who came up the stairs each night to visit after seeing the performance.

Michael wanted me to know that by putting me in the Best Actress category, there was a risk that I might not get an award. As it turned out, I was up against both of the stars of *Chicago,* Chita Rivera and Gwen Verdon, as well as Vivian Reed, who was the lead in *Bubbling Brown Sugar.* I thought it was considerate of Michael to tell me what he was doing, but it really didn't matter to me at that point. Later, I was grateful to him for the efforts he made and appreciated how shrewd he had been.

As the Tony Awards approached in April, the question arose as to whom I was going to go with that night. I assumed that I would be going with Ken, but one day Baayork said to me, "Don't you get it, Donna? You have to go with Michael. You're Broadway's sweethearts." That was the expectation, because the show was so much a part of both our lives. It hadn't really occurred to me before, but the idea of attending with

Michael seemed right and suddenly appealed to me. Of course, I knew that Ken was supposed to be the man of my dreams, so why wouldn't I prefer to attend with him? In the end, it came down to a kind of show business decision. When I brought up the subject with Ken, he was the perfect gentleman about it, deferring to Michael. My sister, Barbara, came with our mother and my dance teacher, Pamela, and like all of us, they were thrilled to see *A Chorus Line* sweep the awards. Everyone seemed so happy for me and for all of us. Yet even as I tried to stay in the moment, accepting the Tony and thanking Michael on national TV, no one, most especially me, could see how events were already spinning out of control.

Chapter 6

❧

A Choreographed Marriage and Other Singular Sensations

After the Tony Awards, the pressure of performing and dealing with all the media attention continued to intensify for those of us in the company. I was at the beck and call of the show's publicists, and there were countless press interviews and public appearances. At the same time, Michael had his own agenda to deal with simply because of the show's staggering success. I remember a picture of us that appeared in the *New York Times*. It showed a gallant Michael beaming with pride as he presented me with a rose. He could be a theatrical showman, but the romance of that gesture was something that he now became keenly intent on acting out in real life.

An unusual sort of courtship ensued while he was assembling the *Chorus Line* touring companies. In addition to the Broadway company, there was to be a national company and an international company. Michael had called upon several of us from the original cast along with Bob Avian to help him work with the new casts. One night Michael took me out to dinner and made a point of repeating his disapproval of what he assumed were my upcoming marriage plans, although I certainly had never told him I was planning on marriage. The way he put it was, "I can't let you marry Ken." That was a stunning thing for him to say, but his style was to make announcements like that rather than express his feelings directly or try to explain them. It would be an understatement for me to say I was even more startled when, a few minutes later, Michael told me point-blank, "Donna, I think we should be together."

As the shock registered, I did feel a certain excitement and I was flattered by his attention, but I also knew Michael well enough by now not to want to have any sort of casual fling with him. I told him so. More than just being cautious, I was afraid of jeopardizing both our friendship and our collaboration. I had seen too many couples who had superficial affairs during shows, and they usually went nowhere, ending with broken hearts and friendships lost. I told Michael that I thought too highly of him to let that happen to us. "I'm a serious person, Michael, and I take you seriously." Then, trying to humor him, I said, "Let's not and say we did." Still, his overture stirred feelings in me, and I was drawn to him more than I wanted to be. Even as unlikely as it might be, I couldn't help but wonder with our long history if something more substantial might be possible for us.

During this time, Ken and I weren't communicating that much. He had started working on the Leonard Bernstein–Alan Jay Lerner musical, *1600 Pennsylvania Avenue,* and when Ken was free, I was working. He had the lead role, but things were not going well for him on that ill-fated show, and the two of us had little time for each other. I was scheduled to leave with *A Chorus Line* for the San Francisco leg of the West Coast tour, which was set to open with the original Broadway cast on May 6, 1976. While I still had feelings for Ken, I didn't have faith anymore in our future together. I started thinking that the upcoming tour would give me an opportunity to withdraw from the relationship and be on my own. As in my childhood, I was planning another escape.

Shortly before I was to leave with the company, Michael redoubled his efforts to overcome my resistance to a romance between us. Over another dinner, he made it clear that he wanted to take care of me, and he offered financial support if I needed money. I thought that was endearing, but I didn't need any sort of handout and only wanted to be compensated fairly for my work on the show. Another time, he took me completely by surprise by telling me that he had been working on himself in therapy every day for a year and a half to be worthy of the kind of relationship that he knew I wanted. This was Michael, my friend, telling me he was willing to make a commitment to me, that he didn't want to lose me, that he loved me and wanted us to be together. "The past is the past," he said.

As strange as it may seem, I never thought of Michael as a gay man. To me, he was always just a man. He was a complicated, very sexual man, but he was still just Michael. I had certainly never met anyone like him. I was beginning to feel myself open up to the possibility of a different kind of relationship with him, but I was still reluctant to meet him halfway. I wondered if I could make him happy. I thought Michael deserved to be happy. Getting to know him better after working with him every day gave me insight. There was no doubt that my feelings for him were very deep.

No other man in my life had ever given me what Michael had given me. He believed in me, fought for me, and created a role for me that would be my passport to a future life and career. And he was saying that he loved me. He seemed so vulnerable and sincere. I still had questions, so I couldn't say yes, absolutely, but I couldn't say no either. I said, "Michael, I love you and I want to try, but I'm not sure." My ambivalence didn't matter to him. At that moment, he was as happy as if I had said yes.

He called me after I got home that night and he sounded so excited, "Honey, we're going to be together and we're going to be happy!" Another pronouncement, I thought, but it made me smile. He wanted to join me in San Francisco to start our lives together as a couple. I have to admit that hearing him talk that way made me feel happy and excited but I was already thinking about the ramifications of this complication in our public lives. A lot of people wouldn't understand and wouldn't be happy for us. But I really had no idea how threatened some people would feel. I thought it would be difficult, perhaps, but it certainly wasn't easy the way things were now.

I know now that part of the attraction for each of us was the need for some security in our lives. We expressed a desire to be the "family" for each other that we never had. We were still living through the disorienting fever-pitch success of A Chorus Line, and we were hoping to find in each other a way to make sense of it all. To some extent, the relationship was to be our shared fortress, but at the same time, glorifying each other as we did was actually a way for each of us to escape from our own difficult realities.

It may be wishful thinking that sometimes has us believing that we can be the personal answer to someone else's happiness. I wasn't without fears and misgivings, but the prospect of seeing this fairy tale come true created the most seductive kind of euphoria. It wasn't as if I had delusions about Michael, but I was finally willing to disregard my fears. I was so tired of being afraid. I sensed a loneliness and unhappiness in him when he wasn't working and I knew that he had difficulty trusting anyone. That was more a source of concern for me than his promiscuity or bisexuality. I remembered a disturbing conversation that we had years ago just after Promises, Promises. I was visiting him at his apartment on 55th Street, and he was in the kitchen, cooking dinner. At one point, he suddenly swung around and came into the living room where I was sitting. He stood there for a moment and then out of nowhere, he said to me, "You know, Donna, there's no such thing as real friendship."

I asked him what he meant, and he said, "People just use each other. I need you, I use you. You need me, you use me. That's what it's all about."

I was disconcerted and said, "Michael, what about really caring for someone and helping that person because you want to? What about sharing and the interdependency of a true friendship? What about love?"

He was unrelenting. "It's just about using! That's what the give-and-take is between people, especially in our business."

Behind that harsh, cynical view of his, I sensed that Michael must have been very hurt, and I felt sorry for him. So the fact that all these years later this same man was now reaching out to me was all the more compelling. I suppose that I had loved him for years without ever having acknowledged it even to myself because he seemed so unattainable. Now there was a part of me ready to celebrate the possibility of having something that I never thought I could have with someone I loved. Yet at the same time, another part of me was saying, *Wait a minute, is this really possible?* There was only one way I was ever going to know, so the risks seemed worthwhile, and since Michael seemed so willing to try, I became more determined than ever to follow through.

Before leaving for San Francisco, I went out with Ken one night and said, "I don't know what's going to happen yet, but I have to make this decision for myself. So when I leave, I'm moving out." I don't think the news came as a surprise to him. I didn't want to hurt him by talking about Michael, and to some extent, the whole situation remained unresolved between us, except for the fact that I was leaving. I only told a few of my close friends what was happening with Michael; it wasn't like either of us was going to announce it to the company. My sister, Barbara, responded with a loving heart, knowing how much Michael was a part of my life, and wanting me to be happy. She never betrayed any reservations she might have had. I think that was probably true with the others with whom I shared the secret as well. I'm sure my friends foresaw danger, but they were supportive because they could tell that I wasn't really asking for advice and wouldn't have listened anyway. One of Michael's assistants, Sue McNair, knew about us, and she later told Michael, "If you don't go out to San Francisco, as soon as Ken's show closes, he'll be out there to get her back."

When I finally left New York, it was all so dizzying and seemed like such an unbelievable whirlwind that I still had doubts whether Michael would actually make the trip west. After we had agreed that we were going to be together, it didn't occur to either of us to discuss how we were actually going to *live* together. What couples don't talk about such things when they plan their future? What would it be like being with each other day in and day out? Of course, I know now that there were some practical areas that we were both happily blocking out, but back then I felt I had no choice. I really felt compelled to see this through with him, but I still thought somehow I might keep the safety net for my heart in place, just in case he changed his mind.

With the help of friends, in San Francisco I rented a charming duplex apartment off a courtyard on Telegraph Hill. Nervously anticipating his arrival, I settled in and started rehearsals. Michael told me when he was coming and I thought I was prepared for him, but on that day as I was rehearsing onstage, all of a sudden there he was, racing down the aisle toward the stage, wearing a suit! I stopped short with what I was doing and just stood there watching him. I was transfixed. I thought, *Oh, my God, he's here and it's happening!*

After rehearsal, we were giddy and went shopping in North Beach and brought back food for a small dinner party that we had quickly planned. We also bought some gorgeous fabrics and draped them all over the bedroom for our first night together. The party to celebrate Michael's arrival and our new home together consisted of only the most intimate of friends. We invited Michel Stuart who played Greg in the show, and was an old friend of Michael's because of his longtime significant relationship with Tommy Tune. Jack Lenny, Michael's devoted agent and his wife, Kim, also came to dinner, and I cooked a turkey. I was just starting to adjust to the fact that maybe, against all odds, we might work as a couple, especially when we had friends who were supportive and happy for us.

The picture of domestic bliss was soon marred that night, however, when Michel Stuart became ill after dinner and begged Michael to let him stay overnight. A blood clot in his leg was acting up again and he couldn't move. "I'll be okay in the morning," he said. I didn't entirely believe him. Michael and I giggled about the situation in our room, but it became less funny when Mr. Stuart kept calling out for Michael to get him water and other sundry things through the night. So Michael and I didn't have the privacy we wanted that first night. But we were in love, and we anticipated the beginning of an idyllic interlude where we would finally be a couple and live our love affair like a pair of starry-eyed newlyweds.

We were both ecstatic living in San Francisco. I was working at night and Michael was watching television and going to movies, having a much earned vacation from the rigors of our show. I would leave him on the couch and return to him on the couch, and I was happy that I could offer such a charming haven for him. We were living in North Beach and enjoyed going shopping together and being with friends after the show. I was so happy then, especially because I could see that I was able to bring some happiness and security into his life.

I started to enjoy that freedom of loving and being loved and not worrying so much all the time, even about what other people thought. Michael encouraged me to go public with our engagement at a press conference before the show opened. When I asked him how I should handle it, he said, "Do it once and get it over with, so you won't have to keep answering those questions." I was asked some awkward questions about my relationship with Ken, and responded by saying that we were "just good friends." The press conference made Michael and me into an instant item, and also made me look a bit foolish. That was how most of the company found out about us.

I knew there were those who must have thought I was crazy to be with him. My ex-husband, Al Schwartz, was the only person who called me and asked, "Why are you marrying Michael? I thought he was gay." At one point, Sammy Williams, who played Paul, came to my dressing room and said with alarm, "What are you doing, Donna? Don't you know he's crazy?" I had a prepared rebuttal, but I appreciated Sammy's concern and his being so direct about it. Most people left us alone. A few friends did ask me why I was marrying him, and I responded simply and honestly that I loved him. There were some who were supportive and thought the match made perfect sense, like Baayork, and my friend Dixie Carter, who married the same man, George Hearn, twice, because she loved him. Many people remained mystified, but I really didn't care what anyone else thought about it, except Michael. I decided that I would make a supreme effort to see it through and make it work. How could I live with myself if I didn't try? I had no idea how much it would cost me to be that cavalier with my feelings.

Just before we opened in San Francisco, *A Chorus Line* won a Pulitzer. The impact of the show continued to be sensational, and we were as well received on the West Coast as we had been in New York. Every performance was sold out. Before leaving town, the producers took out a full-page ad in the *Chronicle* and all of us in the cast signed a thank-you note for the San Francisco audiences. It was unprecedented to send the original Broadway cast of a hit show on the road, rather than just a touring company. People would come up to us in the lobby of the theater and ask if we were really from the original cast. Our next stop was Los Angeles, where we were to spend the summer, and we arrived with the largest advance sale in the city's history.

The pressures mounted for Michael in L.A., partly because Hollywood was now courting him. He had signed a three-picture deal with Universal, and I believe our relationship gave him the secure notion that he was more acceptable in that corporate atmosphere, and not regarded as some boy dancer from New York. I was in love and proud to be with him, happy to provide any comfort I could. He had his own radical but brilliant ideas about how the movie of A Chorus Line should be done to differentiate it from the show, but eventually Michael became frustrated by all the studio politics, and had his lawyer, John Breglio, get him out of the movie deal. Nevertheless, for a while he had an office on the Universal lot and played the Hollywood game of taking meetings and going to dinner parties.

There was one night I shall never forget. When Michael was unable to attend, Leonard Gershe escorted me to a tented outdoor party in Bel-Air at the home of James Stewart. Arriving late because of the show, I was treated like an honored guest, with Mr. Stewart taking me by the hand and walking me from table to table, graciously introducing me to the other guests, including Rosalind Russell, Merle Oberon, and Billy Wilder. Leonard and I sat at Jack Lemmon's table. Having heard I was engaged, Mr. Lemmon gave me a sixpence coin and explained that his wife, Felicia, had put it in her shoe for good luck when they were married. He wanted me to have it, and I was deeply touched by such a personal gift.

Michael and I had moved into an elegant home in Coldwater Canyon that once belonged to Gaylord Hauser, the beauty and nutrition consultant perhaps most famous for his affair with Greta Garbo during the 1930s. As Michael and I plunged back into work, we were living in grand style without yet realizing how little the two of us had in the way of a foundation outside the theater. At the time, we were enjoying what little personal time we had together, but our time was mostly taken up by social obligations with old and new friends.

Our commitment to the relationship was put to the test just before the show opened at the beginning of July. We were still in rehearsals when Ken unexpectedly arrived on the scene. His show in New York had flopped and closed early in May, and just as Sue McNair had predicted, Ken decided to make a dramatic last stand to get me back. I was in the dressing room when he arrived at the theater, and Michael was downstairs rehearsing onstage. Someone came in and told me that Ken was at the stage door and wanted to see me. I was more than a little rattled, but I said, "Let him come in." Moments later, Ken rushed through the door and literally slid across the floor to the chair where I was sitting to embrace me. He was high-strung and emotional in a way that I had never seen him before. It was upsetting, listening to his pleas, and feeling that my heart was breaking also, because I had never said goodbye properly, and he had been such an important part of my life.

I'm not sure what would have happened if Michael hadn't appeared at the door. When he heard that Ken was in the theater, he abruptly left rehearsal and rushed up to the dressing room, completing the awkward triangle. Looking terribly agitated, Michael said, "Let's get out of here." The three of us went to Harry's Bar, which was not the best idea he ever had, and it quickly turned into an uncomfortable and painful scene. It became more about Michael and Ken being territorial, and I was the territory in dispute. I felt like I was watching a dreadful movie and wanted to walk out.

Ultimately, Michael won his claim of ownership, and then Bob Avian arrived to rescue us. After we said our goodbyes, Bob graciously escorted Ken outside and that was the last we saw of him. At that point, I felt so uncomfortable and full of doubts about myself and what I was doing that I almost didn't want to be with anyone. There was to be no further discussion between Michael and me, and that set into motion an unhealthy pattern. The show had to open, and we went back to work.

Although we stayed together and tried to make the best of it, I don't think things were ever quite the same after Los Angeles. When we returned to New York at the end of the summer, life continued at a maddening, hectic pace. We weren't able to spend nearly as much quality time together as we had in California. Michael had to fly to London, so we weren't traveling together. Our new apartment wasn't ready so I lived in a hotel at first. I felt in total disarray. I had to wait for renovations to be completed before I could finally move into a duplex penthouse on Central Park South.

Once Michael returned and we were settled into our new home, our spirits improved. It was a fun place for us to live, with every sort of amenity, including one of the most beautiful views in Manhattan. Claudine, our housekeeper from Los Angeles, came to work for us and Michael was able to secure a studio apartment for her in the building. Things seemed to be coming together, and we were finally able to have some deeper personal conversations about our relationship.

With everything moving forward to a marriage, I remember us having a splendid dinner and afterward sitting in the living room, looking at the view. I was prompted to say, "Michael, I really believe we can conquer anything as long as we love each other. Our love can prevail." I hadn't said this to elicit a specific response from him, but I could feel his affection and his look succeeded in melting me.

I had given Michael an engagement present that he loved: our musical director on *Chorus Line*, Don Pippin, helped me locate a beautiful, antique baby grand player piano. It was stocked with rolls of George Gershwin songs, with Gershwin actually playing. His performance of *Rhapsody in Blue* was one of my favorites. I understood Michael's desire to surround himself with luxury. I knew how hard he worked to live with style. I admired the way he was reaching for a better life. Now that his financial future was finally secure, he was probably the most important figure on Broadway. He wanted to live out his dreams. Even before we left for San Francisco, he had asked me to accompany him on a little errand and wouldn't tell me where he was taking me. The destination that he had in mind turned out to be a Rolls-Royce dealership. He took me inside and had me sit with him in the back seat of a new white Rolls that he was auditioning.

I remember him asking me, "Well, what do you think?" It was like he was asking for my permission. He was like a delighted kid. I thought it was great that he could get so excited over owning something like this, because frankly, I couldn't relate after having lived through Al Schwartz and the Jaguar incident. I told Michael that I thought he should get the car he wanted; he went ahead and bought it. He later had the brilliant costume designer Theoni Aldredge and Broadway's favorite costumer Barbara Matera, design a sable coat for me as an engagement present. It was beautiful, and I loved it, but I was sorry that he told me that it cost as much the car, because even though it was luxurious and kept me warm, I always felt a little uncomfortable wearing it. Eventually, as I became more aware of animal rights, for ethical reasons, I retired it to cold storage.

It was surely no great crime for Michael to reward himself with a lifestyle that was different from anything he had ever known. But he soon became caught up in that world, as if trying to live up to his image of success that was being projected into the world. And for a time, I gladly followed him. The eventual disappointment was probably inevitable, if only because looking for answers to personal happiness in that way is bound to fail. Years later he would say there was "gossip about the Rolls, with no one saying, by the way, that I had never owned a car before, had never owned anything in my life, not a house, a boat, anything, and no one saying I didn't drive and had to hire a driver."

Soon after we moved into the penthouse, he called our housekeeper, Claudine, into the living room for a meeting. Michael sat us down and addressed us like we were both servants, explaining our shared duties in the household. I remember him saying to Claudine, "If Robert Redford comes to dinner, I want you to wear a uniform and be on your best behavior."

He went on and on, sounding like a little mogul. I was caught off guard by his attitude. At first, I thought he was kidding but then I could see through it to some extent. I knew how important Michael felt it was to be successful. He was moving into a new realm of the business. The stakes were higher, but at his core he was still the boy from Buffalo. Claudine was no more prepared for his instructions than I was, and she burst into tears and fled from the room. As soon as Michael realized how ridiculous he sounded, he relented and allowed Claudine to have free rein as far as planning meals and running the household. My job was still in question.

One day, seemingly out of the blue, Michael decided that our wedding was going to take place in Paris. My attitude was "Fine. Whatever you want, Michael." I reminded myself of a piece of ancient wisdom that I had heard many times when I was growing up, that the first year of marriage was always the toughest. I figured our clock was already ticking. The wedding was to be a special affair, one worthy of being called a Michael Bennett production.

Michael and I were married in the Bureau de Mariages in Montmartre, on December 4, 1976. Neither of our families attended, and the ceremony was in French, which I later thought was rather convenient for Michael, since he didn't speak the language and most likely found it less threatening and less real. The best man was French actor Jean-Pierre Cassel, who was to play Zach in the London production of *A Chorus Line*. His wife, Sabine, was my maid of honor. Michael adored both of them; I met them with Michael when he took me to Paris the first time. Sometimes, Michael flirted openly with Sabine and I would get jealous even though I tried not to show it. Once, I brought it to his attention and he appeased me by telling me that she fancied him and was feeling a little jealous. He explained that to make her feel better he had said to her, "I'm only marrying Donna because you're already married."

In spite of the up-and-down ride, I was getting used to Michael, and the day of our ceremony was blissful. The Cassels gave us a lovely wedding supper at their home in Montmartre. We stayed in a magnificent suite at the Plaza Athénée and were taken everywhere by Sabine and Jean-Pierre. It was a heady time, even though I started sensing some signs of uncertainty on Michael's part. He could be moody, and I was too reactive. I couldn't face my own insecurity and misgivings, so I pushed these thoughts and feelings away by continuing to rationalize and excuse his behavior.

After returning to New York, I went back into the show, but Michael had no immediate new project. He fell into dark moods during which I couldn't reach him. We were both probably drinking too much wine for our own good. I know I was, but it was unusual to ever see Michael out of control. He had an incredible constitution. Years later his indulgence with drugs would be made public, but in the 1970s in our circle of friends, certain drugs, like marijuana, in moderation, were socially acceptable. Everybody experimented to some degree, and eventually you had to sort things out for yourself.

I don't mean to condone this kind of behavior, nor do I mean to rationalize, but I really never judged Michael. I was too uninformed then to know the damage that abusing drugs can do to one's health and to one's relationships. Unlike the stories I heard about him much later, Michael always seemed to be in charge, and he was capable and professional when he needed to be. Having a dancer's discipline was my good fortune, and having to do eight shows a week, thankfully, kept me on track during that time. Also, I soon realized that any desire for us to have an intimate and meaningful discussion while imbibing alcohol, was futile.

Our sex life was never a problem for us, but there were other areas of intimacy that were being shortchanged and that were difficult for us to talk about. Our inability to achieve the emotional intimacy and trust we both wanted was the biggest problem. I thought at times that I was to blame, that I was somehow falling short of what Michael wanted in a partner. It didn't help us when his mother, Helen, called at all hours of the night, crying and complaining to Michael that now he was married, she was afraid she would never see him again. He would roll his eyes at me while he talked to her, as if to say, "Look what I have to put up with." But he would never get her off the phone. I remember thinking, *What chance do I have with her in the picture?*

I also started seeing how old-world Italian he really was with his outlook about marriage and family. At one point, in frustration, he said to me, "Make up your mind, Donna! Do you want to be a star? Or do you want to be a wife?"

I insisted, "What's wrong with being both? Why do I have to choose?"

As newlyweds, we were the blind leading the blind, often making things incredibly difficult for each other, even with the best of intentions. I missed having someone with whom I could confide. I had stopped going to therapy after we were married because I wanted Michael to be my significant other, not the doctor. I have this image of my therapist hanging up the phone after my call canceling my sessions and saying woefully to himself, "Oh, dear." I remember one night in particular after Claudine had served us dinner and gone home. We were sitting at the glass table in our glass dining room, looking out at that fabulous view of the city as we started our first course. Michael was pensive, and I was quiet, not wanting to bring up anything that might annoy him. He suddenly looked up at me, and all he said was "It's hard, isn't it?"

His question put a lump in my throat, and I told him, "Yes, it is." Neither of us said another word about it. I think what he was really trying to tell me was, "I don't know what to do with this. It's painful, and I don't know how to make this work." I know that's what I was thinking, but I was afraid to speak. The moment seemed so fragile, and I was so used to deferring to Michael and tiptoeing around his moods that I felt powerless. But I still wasn't willing to give up on him or on us. I was desperate to figure out what I could do to make him happy again. I remember that Michael's father, Salvatore DiFiglia, once encouraged me to have children. Now he was very old-world Italian in his thinking, and he suggested that having children was the only way that I would hold on to Michael. But we didn't marry each other to have children. We married to have a relationship, and that was proving to be more of a challenge than either of us ever imagined.

The situation seemed to improve for us that winter just before Michael was to make a trip to London. The international company of *A Chorus Line* had been playing at the Drury Lane Theatre since July, and the production was the first musical to win London's Laurence Olivier Award (then called the Society of West End Theatre Award). The international cast was about to be replaced by a British Equity cast, and Michael had to be there to oversee the production.

The night before he left, he made an effort to reach out to me again. It was one of our better nights and the first time in a long time that he initiated a discussion. He went so far as to tell me how much he appreciated me and how much he was going to miss me. I started feeling like there might be some sliver of hope for us after all. Within a couple of weeks, Michael called from London and told me that he needed my help. He wanted me to join him right away, and I was only too happy to fly over to be with him and to have the opportunity to show him how much I loved him.

But the situation in London was quickly turning into a full-blown *Chorus Line* crisis. Michael had fired the show's Cassie, who was to have been played by Elizabeth Seal. Elizabeth had won acclaim in the 1958 London production of *Irma La Douce,* but Michael didn't feel she had the right qualities to make the role of Cassie work. To replace her, he hired a young dancer named Petra Siniawski. Michael wanted me to dance in five previews to keep the show going while giving Petra time to learn the role.

Michael made it clear to everyone in the show that I wasn't there to replace anyone, but only to help with Petra's preparation. British Equity approved the plan, but once it was announced in the press, there was an explosion of protest from some in the theater community who resented this latest American invasion. There was a rumor I heard later that a prominent performer paid unemployed actors one pound if they showed up at British Equity to vote against this American actress who was replacing a Brit. There was no representation of the facts or of my history in previous shows in the West End, and never an acknowledgment that I was after all an actress in my own right. I was portrayed simply as the "director's wife," who was brought over from America to take over the role. In the British press, President Jimmy Carter was buried on the fourth page during his inauguration, while I was on the front page for three days running.

The atmosphere in London was already extremely hostile when I arrived, and I was hardly prepared for what I was walking into. I found Michael and Bob Avian under siege, holed up in a hotel. It was like walking into a scary movie, with the two of them looking under the door at shadows when anyone passed in the hallway. When Michael fired Elizabeth, who was much loved by the theater community, there was an uproar in the press. It was illegal to fire anyone in this social democracy, so a settlement was reached. Michael could be paranoid at times, but in this case his fears seemed to be well founded. There had been death threats, after which he and Bob had hired a chauffeur who served as a bodyguard. We were like prisoners in the hotel and rarely went out anywhere except to the theater.

One night after rehearsing, Michael insisted that I go out with him and Bob to attend a dinner with London producer Michael White. I was exhausted and told Michael, "I can't. I just can't." But I knew that I had to, so I tried to rally myself for them. When the three of us came out of the theater, we were met by a couple dozen British paparazzi. I was accustomed by now to being photographed, but not by photographers who rushed at you, pushing and shoving. A melee ensued, and I found myself separated from Michael and Bob. I was alone and in total panic. By the time the two of them came back and led me away, I was in tears, practically breaking down. At that point, Michael became enraged at me, furious that I had lost my composure. In his mind, my loss of control somehow meant that I was giving up rather than fighting back. I was supposed to be there *for him,* and I let him down.

Michael was in a career crisis and stretched to the limit. I could tell that he was concerned for me after that incident, but he couldn't deal with me directly, and I really needed that support from him. I was feeling the head-on collision of my personal and professional lives. Elaine Stritch happened to be in London, and while Michael was at the theater, he asked her to go to the hotel "to cheer me up." Elaine was a dear and tried to help, but even she couldn't remedy the dread I was feeling. I carried on with the work, sneaking into the basement of the theater to coach Petra, and when my job was done, I was promptly sent home to New York to go back in the show.

That was the beginning of the end, and it was devastating for both of us. During a performance on February 4, 1977, I sustained a back injury, and after the show, Donald Pippin had to carry me out of the theater. My injury was serious enough to prevent me from returning to the show, and I thought that was such a sad way for my *Chorus Line* experience to end.

Michael seemed to bring some of his paranoia with him back to Manhattan. Looking back, I can see now that he was agonizing about his failure in London and his failure with me, and taking it out on me. He was contentious, and would say things just to wound me, but his silences were even worse. At one point, I told him, "I'll do anything, whatever you want, whatever you say. Just tell me. Talk to me, Michael."

And he said, "The one cardinal sin you committed was that you made me feel. And you have a flaw, which is . . ."

He hesitated, and I said, "What flaw? Tell me! I'll change. I know I'm not perfect."

Then he told me, "Your flaw is that you love me."

That was a battle I couldn't win. I could no longer keep up the front, but he was going through something that was truly beyond my capacity to understand

Out of desperation, I prevailed upon him to go with me to visit my therapist. The idea was for us to find a way to talk. He went reluctantly. As soon as the session began, he became guarded and distant. He was going through the motions, but it became clear that Michael did not want to talk. He just bridled and closed himself off. I was resentful, and didn't help the situation when we left the office. He said to me, "The car is waiting." But I told him I wanted to be alone and would rather walk home, so he took the car and I traipsed back to Central Park South.

A short time later, Michael had to make a trip to Australia for the opening of the international *Chorus Line* troupe in Sydney. Before he left, he was openly hostile and instructed his assistants in his office, "Keep her away from me." In the past, I had always known where he was traveling and what he was doing, but when he took off for Sydney, he left orders for his staff not to tell me where he was and not to allow me to contact him. At a certain point, I exploded and told one of his assistants, "Look, I'm not an employee here. I'm his wife! It's my responsibility to know where Michael is."

Almost as soon as Michael returned from his trip, he flew off again to San Francisco. I knew I couldn't live this way, and I knew that he couldn't either. He had been invited by writer George Furth to help doctor *The Act,* a Liza Minnelli vehicle that was in trouble out of town. The show was under the direction of Martin Scorsese, who had never staged a musical and eventually had to be replaced by Gower Champion. In the end, Michael didn't actually work on the show except to give hours of notes after seeing a performance. He returned to New York full of himself, and he started taunting me again, as if forcing my hand and testing me to see when I would break.

At that point, I realized that we were beyond working it out. Months before, I had confided in a friend, who told me, "Your trouble is you wear your heart on your sleeve all the time, Donna, so every time he says something mean, it goes to the quick." That was true, but at that time in my life, I had no objectivity whatsoever and didn't know how to be any other way. I took everything that Michael said literally.

At wit's end, I finally went to Michael and told him, "Look, I don't think I was meant to have a miserable life, and I don't think I was put here on earth to make you miserable. Why did you marry me? Please just tell me. Why did you do it?"

I remember he was standing across the room. After a moment, he said, "It was a whim. It seemed like a good idea at the time." I saw through that too. He was trying to hurt me and it worked.

That was hardly the end of it. In an interview that Michael gave the following year, he recalled, "I really tried in my marriage . . . I really, truly tried. We were chorus kids together. We grew up the same way, dancing school darlings, lessons in tap, Spanish dance, the schmear. We did shows together, and she was my Cassie. I loved Donna. And I needed someone, and I thought we could work out whatever problems we might have. I was wrong. I couldn't. She couldn't. . . . It was very painful for me, for her, for our friends. We tried to live up to the image. We got a Central Park penthouse . . . but I was never very happy there."

Michael moved in with Bob Avian, who had an apartment downtown on 8th Street. I stayed in our penthouse and went back into therapy to try to understand what had happened. That was going to take me years to figure out, not yet realizing that I focused on Michael to avoid focusing on myself. My therapist told me bluntly, "You were trying to save the marriage and you kept trying beyond the point where there could be any hope. How many times can you allow yourself to be kicked in the head?"

But there were still more kicks to come. Several months after Michael moved out, he called and came by to see me. My sister, Barbara, was staying with me some of the time since I was having difficulty being alone. He told me that living in Bob's apartment was driving him out of his mind. A little dog upstairs was keeping him awake at night, and he was apparently having terrible fits and literally tearing telephones off the walls. As he relayed this to me, he was practically in tears. He didn't want to move into a hotel, so he begged me to move out and give him the penthouse so he could do his work. Once again I fell for the act and deferred to him. I said, "All right, Michael, I'll move. But I'll need your help because I don't have a job." I was still convalescing with my back injury.

"Don't worry," he assured me. "I'll take care of you."

With Michael's aid, I soon moved with my sister into a two-bedroom apartment in the nearby Essex Hotel, and he moved back into the penthouse. I knew now there was no going back, and that I was going to have to find a way to survive on my own. One night a short time later, I returned to the Essex and wasn't allowed into the suite. Michael had me locked out. It was an underhanded trick, of course, but this was Michael's way of pushing me to the brink so I would give in to his terms for the divorce. It was now in the lawyers' hands and I was given a small living allowance awarded by the court until the divorce could be finalized. That battle went on for another year. During that time, I moved around like a vagabond, sleeping on friends' couches and staying with my sister, sometimes in hotels. "Remember the Drake," as in the Drake Hotel, is our private expression for reminding each other not to lose hope when life seems difficult. Because if we could get through "the time at the Drake Hotel," we can get through anything. Eventually, I borrowed some money and found a sublet in the West Village. Shame and a sense of failure were now my constant companions.

Michael undoubtedly suffered as well, and his state of mind was increasingly questionable. He was back into his promiscuous mode, and ironically, he started an affair with Sabine Cassel that would break up her marriage. She moved into the apartment with Michael on Central

Park South, but eventually, she and Michael would break up as well. He gave an interview to biographer Kevin Kelly in September of 1978 while he was working on a new show, *Ballroom*. Michael said, "You wanna hear about my paranoia? I'll tell you about my paranoia. . . . Look, I had a nervous breakdown in November [1977]. I got this crazy idea that somehow, unknown to me, I was a protégé of the Mafia, that they owned me, had owned me from birth in Buffalo, that my parents were in on it, even my dancing-school teacher, and that I owed everything— even critics' reviews!—to the Mafia. I've gotten over some of that, worked it out with my analyst. I'm a lot less manic."

Michael went on to explain how he had invested his own money in *Ballroom* (a musical based on Jerome Kass's 1975 teleplay, *Queen of the Stardust Ballroom*). "With the help of Bernie Jacobs and the Shubert Organization, I sat down and figured out how I could own *Ballroom*. I got $1.5 million from Morgan Guaranty by signing over to them every-thing I had, the building I owned on Broadway and East Nineteenth, my workshop, my van. What it comes down to is: a bank is backing a Broadway show. What it also comes down to is my feeling that this is 'Get Michael time.'"

Apparently for Michael, it was also "Get Donna out of the way time." With *Ballroom* in the works and with so much riding on it, he decided the time had come to resolve the divorce. Only our lawyers were com-municating, and they were not coming to terms easily. I was expected to walk away without much support, in fact, nothing. I didn't need much, but I needed something until I could get back on my feet. I didn't understand why it was taking so long, and I really felt that at this time Michael and I should be able to sit down and work these things out with a mediator. There was talk about us having to go to court and nobody was happy about that, including me. At this point, Bernie Jacobs phoned and asked to meet with me. Essentially acting as Michael's busi-ness partner, Bernie had a large investment in *Ballroom* and wanted Michael to make it work.

Bernie had papers that he wanted me to sign, and I had a sense of foreboding about our meeting. Up until this time, I had always been able to maintain what I thought was a healthy separation between my personal and professional lives. However chaotic my personal affairs were at times, I could always depend on the work. It was through the work that I found my identity and respect. I prided myself on my professional ethics, and earned the respect of my peers by always working as hard as I could and keeping my standards high. Now the borders were blurring, and I found myself feeling the threat of not having either work or security. Filled with anxiety, and realizing I had nothing to fall back on, I visited Bernie at his office.

When I walked in, Bernie immediately embraced me and tried to put me at ease. I had always liked Bernie and responded to his warmth. Even though he was the all-powerful Shubert Organization, and could be very tough in his business dealings, I had also seen his gentler side when he was with his family. I believed him when he said, "You and Michael have given me some of my greatest experiences in the theater. You are both good people and shouldn't have to go through this mess." I told him that I was not fighting the divorce and also wanted it to be resolved, but in a more human way.

I explained how hurt and upset I was at Michael's refusal to talk to me, and I mentioned the indirect (and not so indirect) hostility that I was experiencing from Michael and some of the people working for him. In the face of what was quickly becoming my lost dignity, I appealed to him. "I just need to talk to Michael, Bernie. I know we can work anything out if we just sit down and talk."

We discussed my other needs, like getting a place to live. Bernie told me, "I'm going to help you get an apartment in the building where my wife and I have a place, on Park Avenue and 70th Street. Bess Myerson wants it for her daughter, but I think we can get it for you." Then he reassured me, saying, "We'll have dinner, the three of us, you and Michael and I. Go ahead and sign the papers, and I'll get you together with Michael."

At that point, I essentially signed away any rights I had in the marriage, not that I wanted anything from Michael. I never even asked for the wedding gifts. They always struck me as more business than personal anyway. There were some that had been given to Michael by his associates, like crystal and silver from the Shuberts, and china from Bob

Avian. I did take a crystal vase that Joe Papp had given us and a glass cat sculpture from Ed Kleban. Our marriage lasted a little over a year, with the divorce finalized in 1979.

As it turned out, there was to be no dinner with Michael. But Bernie was true to his word as far as getting me the apartment in his building, though I wasn't able to move in for almost a year. Eventually, I also received a nominal monetary settlement and a limited monthly stipend, along with a one-time insurance compensation payment of $20,000 for the back injury that prevented me from dancing for a few months, and caused me to lose my job. But my inability to find paying work was causing some serious financial hardship. My professional life had always been a safety net, but my career had somehow come to a sudden halt.

I thought it was strange that even with my success in *A Chorus Line,* after our marriage broke up, not only was I not able to get a job, I wasn't able to get a single important audition for almost two years, even for parts that at the very least I should have been sent up for. It could have been a coincidence, but I didn't think so. I was reminded of a low point earlier in my career when I auditioned for a part in *Pippin.* The producers were actually looking for a "Donna McKechnie type," but as it turned out, apparently, I wasn't right for the role. They wanted my "type," not me. At the time, I appeared to be too young for that character, I was told. Now it seemed I wasn't right for any role.

What was really happening to me? Was my emotional pain distorting my perceptions? My struggle with low self-esteem was hindering my ability to audition. Trying to rise above my depression and sadness with a forced smile and feigned positive energy was unsettling and exhausting. There were a couple of times when I felt so right for a role that I called and begged my agent to pursue the audition again. He called back and told me, "They know you, Donna, and they like you, but you're just not right." I would have had a better chance getting an audition if I had been the kid nobody knew who just got off the bus.

Michael had made his feelings about me clear within the tight-knit family of the New York theater community and he was shutting me out. That was how he operated, by slamming the door or turning the page and saying, "She's last-year." But in my case, it seemed that everyone in the business was following suit.

There were only a few times when I was offered work by friends, and I jumped at the chance. At the end of 1977, I was invited to dance at the Brooklyn Academy of Music in a modern ballet, *The Spy,* which was being choreographed by Lynn Taylor Corbett, an ex–show dancer but now a blossoming choreographer, whom I had known for years. The ballet was based on Anaïs Nin's novel *A Spy in the House of Love,* set to music composed by Judith Lander. The piece was being co-produced by another friend of mine, Lynn Simonson, who was a world-class dancer and teacher.

As we approached the technical rehearsal, I was told that the producers had run out of money and were going to have to cancel. I wrote them a check for $6,000, not that I could afford it, but I couldn't face the alternative. Though I was struggling with the work, once again, it was the only thing keeping me together emotionally. So I pushed myself through each of the performances, thinking if it were not a job well done, at least I had seen it through to completion.

At the beginning of 1978, I was featured with Leslie Uggams on *The Kraft Music Hall 7th Anniversary Special,* a ninety-minute TV variety show. It was a godsend not to have to audition, thanks to an old friend, Gary Smith, who was the producer. The director was Dwight Hemion, the choreographer was Ron Field, and my partner for one segment was Don Correia. Unlike the experience with Ron in *On the Town,* this time he brilliantly staged and choreographed a musical storyline that followed my career from chorus girl to the cover of *Newsweek.* Except for the host, Bob Hope, these were all people I had worked with before and respected tremendously. Peter Matz was the musical director, and Bill Byers created the dance arrangements. I loved them both. Bill had orchestrated the musical arrangement for my number in *A Chorus Line.*

I performed "Long Ago and Far Away." The number was a wonderful blending of music, text, song, and dance, and the experience was a joy from beginning to end. I especially loved the ending. There was a long shot of me filmed from high above, and I was sitting on the seat directly behind the TV camera as I sang the big ending of the song. The camera that I was sitting on was attached to the long arm of a cherry picker, and as I was about to finish, the camera zoomed up quickly to the camera above, so I ended singing right into the lens. That was such an exciting effect, and I was thrilled by the whole sequence. I returned to New York filled with hope and a new validation, thinking maybe I would be okay after all.

That summer the *New York Times* ran a story under the headline, "Does a Smash Hit Guarantee a Performer's Future?" The run of *A Chorus Line* had already surpassed 1,000 performances that year. The writer asked members of the original cast if being in such a hit show had "typecast them and sealed them into an artistic prison." What a pointed question that was. Asked to comment on my marriage to Michael, I said, "I think it's too easy and too early to say it was a mistake. Some days I think it was. Other days I don't. I'm still too close to comprehend it all."

I didn't mention the difficulties I had been having finding work, except to say, "I think it's obvious that I'm sad, but I would be even more depressed if I didn't have my work. What I got from *A Chorus Line* is that for the first time in my life I feel like a grown-up. You couldn't go through all I've experienced in the last three years and not grow up." I had to make quite an effort to sound that reasonable.

A short while later, I received a bizarre telephone call from Michael. It was a one-sided conversation, and he was intent on sharing with me his feelings about the progress of *Ballroom,* as if it were of the utmost importance for me to know how he was doing. He said, "I think I've figured it out. It's going to be okay. I can see the light at the end of the tunnel now, honey."

Honey? He must have been drunk. His use of that word surprised me, and I wasn't going to allow myself to be pulled into whatever scheme he had in mind. After saying how very happy I was for him that things were going well, I told him to take care and said good night. I wouldn't hear from him again for several years.

At this time I was living in a sublet at Fifth Avenue and 8th Street, still waiting for the divorce to be finalized. It felt like I was in purgatory, and I didn't want to burden my friends with my grief and complaints. I was going to therapy sessions three times a week, and that at least kept me on some kind of schedule, if not moving forward. Among the few blessings in my life, I counted my old friends Larry Moss and his wife at the time, Susan Slavin. Together, we studied acting with Warren Robertson.

The work I did at Warren's studio enhanced the technical scene-study classes that I took with Uta Hagen at the Herbert Berghof Studio. Uta wanted us to experience the character's emotional life, but her approach was from the outside-in. She would say, referring to our tears, "I don't care about the gook coming from your eyes. That will come or not. I want to see the scene played fully with intention." In contrast, Warren's exercises worked from the inside-out, in that they supplied the psychological tools (words with a personal connection) to tap into a deeper emotional expression without the boundaries of a scene. Then the performance could be shaped with our choices to meet the exact conditions of any given scene or character. This process enabled me to break down my inhibitions in a shared environment, inhibitions which had kept me from bringing a fully realized emotional life to a character. Warren's teaching provided a great complement to the work I did in Uta's classes.

Larry and Susan have since divorced, but both have gone on to have distinguished careers in the theater, writing, directing, producing, and teaching. Larry had been a supportive confidant when I first broke up with Ken Howard and even referred me to a therapist. While my life was in limbo in the late 1970s, Larry was co-starring on Broadway in Cy Coleman's *I Love My Wife*. I found solace listening to him confide about the stress and difficulties he was having on that show. Nobody really understands what it is to do eight shows a week until you've had the experience.

Larry and Susan had a network of friends who in turn became my friends. We were bonded by our beliefs and quests for emotional and spiritual health, while pursuing our acting and musical theater careers. This network evolved naturally into a peer support group, with Larry and Susan taking the lead. Some people came and went over the years, but the nucleus of friends included Pam Shaw, Jane Summerhays, Ron Perlman, Carol Demas, Ron Young, Ian Herman, and Bob Goldstone. We would usually meet once a week in the evening, usually at Carol's apartment, and each of us would have individual time in front of the group, working through inhibitions with acting exercises and music.

Our primary goal was to improve as musical performers. We brought in material of our own choice to work on, whether for an audition or a musical that we were in at the time. We emphasized the process rather than the result, so there was to be no applause. It was important for each of us to have this kind of safe place to grow and extend ourselves. Without the demand for a finished product, we were able to relax, and more easily arrive at spontaneous creative choices.

Each of us brought in things that were going on in our lives that we were able to channel and exorcise through our work. I couldn't imagine a healthier way to deal with neuroses and inner conflicts. The atmosphere was always one of mutual trust; the process made for exciting theater. It wasn't therapy but it was highly therapeutic for all of us. Looking back, I can see how the group influenced me in all the areas that I later pursued with my career, from performing to teaching, writing, choreographing, and directing. My life started improving as I met new friends. There were other supportive people who became important to me, including Benay Venuta, Judy Gordon, and Steven Greenberg.

With insights derived from the group, I started making connections for myself, and at a certain point realized how one loss could trigger another. Peeling away the layers of my unresolved feelings, I traveled back in time to what seemed to be the original loss, which was related to my fears of abandonment and intimacy. It was exciting to be able to confide with others in the group and share breakthroughs like that. No longer depending on Michael for approval, and finally disentangling my identity from his, I was feeling less like a victim. I knew I had to take charge of my personal happiness, but that was an ongoing challenge. I also realized that it wasn't just the failure of the marriage that was so crushing, but the loss of a friendship that I thought had been based on genuine love and respect.

I remember complaining one time to one of my friends in the group about my not getting work. He said, "Michael can't stop you from having a career, Donna. I think you're being a little paranoid."

I was defensive and told him, "You don't understand. Even if he hasn't put out an explicit memo about me, when Michael is doing business, I know that he's bandying my name around in a very negative way. It gets back to me. And nobody's going to hire me who has any association with him now or who wants to have the opportunity to work with him in the future."

Even my therapist seemed perplexed by the situation, and he asked me, "Why is Michael so intent on demeaning you?" I had no answer at the time. Once the divorce was settled, I had no contact with him, and I certainly didn't pose a threat, so I couldn't fathom why I was still the target of his hostility.

I had no desire to make any trouble for Michael, but more importantly, I didn't want to make any more trouble for myself. My unwillingness to fight may have provoked Michael's continued animosity toward me. My lawyer once speculated that Michael's outrage and attacks seemed to be based on his own feelings of guilt. I'll never know for sure. Given Michael's pattern with those whom he left, I later felt that he might have been friendlier toward me if I had given him a hard time and vented my feelings about the way I was being treated. That might have been a healthier tack for me to take, because as I was soon to discover, the worst was yet to come.

Chapter 7

———— ❧ ————

MASOCHIST'S LAMENT

During the down times in the aftermath of the divorce, I started to show all of the signs of clinical depression. I was experiencing insomnia, fatigue, and mood swings. After nights when I was able to sleep, I found it difficult to get up in the morning. Why get up to face another joyless day? I rarely went to class, and schedules were more and more impossible to keep. Exercise called for deep breathing, which caused feelings to surface that I wasn't able to control. I would suddenly just burst into tears at the most unlikely times.

Being alone in this condition was unbearable. My nerves were constantly on edge, and I would eat to calm myself. The weight gain that came with overeating and my not being in the best physical condition further contributed to the vicious circle of depression. In the past, I had always been able to call on the willful part of me to pull myself up and get out the door. The survival instinct that sustained the runaway girl in me year after year wasn't there anymore. The friends I trusted enough to confide in always gave loving advice, which I appreciated but wasn't yet able to put into practice. That seemed like yet another failure. I could understand it all intellectually, but I still wasn't able to grasp the deeper emotional issues. I couldn't see how I was abandoning myself day by day.

Although battling my depression made it difficult to apply myself to work, I tried as much as possible during 1978 to organize and produce what was eventually to be my own one-woman show. This project began as a cabaret act that included songs from the Broadway shows I had done as well as lighthearted references to the ups and downs of my life and career. While the revue was to some extent autobiographical, the work was also a way for me *not* to deal with my feelings. I was still trying to escape my sense of failure after the divorce. What do I do when I'm down? I get busy and try to be creative and do something on the stage. But before the show ever made its debut, my life took a new and harrowing turn.

Gwen Verdon once told me that every dancer dies twice, the first time when age, or in some cases physical infirmity, forces a dancer into early retirement. I thought my time had come. Instead of being uplifted by having a new home and the opportunity to make a fresh start, I encountered an obstacle that I could never have imagined for myself even on my worst day.

Most dancers have a ritual for dealing with pain. In the same way that we dance through our injuries, living with stiffness and discomfort becomes part of the daily routine, and so it was for me. But the intensity and duration of the pain I was experiencing began to change. Ordinarily when I would get out of bed in the morning, there would always be some degree of soreness from the strenuous dance classes or rehearsals the day before. I would throw my legs over the side of the bed and slowly do a demi-plié, a little knee bend rising to an upright position to find my center balance. I would then do some gentle stretches to get the blood circulating, and slowly I would feel more limber.

I had inherited less than perfect feet. Besides being naturally flat, I think I was born with bunions. When I was a teenager, they got worse from wearing pointe shoes for my ballet training. So my feet *always* hurt. I got used to the pain, like a fact of life. Usually most of the pain would subside over the course of the day, or if not, like most dancers, I would just go into denial and work through it. But in the winter of that year, I started to notice that the pain and stiffness weren't going away as easily.

I wasn't dancing as much at the time. I was taking dance classes whenever I could, but I was devoting more of my time to my singing and the work I did with my peer group. I was trying to carry on and enjoy myself, but the problem with my feet was worsening. A subtle swelling was beginning to affect my joints. Initially, I passed it off as water retention. I first noticed the problem in my feet, and then in my knees, elbows, fingers, and toes. I was definitely not feeling well, but I was still managing to push both the physical and emotional pain away, not really allowing my condition to register consciously as something to be concerned or alarmed about.

When one of my girlfriends, Sandy Deetz, invited me to spend a long weekend with her in Florida, I was happy to accept her offer, thinking that a little break might be good for me. Sandy was a great pal, someone I had known since the time of my first marriage, and she had a new condo on the water she wanted to show off. On my first night we went out to a club where she was a member, and I met the fellow she was seeing at the time, who happened to be a doctor. On the second day of my visit, my hands became swollen, red, and inflamed. My fingers blew up so much that even I had to take notice. That day I went to see the doctor my friend was dating. He did a blood test and later told me there was an elevated rheumatoid factor in my blood. That meant it was likely I had rheumatoid arthritis. I told him I didn't even know what that was. I asked him, "What can I do about it?"

He told me, "Well, not too much right now. Take some aspirin or Bufferin for the time being." He advised me to see a specialist when I returned to New York if there was no improvement.

After returning home, I realized that something had to be terribly wrong. I was in agony, and found it difficult to move or even sit without pain. I was only able to get around very slowly, and I was conscious of every step. In desperation, I made an appointment to see a rheumatologist, Dr. King, who was the best specialist I could find. Highly regarded in the field, Dr. King had his own clinic in the East 70s and did his own blood work and X-rays. It was like he had his own little private hospital. He was an unusually caring doctor and I liked him immediately. Dr. King was first-rate and also quite expensive, but money was the last thing I was thinking about.

After our first meeting, I felt I was in good hands and my spirits lifted temporarily. I had my blood tested again and X-rays were taken, and then came a moment I will never forget. On my second visit to the clinic, I was sitting in Dr. King's examination room waiting for him to come back with the results of my tests. When he walked into the room, I could tell by his demeanor that he didn't have good news. He told me, "I'm afraid you do have rheumatoid arthritis, and it's not going to go away."

I said, "Well, is there something I can take? What can I do about it? I'm a dancer!"

He said, "Forget about dancing. Eventually, you won't be able to walk." Perhaps in order to impress upon me the seriousness of my condition, he advised me to check into nursing care. He told me that in the worst-case scenario, I would need a twenty-four-hour nurse.

That was a staggering thing to hear. Dr. King kept talking and I tried to concentrate on what he was saying, but there was this fierce declaration inside me: *No, no, no!* It was as if I were yelling inside my brain. I even saw a big NO like a billboard in my mind's eye. I just couldn't accept what he was saying. With my heart racing, I tried to say calmly, "But Dr. King, there has got to be something I can do."

I remember thinking how reasonable and unemotional I sounded, while my body was going through all of these physiological changes as the shock registered. I said, "There must be something I can take for it. I mean, this is the age of technology and medical miracles." He told me that he had used gold injections and cortisone. Now this was quite a while ago, and at that time those treatments were somewhat experimental. Even though I knew my case could become more severe, I was reluctant to think about metal injections, and knew instinctively I wanted to stay away from drugs. I had always taken a more holistic approach to medicine.

Dr. King told me he was going to put me on Bufferin; I was to take three Bufferin tablets six times a day. Buffered aspirin seemed to me relatively safe, though I didn't understand how it could be effective. Dr. King was straightforward: it would help and it was the best option we had to work with.

When I left the clinic, I felt too alone and too frightened to cry. I went back to my apartment and methodically tried to think the situation through in practical terms. It didn't take me long to come to the realization that I had no future if I didn't find a way out. I didn't have a lot of money, only the monthly stipend from the divorce settlement that covered my expenses, and that would end after three years. I did have royalties from *A Chorus Line,* but that only amounted to a few thousand dollars a year, and how long could I depend on that? My mortgage payments were paid for a few months, and I had some money to live on while I wasn't working. But that would only last a short time. Beyond that, I knew I was going to have to work to make ends meet. I couldn't afford to be sick. I tried to fend off the panic by telling myself, *I'll just have to keep doing what I'm doing and find another way.*

Because of the stigma attached to having a chronic illness in show business, I kept it to myself, a secret that I shared with only a few close friends. I felt very isolated, and the symptoms were increasingly difficult to hide. I did tell my sister, though reluctantly. As the big sister, I still felt that impulse to protect Barbara, to project an image of confidence and independence. She continued to stay with me from time to time, and that went on for quite a while. In my Park Avenue apartment, I went through what I now call the "down-in-the-depths on the 90th floor" syndrome, after the Cole Porter song. I was afraid to be alone. Barbara had never seen me like this before, and it frightened her. She made many sacrifices with her own life to try to help me through this crisis.

There were mornings when Barbara had to help me get out of bed. The disease was now affecting my whole body, including my spine and neck, and it took so long to get anywhere that I hardly moved. I read self-help books and went back to therapy until I was no longer able to make the trip. The pain was the most severe I had ever experienced. It felt like razor blades were slicing into my knuckles and joints every time I moved them. My physical anguish reached the point where I didn't think I could live with it.

I remember one day yelling out for my sister, who was in the other room. It took so much energy to shout, "Barbara, can't you hear me? I need some water." The effort to raise my voice affected all the muscles and bones in my neck. Barbara came running in and leaned against the bedroom door. She looked at me and her eyes were full of tears. I looked at her and just could not stand what I was doing to her and to myself. I could now comprehend how elderly, bedridden people feel such fear when they are unable to take care of themselves. My Grandfather Dillard had been that way when he was dying of emphysema. He seemed cranky all the time, always shouting orders to Gladys to get him things that he couldn't get himself. He was very different from the smiling, good-natured grandfather I remembered as a girl.

I don't believe in suicide, but I no longer judge people harshly who take their own lives. When the agony is that great, I can understand how a person would do anything to put an end to it. It was soon after that incident with my sister that I started to have thoughts about ending my own life. These dark thoughts ran against my basic nature, but I saw no future for myself, and I knew I couldn't continue to live this way. What purpose in life had I to fulfill at this point?

I imagined myself walking to the window and climbing up on the ledge. I knew that I could do it, but I had to make sure no one was walking on the street below me. I was trying to be practical. My apartment was on the seventh floor, so I figured my death would be immediate and I probably wouldn't feel anything. But in that split second between the mental command and actually putting one foot in front of the other, I realized that I couldn't do it. My emotions flooded over me, and I sobbed and sobbed. I told myself, *If you can't do it, you're going to have to find a way to live.* Whether I ever danced again made no difference at this point. I just had to think about living and not dying. That awareness was born out of sheer desperation, but it somehow seemed to push me in a better mental direction.

In the past when I was alone, I would have music playing, or I would hum and sing, but not since the onset of my illness. I was living in silence. I wouldn't listen to music. It was too painful to hear the strains of a beautiful song. But even under such dismal circumstances, there came a day when my sense of humor returned, and I thought that was a very good sign.

My sister was out of the apartment and I had to make a trip to the bathroom on my own. I remember how much it hurt getting out of bed.

Then I had to inch my way along the wall, leaning against it with my back and shoulders. The journey seemed endless. When I finally made it into the bathroom, I was struck by how pathetic my situation was. I stood over the toilet, knowing how much it would hurt to bend my knees, so I made sure that I was positioned directly over the seat, and prepared to let myself drop. I figured if I did it quickly, it wouldn't hurt as much.

At that moment, it was as if I was outside of myself and watching this scene. My descent was jarring and anything but graceful. There was a crashing thud as the marble tiles in the bathroom reverberated with the sound. I had to laugh out loud, because I saw the absurdity in that image of me, the dancer, throwing herself onto the toilet. It was just too funny, and I laughed until I cried. It was a cathartic shift that gave me hope, and I knew that somehow I was going to have to find a solution to this horrid predicament.

One of my friends in my peer group, Susan Slavin, eventually found another doctor for me to go to. Susan told me she had gone to him for low blood sugar, and his treatment was effective. I might not have agreed to see him if I hadn't been so desperate, because he sounded so unconventional. But I trusted Susan because she was a very bright and sensitive woman, and she had done her research. She told me, "His name is Dr. Sam Getlen. He's well-known and people come from all over the world to see him. He has a waiting list of six months to a year. I'm going to call and see if he can take you right away." Her tenacity prevailed, and Dr. Getlen soon agreed to see me.

Susan and I rented a car and she drove me to Trenton, New Jersey. We had to make the trip at night because Dr. Getlen only saw patients between the hours of 10:00 P.M. and 5:00 A.M. We pulled up in front of a spooky-looking old dark house. It had a lot of turrets on the roof, like the House of the Seven Gables. The neighborhood was run-down. I remember we parked next to a high-chain link fence that ran along the whole street. It didn't make for an inspiring first impression, but I thought, if nothing else, it will be an adventure.

With her support, Susan gave me courage. She helped me out of the car, and I hobbled up the stairs into the house. The place was shabby. A naked glaring white lightbulb hung from the ceiling and the walls were painted a shiny yellow but were clean. Dr. Getlen greeted us right away. He was a slight man, about five-four, and stooped with age. Actually, he was ninety-five years old. He had a shiny bald head with a little fuzz at the sides, and a very sweet face with the most beautiful skin. He wore an ordinary shirt and slacks rather than a doctor's white coat. He took my hand, and his skin was so soft and smooth that it felt like a baby's. His confidence put me at ease. Without further ado, he invited me into his examining room, and had Susan wait outside.

After I sat on the examining table, he gave me a pencil and a pad, and took the stool and urine samples he had requested behind the partition. For the next twenty minutes, he stayed behind the partition and gave me directives. He said, "I'm going to give you a yes list and a no list for your diet, and you just write this down." I started to ask something, and this sweet little man got very tough all of a sudden. "Just do what I say," he said, "and no fussin'!"

I said, "Yes, Doctor, but—"

He interrupted me, saying, "I said no fussin'. Just write it down."

I followed his instructions. His manner made more sense to me later because I realized that people would come to him in pain, and their anxiety made it difficult for them to hear or comprehend the information that he needed to give them. I would later learn that anxiety also wreaks havoc with your blood sugar. Dr. Getlen couldn't possibly explain everything he knew about the body's chemistry while answering his patients' questions. There was too much to absorb all at once.

I continued to write as fast as I could, taking down everything the voice behind the partition was telling me, no matter how unorthodox it all seemed. Why did he see patients only in the wee hours? There was a reason physiologically, but that was also something I would learn later.

So I wrote down his yes list and no list for food, vitamins, and behavior. This began with mega-vitamin therapy. I was to take certain vitamins every few hours during the day. These included complex B, C, E, and others. Over time, I would be able to wean myself off the high doses. I was to take alfalfa for the pain. As I understood it, my disease was the result of a toxic condition that I could reverse by balancing my metabolism and lifestyle. This process involved a cleansing or elimination diet. No red meat, no coffee, no alcohol, no sugar, no butter, no white flour, no milk products, no processed foods, no canned food, no tap water, no nightshade plants like tomato, potato, eggplant, green pepper. He also excluded bananas and most citrus fruits.

The yes list included whole foods only, herbal tea, bottled or filtered water, and olive oil instead of butter. The only canned product I could have was tuna packed in water. I was also allowed chicken, turkey, fish without the skin, rye and oat grains, alfalfa, some herbs, and sweet potatoes or yams. Dr. Getlen said, "Stay away from *yellow* and *orange*. Sweet potatoes and yams are the exception. You want only green vegetables." I could also have lemon, the only citrus, and fruits like apples, berries, and peaches. At first, I was to eat 60 percent raw foods and 40 percent steamed or cooked. Later, I could reverse that ratio.

Dr. Getlen also advised me, "When you do anything that feels good, like if you take a warm bath, anything you enjoy, I want you to say out loud, 'This feels good!'" He spoke to me as if I were a child likely to misbehave. "And stay away from loud people. No fussin' with anyone. Don't get into confrontations or fights." I wrote down every word. He finally said, "Be patient. If you follow these instructions, in three weeks the pain should start to subside, and in six weeks you should be able to walk and get around better. Then you can start some light exercise without overdoing it. In six months, you should be able to exercise again."

I said, "I'm a dancer. Will I be able to dance again?"

He thought for a moment and said, "You could possibly be dancing again in one year."

Of course, I was happy to hear that, but I couldn't really believe it. Dr. Getlen told me that he had worked for thirty years as a traditional medical doctor, but that he had changed his practice. He explained his reason for adopting his unusual approach by saying, "I just got tired of burying my patients." Then he showed me several large bound books. They were scrapbooks, and he put one on my lap and showed me page after page of the hundreds of letters he had received from patients over the years. They included people he had treated for arthritis, cancer, multiple sclerosis, and other diseases that he described as stress-related.

"My patients all write to me and tell me how they improve. That's what I want you to do. Write me a letter when you're feeling better."

Before I left, I asked, "How much do I owe you?"

He said, "Eighteen dollars."

I didn't think I heard him correctly. He repeated himself and explained that the number eighteen represented the sign of life in Hebrew.

I promised that I would write to him when I was well again. I believed in the power of suggestion, but his regimen was more than that. He gave me something I could do. I didn't have to feel impotent anymore. The letters of success and gratitude that he had received from other patients also encouraged me.

Dr. Getlen's fee may have been cheap at $18, but the vitamins he prescribed were very expensive. Initially I was taking about sixty pills a day while drinking lemon juice and cleansing my system. Each night I had to squeeze lemon juice to the top of an eight-ounce glass, then put five raisins in the bottom of it. This concoction had to sit overnight with a paper towel over it. I drank that each morning before having anything else.

I remember I was living on broth made with vegetables like green beans, squash, and parsley. I would boil vegetables, and toss the pulp. And I had jars and jars of this potassium drink that I slugged all day long. I devoted all my energy just to taking care of myself; I was barely able to get around to shop and cook. My voice had suffered as well, so I knew I was really going to have to work on my entire instrument if I was ever going to get back into shape. I rested a lot and tried to stay quiet and I watched *Mister Rogers* on TV. I was impatient and didn't quite believe that Dr. Getlen's plan would actually work, but I tried to be optimistic, and allow for that possibility. It was really all that I had to hang on to. Eventually, I would introduce other foods into my diet, but only slowly and in moderation. These included yogurt, cheese, tomatoes, a little butter, brown rice, coffee, and bananas. Now, if I do sometimes partake from the no list, I focus on balance and moderation.

Slowly, I noticed some improvement. After three weeks, I started feeling the pain subside as he had predicted, and I was filled with hope. It inspired me, and I was all the more determined to follow through. I also started seeing a new psychiatrist my friend Susan found for me. Dr. De la Vega was a Freudian psychiatrist and neurosurgeon who specialized in clinical depression. He didn't buy Dr. Getlen's radical approach entirely, but he didn't try to discourage me. He didn't mind the diet, but had reservations about the vitamin therapy. Dr. De la Vega was more of the school that views rheumatoid arthritis as a physical disease, and once you have it, it's irreversible and you will always have it. He did, of course, recognize the powerful connection between emotional and physical life, and how emotions can affect the body. As far as my emotional life was concerned, he tried to help me connect, and deal with my grief and anger. I was still a long way from getting to the bottom of things. I discovered a book called *There Is a Cure for Arthritis,* by Dr. Paavo Airola. It started me on a path of self-education about alternative medicine, alkaline-base metabolism, and mind-body connection.

When I felt well enough to start doing physical therapy, I had a yoga teacher come to my home, because I still couldn't get around easily, and I was also still paranoid about being seen in my condition. So the teacher came to my apartment, and at first I could hardly do any of the exercises. I wasn't able to put pressure or weight on my arms or legs. But I kept at it, and there was gradual improvement, with some days better than others. I'm certainly not a medical expert, but I do know that my experience with the condition was a slow process of recovery that required many months. There was more than one factor that eventually led me back to health, including both the dietary changes and the exorcism of various psychological demons, a process carried out over time through analysis. I took the stance that if a troubled mind got me into this ordeal, then a healthy mind could get me out of it.

By the spring of 1979, I was feeling relief and walking, and I went back to Dr. King. I wanted him to see my recovery because I thought it was fairly remarkable. Dr. King was impressed, and where other doctors might have said it was a fluke, he said, "It's amazing! I'm just so happy to see you walking again. Please give me this doctor's name, and I'll refer patients to him, those whom I can't help." I admired Dr. King for having such an open-minded and caring attitude. As an aside, I should note that there are about one hundred kinds of arthriris, and everyone's chemistry is different. I can't presume to have the answer for all people suffering with this condition, but I do believe there may be thousands of people with cases similar enough to mine, who do not have to live in pain. With lifestyle adjustments and education about alternative medicine, many people can surely be helped if not cured completely, as I was eventually.

Meanwhile, I was making enough progress to take on a role in a play called *Wine Untouched*, which was produced off-Broadway at the Harold Clurman Theatre. I figured I could get away with it since this was an acting role without any dancing or singing . The play was a translation based on a Norwegian work by Björg Vik. The story involved the poignant reunion of five women who had been childhood friends and who came together in their midlife years. I was to play Lillian, a downtrodden housewife with four children. The other roles were performed by a terrific cast comprised of Glenn Close, Swoosie Kurtz, Patricia Elliott, and my friend Susan Slavin. We were directed by Lynne Guerra, and I managed to get through rehearsals without succumbing to my condition. The opening took place June 18, 1979, and we ran only fourteen performances. The show was not particularly well received by the critics, and for my part, I was still limited physically and had probably tried to come back too early. As was my nature, I was being overly demanding of myself.

Even though my condition had improved enough for me to be able to perform in a straight dramatic play, I wasn't yet able to take dance classes. I worked on my singing with Paul Gavert, the voice teacher who prepared me for my role in *A Chorus Line*. Paul became a voice coach for many dancers who came into the show because Michael was so impressed with the work we did. My voice was a challenge because there was still so much tension in my body caused by the arthritis; when I tried to sing, the muscles in my back, chest, and throat would tighten up. As a result, I felt great fatigue. To sing properly requires a lot of strength and stamina. I was straining my vocal cords, and at times I lost my voice entirely.

I was still seeing Dr. De la Vega, and he was trying to get me to express my anger. He said, "If you don't let out your anger, you're going to get sick, or sicker. That's why you've lost your voice." He was deliberately trying to provoke me by demanding that I yell at him and call him names. But I just couldn't do it. He was right that I was angry. I was hurt and holding it all in, but my way of dealing with these emotions was to go to the ballet barre and start taking class again. By the end of the year, I also went back to working on my show. In reality I was staying at arm's length from myself. I didn't have enough of a loving relationship with myself at that point to fight all that resistance.

The truth was I was barely hanging on, and still had to spend periods convalescing. I wasn't invited to the earliest *Chorus Line* gala reunions, to me it was just another sign that wherever Michael was, I was not welcome. I started getting phone calls from him every once in a while late at night. This went on intermittently for several years. One time he called on December 4, and began the conversation with, "Happy Anniversary!" After hanging up the phone, I burst into tears. I thought it was a perverse and cruel joke. After thinking about it, I realized that he probably didn't think there was anything wrong with saying that. His behavior seemed so bizarre that it probably had nothing to do with me. Later, I thought he was actually trying to reach out, and took that as an underhanded compliment. But he never asked me how I was, or what I was doing. There was no empathy. I suppose he might have been trying to torture me, but I think it was more likely that his need to contact me stemmed from his own desperate state. I could relate to that. I also remembered how our similarities brought us together in the past.

I remember one time when I was in Los Angeles, living in a house that I could barely afford. I was still struggling with my condition and not working, and I got a call from Michael out of the blue. He told me he had just bought a house in East Hampton. It was as if he was trying to share his happiness with me, and wanted me to celebrate with him. He said, "You wouldn't believe it! I have this beautiful house and I'm sitting here on the porch. It's so wonderful, and I'm painting all the antique wicker furniture white."

All I could say was, "I'm happy for you, Michael. It sounds wonderful." He might have been stoned. He was working on a new show, *Scandals*, and he tried to share his feelings about the work as he had in the past. I was struggling financially, but I wasn't about to share any of that with him. I wouldn't hear from him for months, and then he would call again. It made no sense except that he was trying to find some kind of reassurance, because that was the role I had always played. I did call and ask for a loan once. I hated making that call. I was no longer getting alimony and I needed to pay taxes and doctor fees. He was very good about it and in an easy way he said to call his business manager. I received a few thousand dollars—half the amount I asked for—in three or four payments, and then the money stopped. I never called back. I felt that I had embarrassed myself enough.

Back in New York, I was trying to put together more than a cabaret show. I was working with Bobby Thomas, who did my musical arrangements. He had been Michael's drummer and friend for about twenty years, and was a life raft for me in a way, because I was all at sea. I was pleased that he didn't allow Michael to discourage him from working with me.

As the story elements of my show evolved, it became the journey of a woman (like me) who went through marriage and divorce, and then marriage and divorce yet again. I did it out of my own confusion and need to understand, but I soon had to admit that I was in no condition to take on that much work. I had been rehearsing every day, and I hired several male dancers. Paying for this rehearsal time had stretched my resources to the limit. There really was no show yet. I wasn't making any money and found I couldn't afford to keep employing people. So the project had to be put on hold for a few years.

At the beginning of 1980, I came to be represented by Jack Rollins of the Rollins-Jaffe Company, who produced Woody Allen's movies. He was based in New York, and I had given him a tape of some of the songs that were in my show. Jack was always supportive and he arranged for me to tour that spring. Playing at clubs like Les Mouches in New York and similar venues in Atlanta, Chicago, and San Francisco, I had to scale the show down to songs and cue lines, working on it along the way.

I traveled with a great stage manager, Janet Beroza, and, on and off, several musicians, including singer Lori Jaroslow. I sang a number of Sondheim pieces, some pop numbers, and "The Music and the Mirror" from *A Chorus Line.* Marvin Hamlisch's "Inside the Music," which had been cut from *Chorus Line,* became a cornerstone of my show. Even though it wasn't right originally and had to be cut, it was effective enough for me that I was eventually able to build a whole show around it.

We opened the tour during March at a dinner theater in Peekskill, New York, and that was the first time I performed the show in front of an audience. We rehearsed in the mornings, I took dance classes in the afternoon, and then I went to the theater each night. Interviewed at the time, I said, "I've never done anything like this before, and I really enjoy the conducive environment, as well as the warm, friendly audience. It's almost as though you can reach out and touch them." That was actually a lie. I was exhausted from singing to people who were more interested in eating their dinners.

And there were many nights I felt like I couldn't touch anyone or do anything right. But Jack was encouraging. He would tell me things like, "I remember for about eighteen months when he was starting out, Woody went out there and flopped." He was trying to make me feel better, because my show wasn't working, and I was literally quaking with each performance. This was a time in my life when it was painful to even hear my name because I just didn't know who I was anymore. There was that split second after hearing my name announced as the show began that I would say to myself, "What am I doing? Am I crazy? I shouldn't be out in front of people. I should be in bed!"

I can laugh at it now, but I kept flogging away at myself, always criticizing. The following summer Jack arranged for me to join the Kenley Players summer stock company in Akron, Ohio, playing Sally Bowles in the John Kander and Fred Ebb musical *Cabaret.* The part of the Emcee was performed marvelously by Billy Crystal, who at that time was appearing as the gay stepson in the TV comedy *Soap.* For me, the experience was all about working back into shape and rebuilding some confidence.

Because Jack and his partner, Charles Jaffe, were fairly influential movie producers, sometimes people would put pressure on me by saying, "Oh my God, you're with them! Why don't they put you in a movie?" But I was just starting over, and I was simply grateful to have the chance to work. One time Jack wanted to have director Joe Layton help me put a show together. We met, but Joe was tied up for a year directing *Barnum*, as well as doing other projects. I figured at least someone was trying to get me work. Jack gave me hope that I still had a future.

At the end of 1980, I got a job to go to Chicago with *I'm Getting My Act Together and Taking It on the Road*. The book and lyrics of this musical were written by Gretchen Cryer; Nancy Ford was the composer. Gretchen had originally opened the show, followed by Phyllis Newman. I was replacing Phyllis. It was one of the first women's liberation shows and had a successful run with the Shakespeare Festival in 1978, then continued at Circle in the Square. The show was about a woman with a nightclub act, working through her divorce and relationships—not unlike the show that I had been putting together. We were to play at the Water Tower Theatre, and I remember I arrived on the night that John Lennon was shot, December 8, 1980. It affected me more than I could ever imagine. He was a symbol of hope for me and millions of others.

I was given a beautiful apartment off Michigan Avenue. It was all glass and overlooked the city. I stayed there through the winter, and I had a lovely kitchen where I continued my daily routine of mixing potassium drinks and boiling pots of vegetables.

Physically, I was still aching, but I was happy to be working again. I remember a friend came to see me in the show, and afterward she asked, "What's wrong with your knees?" I said, "What do you mean?" In the show there was a ramp, a kind of runway that went from the proscenium into the audience, where scenes could be played. The ramp was a few feet high, and I had to step down and step up, which would have been easy if the pain in my joints wasn't hindering me. My friend pointed out that each time I stepped down, my shoulders lifted up to my ears. I had been unaware that I was compensating that way, so I simply made a mental note, and after that I kept my shoulders down.

The show was successful and ran several months. When we closed, since I was halfway across the country, I said to myself, "Why don't I keep going? What is there for me back in New York?" So I moved on to

Los Angeles in 1981 and found a place to live in the Hollywood Hills on Gower Street. It was a whirlwind move that started a new phase of my life. Rollins and Jaffe had an office out there, so I thought I would have better representation this time and thus moved with a buoyant sense of confidence. It was like I was a new girl in town again, though of course some people knew me or remembered me from my earlier visits.

I first did a short run of a play called *Table Settings,* a comedy about Jewish families written by James Lapine, who later collaborated with Stephen Sondheim on *Into the Woods* and *Sunday in the Park with George.* After *Table Settings* closed, I was cast in an Aaron Spelling TV film called *Twirl.* I'll never forget when I met Aaron Spelling in his office, and he stood up to greet me. It was just a little gesture of courtesy on his part, but I thought, *Why is he getting up?* He told me how much he liked my work. I was slow to see what a gentleman he was. A lot of people in L.A. in his position weren't as classy.

I was impressed by Mr. Spelling and started feeling like maybe I wasn't invisible after all; maybe I could hold my own here. It was foreign and intimidating to go into those plush offices, but I started thinking that I was capable of sitting down and having an interview, as opposed to having a reading for a part where you're really up there doing it. People would give me suggestions for auditioning, like "you've got to be in character," but that had never been my way of working. I was always Donna first. I was never in character when I walked through the door. So L.A. was a big adjustment for me in terms of bearing and audition technique.

Twirl was a drama about a teenage baton-twirling contest. The movie was directed by Gus Trikonis, who had played Action in the original production of *West Side Story.* In *Twirl,* I had a wonderful role as a mother, and Missy Gold had the part of my baton-twirling daughter. Heather Locklear was just starting out, and she had a role in the film as well. Heather was very pretty and confident. She has been enormously successful over the years, and I have always enjoyed watching her as she goes from show to show. A lot of people can't do that, and I admire her for having that kind of focus.

The following year I played Debra in the second episode of *Cheers,* which was directed by my old friend James Burrows, who went on to direct *Friends* and *Will and Grace*. I also did a Pontiac industrial show in L.A. called *Showstoppers*. That was quite an extravaganza, choreographed by Walter Painter, who had worked in TV and movies and later staged *City of Angels* on Broadway. He had also worked as a dancer in *Billie*. I was headlined in the Pontiac show and did numbers from several musicals, including *West Side Story* and *A Chorus Line*. Donald O'Connor came to see us during rehearsals and thrilled us all. During the show, I met a stunt driver named Roger. He was charming, funny, and handsome, and this was to become an important relationship for me, the first since Michael.

I did very well this time on the West Coast, and life was good to me. I worked on several episodes of *Fame, Family Ties, Scarecrow and Mrs. King*, and later a TV movie with Ben Vereen called *Breakin' Through*. My home on Gower was nothing fancy, but it was an adorable duplex with a little deck overlooking the hills. I was going to class and studying again, and I started connecting and networking with my peers. My brother, Ron, soon came to live with me while he was going to school at UCLA. I hadn't spent much time with him in the last ten years, and I enjoyed getting to know him again, now that he was growing up. While I had recovered my confidence, I was only doing jobs that were within my grasp. Still, I started feeling at last like I was going to survive. Even my relationship with my mother was improving. She had moved to San Diego, and we were able to spend enjoyable times together.

I started analysis with a Los Angeles psychiatrist named Jerome Saperstein, who was like a loving grandfather. I was referred to him by my doctor in New York because Dr. Saperstein treated clinical depression, though his approach was different from that of the other therapists I had seen. When I first met him, he was about seventy and initially said he wasn't taking on anyone new. But he finally agreed to see me. After we talked for a while in his office, he said, "I'm going to take you because I think we could get some work done, because I think there's a connection that I'm making and that you're making." He always talked about the chemistry between us in the Freudian terms of I and thou. It was never "You need me," or "I think I can help you." Rather, he would say, "I think we can do this," and that set the tone for what we could accomplish.

I learned more about the technical aspects of analysis, like transference and projection, but most importantly, over time I learned how to love and accept myself and how to trust another person. I knew very little about Dr. Saperstein personally. We never met socially; our relationship was confined to that one room. When he talked, I could sense that words were important to him, as he always chose them carefully. He was the kind of man who, when he looked at me, made me feel like he was really seeing me. He didn't just listen—he heard and cared about what I had to say.

I suppose I needed to be talked to like a two-year-old at times, because I really was a frightened child who was acting out in a panic of anxieties. Sometimes I would get impatient with him, and I would think, *I got it, okay, can you talk a little faster.* But after a while, each of our sessions was like enjoying a warm embrace. He instilled such a great feeling of comfort. Still, analysis can also get sticky—what I call the grinding process—when long-repressed emotions inside of you come to the surface. I realized why many people quit before they finish, why they can only tolerate so much self-knowledge at a given time. It's a case of one step forward, and sometimes several steps back. I never discounted the progress I made with other therapists. In my mind, they worked hand in hand.

What I learned was there are certain aspects in our behavior that have nothing to do with the reality of here and now. They are related to the past, and to that unique relationship that you have with yourself and your family. And the more you distance yourself by projecting and acting out, the more difficult it becomes to find the core reality, what really makes one tick. I think addressing those issues was what enabled me to finally heal emotionally and physically more completely. I told Dr. Saperstein about the guilty feelings I had, and about not being able to express my anger and the irrational fear about separating from my parents. Saperstein worked from the principle "Go to the love first." That became one of my mantras, *Go where the love is.* The idea was to find trust and then entitlement.

With that Calvinist sensibility in my background, as I've said, there was always criticism in the air while I was growing up, and I brought that with me into everything, along with that dancer's masochistic quest that has us ever striving for unattainable perfection. I was raised to believe if it doesn't hurt, you're not doing it right. Nothing is ever good enough—where is the love in that?

It was painful to realize how low my self-esteem had been, how I had been in denial so much of my life, and how I allowed myself to be ruled by those early feelings of abandonment. I felt that I was living out a prophecy my father had given me when he was angry and hurt and unfulfilled. Dr. Saperstein encouraged me, in a sense, to be a new parent to myself. He enabled me to establish a new accepting relationship with myself, and with him, and it wasn't just in theory. I felt that change deeply and my hard-won knowledge allowed me to take the baby steps of growing again.

I experienced a kind of rebirth through understanding the emotional and psychological aspects of my arthritis and came to see the disease as a physical manifestation of the conflicts I carried inside me. Dr. Saperstein once explained this to me in choreographic terms, by putting his two pinkies together and trying to pull them apart. That image made a great deal of sense, suggesting that such a destructive process had been undermining my emotional life. It seemed that I had been pulling myself apart that way for years, and that a personal tug-of-war finally manifested itself as a physical condition in my joints.

He demonstrated another piece of "choreography" that I loved for its simplicity and metaphorical significance. He showed me how a mother wraps her arms around you, her child, until a time comes when the father must save you from her embrace. The father puts one arm around your shoulder and extends his other arm in front of you, showing you the world. Then, you are free to go into the world with your parents' love and blessing, and with that sense of security, you are able to become a person in your own right.

With newfound confidence, I remember going back to New York briefly in 1983 for the reunion gala of *A Chorus Line*. My participation was Michael's doing; he called me personally. His gesture was important because it signified that it was indeed personal, but also about business, and that's how we would proceed with our relationship. That was fine with me. I don't think there had been any profound change of heart so much as his realization that my returning to the role of Cassie that one night and being part of the celebration would be good for the show, and good for business.

I was happy to have been invited because that show was such an important part of my life, and everyone in that cast was important to me as well. I wanted to be there with them to celebrate its success. The occasion marked the show's record-breaking 3,389th performance. There were photos taken of Michael and me that seemed to suggest that some sort of reconciliation had taken place.

At one point he had me in a clutch, with his face next to my ear. It unnerved me at first to feel that kind of closeness with him, even though we were posing for a group of photographers. While the onslaught of clicking cameras continued he whispered in my ear, "Why would I get Ann-Margret when I could have you?" I thought for a minute, then realized he was referring to a property that I heard he was thinking of developing for Ann-Margret, based on the Doris Day movie *Love Me or Leave Me*. Ironically, this was a project I suggested to him when we were married, to option as a next show for me. I'm not saying he was now being phony, but it was about business, though it came across like pillow talk. I was actually amused, and to this day, whenever I see that photograph, I can't help but smile. I knew that my being there was important to Michael. I believe he took my return to mean I was apologizing or saying everything was okay. I was making him look good, and in his eyes, this was my way of making up.

Obviously, I worked hard at trying to interpret Michael's behavior. His way of giving me information was never direct or personal; it was about other people. He told me how he felt bad about the way he had treated his girlfriend in *Follies,* and how she had pounded on his door, crying. He was on the other side and he wouldn't answer. Then he said, "But eventually they always come back, and it's okay. They all forgive me. They all want me to like them. They all want to be in show business." That was his attitude, and an often repeated refrain. It was his way of telling me how he handled things, and it was totally contemptuous.

So I showed up and rehearsed. Having turned forty, I was an older Cassie, but perhaps a little wiser as well. Michael was graceful, but he couldn't say anything to me of any substance. He generously arranged for Theoni Aldredge to design a lovely party dress for me, with our other friend Barbara Matera, whipping it up like a beautiful soufflé. We rehearsed some of the scenes in the rehearsal rooms of his building at 890 Broadway. As always, Bob Avian was working right beside him, and of course, Michael had other assistants working for him as well.

One of the tasks was to restage "The Music and the Mirror" with ten additional Cassies in the number. The entire cast was to include hundreds of past *Chorus Line* performers from all of the companies, some of which were still on tour. As I recall, the only company unable to participate was the one in London. Bringing all these casts together in the production was Michael at his best. The concept was pure genius. It was also a great reunion for all of us originals, plus all our friends who had been in other companies.

This gala was the biggest, grandest theater party of the decade. The whole of Shubert Alley was covered in a white tent, and champagne and hors d'oeuvres were served. The dressing rooms upstairs in the Booth Theatre absorbed the overflow of dancers from the Shubert, who were changing costumes and then running back to the Shubert to make their cues. The whole week was rich with emotion, as everyone dashed by each other in the halls or staircases, on their way to different rehearsals, with only enough time to touch each other. We all laughed and cried the whole week. The entire event was well planned and executed, and I was elated to be back.

Throughout the show, Michael played on juxtaposing the dancers from the original cast with the other dancers who followed us. Some whole scenes and songs were performed in different languages, such as Japanese and German. Robin Wagner had the stage braced in order to support three hundred dancers, while Tharon Musser hung lights above all the aisles, including the ones in the balcony, in order to capture the last kick line, when dancers in the aisles reflected the dancers on the stage. That was my favorite moment in the whole glorious night: doing the jump kicks, and then taking off my top hat to the dancers in the balcony as they took their hats off to us on the stage.

After the performance, Michael very appropriately brought wardrobe mistress Alyce Gilbert out to take a bow, an honor for her after so many years of devotion to the show. The gala night was not just a unique triumph for the show and for all of us, but for all of Broadway, and everyone in our theater community. But it was especially Michael's triumph, and he received the standing ovation he truly deserved. I couldn't have been happier for him.

With my one-night success, I left New York feeling freer and happier than I had in quite a while, and I was eager to get home. My finances had been a mess for some time, with taxes and therapy fees, and no steady employment. Nevertheless, in the next couple of years after my return to L.A. I was able to acquire an income property in Laguna Beach, thanks to my good friend from *Company,* Teri Ralston. She had become my real estate agent, and with her help I also bought a three-bedroom house in Studio City, a single-level ranch on a corner lot. It was gorgeous, with fruit trees in the back.

Roger helped me take care of that place. I really enjoyed living in a house, like a quote-unquote normal person. Having a yard was like living in paradise. I became involved in a very creative and fun project, co-produced with Teri Ralston and Pam Myers, along with three other people we liked and admired: our conductor and arranger, Paul Horner, Michael Byers, and Tucker Smith, who had appeared on the stage and in the movie of *West Side Story.*

Let Me Sing and I'm Happy told the story of Tin Pan Alley up until the time of *Porgy and Bess*, with the music of Gershwin, Kern, and Berlin. We rented a little storefront theater in Burbank, rearranged the bleacher seating, painted the whole place dark blue, and hung black curtains. Teri was the director and I was the choreographer. What a great time I had performing with friends on that show and singing those fabulous songs. The audiences loved it, and I was delighted one night when Buddy Ebsen came to the show.

Roger and I broke up eventually because he was ready to settle down and I wasn't. He had an ambition to create his own business and a desire to make the commitment to share it with someone he loved. I loved him and supported his decisions, but I didn't trust that I could be there for him because of my profession. The fact that I was beyond my childbearing years was also a consideration for me. He argued that he didn't want children. In fact, he was famous for saying he "hated" kids. He was a very funny guy and he would crack me up when we were in some public place like a supermarket where a baby would start screaming and Roger would make a face and quickly walk away.

Breaking off with him was one of the most unselfish things I've ever done because I really didn't want to do it. But I had an instinct that someday he might change his mind about wanting to have a family of his own. As it turned out, I was right. Since that time, he did get married, happily has two beautiful children, and is a great father. So I look at that turn of events with great satisfaction.

After the breakup, my world was looking a little grim again and I had a very neurotic affair. It was like the backlash to all my good therapy. When you get down to the nitty-gritty of analysis, sometimes there's a reaction like that. I was frightened and started running again. There were some professional tensions that came up as well. Even while I was living in L.A. and working on television projects, I continued trying to pursue theater. At one point, I became part of a special theatrical project, and that led to an unsettling run-in with one of my agents.

I had been cast in a show called *Get Happy,* which was based on the songs of Harold Arlen. The show was directed and choreographed by Tony Stevens, and my friend Pam Myers was in the cast. While I was in rehearsals, my agent told me that he had arranged an audition for me for a TV episode. I had to tell him, "I can't, I have my dress rehearsal for *Get Happy.*"

He challenged me, saying, "Well, Donna, what are you doing out here? Why are you out here—to do theater in L.A.?"

I told him, "Any other time, any other day, I could do the audition. But it's my dress rehearsal!" My sense of professional responsibility wouldn't allow me to let down my fellow cast members. I believed that with every fiber of my being, and I couldn't imagine missing a dress rehearsal. But still, the confrontation with my agent was unnerving, and afterward I had to ask myself once again, *What am I doing here? Where should I be?*

That dilemma more or less reflected my state of mind, until I received a telephone call in 1985 from Baayork Lee, who gave me a reason to dance again. That call would set me on a long journey back to Broadway—by way of Tokyo and Paris and many points in between.

Chapter 8

———— ❧ ————

SWEET CHARITY

Baayork was about to direct a new touring company of *A Chorus Line,* and she called to invite me to return to the role of Cassie. The first leg of the tour would take place in the summer of 1985, and that would be a prelude for a more ambitious effort the following year that would take me to Japan for the first time and then back to Los Angeles for another run there. Except for the night of the reunion gala in 1983, I had been away from the show for almost nine years. I was thrilled by the prospect of returning, and also deeply touched that Baayork had confidence in me. Since recovering from my illness, I hadn't undertaken a role as demanding as Cassie, and now at the age of forty-four, I knew that I was going to have to work hard to get back into the kind of shape that would allow me to perform that part eight times a week.

I was determined to be more careful with myself as I worked up to the demands of the show. I couldn't rely on muscle memory very much after being away so long. I could no longer assume anything about my body, and I was essentially forced to show a new respect for it in the way that I worked and conditioned myself.

My aerobic exercise at the gym had kept me somewhat fit, but now I would be using different muscles in different ways, no matter how much of the show I actually remembered. I was determined not to fall prey to the kind of injury that happens all too often to dancers in rehearsals—when you work for hours, learning where the weight goes, and how much effort to make for the right momentum that you need to do difficult steps. You spend hours going over choreography that, during a performance, you might only do once. And after all, I would be learning to use my body all over again, because I had changed, physically and mentally. I was bringing a new person to the part with new information, and I wanted to have a successful, healthy run.

I had about two months before I had to leave for rehearsals in New York, and I wanted to be smart about my preparation. I did a lot of strength and flexibility training with Bikram yoga and Pilates exercises. I was all over the place with dance classes, studying with Joe Tremaine, Stanley Holden's school, and a little ballet studio on Moorpark. After not dancing for such a long time, the sensation of moving and finding my balance and coordination was different. One positive change was that I was more thoughtful about my approach, and I was breathing more effectively. The hardest thing was to be patient with slow progress. I had to be gentle and loving with myself. That was definitely a new muscle for me to exercise. I had a newfound sense of relaxation that made the physical experience of dancing even better for me, though it would take time to completely trust this approach.

Years before, when I saw Lena Horne in concert, I had learned the lesson that trust is an essential aspect of artistry. My friend Larry Moss and I attended her historic one-woman show, and Lena demonstrated that kind of trust by singing "Stormy Weather" at the end of the first act and again at the end of the show. The first time was impeccable, perfect in every way. When she finished, Larry and I were enthralled and cheered loudly with the rest of the audience. When she sang the song again at the close, she prefaced it by saying that it took her twenty years to learn how to sing a ballad. Then she started singing with such an emotional intensity that we were held transfixed as we experienced everything she was feeling.

Her body responded with an abandon we hadn't seen before, and the interpretation followed. Her performance was impossible to analyze at the time because we had been transported. Our cheering screams were even louder this time. What a magnificent way to experience the point she was making about artistry, and not just about singing but about life, humanity, integrity, and trust. They say an actor's trust in the artistic process takes about twenty years to develop. Maybe I was on schedule after all.

As I began preparing to return to *A Chorus Line,* I quickly discovered that the role of Cassie was now as much of a psychological challenge as a physical one. I had a very different relationship with the character. This was an alien feeling at first because I felt less fragmented as a person, and in a way, less like Cassie. All the work I had done on myself through analysis had made me more acutely aware of the dynamic of good and bad in the relationships I had with my dancing, with Michael, my family, and myself.

So I went into these rehearsals being more of a whole person and having boundaries that I didn't have before. Having to make choices, and new choices that I had never made before in that role, gave me an exhilarating freedom as an actress. I really experienced a new sensation by sculpting the character from the *outside in,* as well as from the *inside out.* I wasn't living in anxiety as I did when I first did the role, but that frame of reference was at my fingertips. That was the strangest feeling, because I was Cassie, and yet I wasn't anymore. She was a reflection of that feverish time when we were living day in and day out in rehearsals, making our personal stories come to life on the stage. My emotional distance from the character now allowed me to breathe and relax into the role. I could be the actress, leave the part in the dressing room after the show, and then go out to dinner with friends and have fun.

With maturity, my sense of self had a new meaning. I wasn't identifying as much with my ambition, but who I was and what I felt, which were separate from dancing and performing. I had always been happy when I was working, and dancing was such an important part of me, but I came to realize that it was *only a part of me.* In the past, when I wasn't working, I either felt invisible or depressed. Too many times that had caused me to fly into unsuitable relationships, looking for the reassurance I needed.

It had taken years of therapy and a disease that stopped me in my tracks for me to begin to unravel the mystery of why I felt so unlovable and so undeserving. I now wanted more than anything to rewrite my history, to really know in my heart that there was more to me than what I did in the theater. It was easy for me to see this in other people. When I was in my peer group, or later, when I taught at HB Studio in New York, I witnessed the beauty of each person when they were at their most vulnerable, when they were just being human. I could also see the reluctance of everyone in class to embrace the good qualities they possessed. I've come to believe that most of us who go into show business tend to criticize ourselves too much.

I had come so far, but I wasn't quite there yet. I did have a better appreciation of my life, having come through both the arthritis and depression, both of which had affected me on so many levels. I had an opportunity now to tackle this role and this show with a new integrity. And with so much experience behind me, I know my acting had improved, and certainly my singing was better. I also felt that my dancing improved.

I am reminded of a cherished quote by Mikhail Baryshnikov. "When a dancer comes onstage, he is not just a blank slate that the choreographer has written on. Behind him he has all the decisions he has made in his life. . . . Each time he has chosen, and in what he is onstage, you see the result of those choices. You are looking at the person he is, the person who, at this point, he cannot help but be."

I believe it can be true that as we get older we do improve as performers. Our jumps may not be as high, but there is a tradeoff that gives us more dramatic depth. It's a different kind of strength and endurance that we cultivate over time. I know that as an actress I was eventually able to make the role as natural and organic as I had before. Cassie's emotional condition in the show still had that life-or-death edge to it, but Donna's did not. Now I had to *act,* and that was fun, which is an ideal goal for any actor—to be able to enjoy the work, to have fun with it, even when playing tragedy.

Of course, other perceptions of mine were still changing, and I was still in flux. On tour, I was initially afraid to dance with the abandon that

I had in the past. I was being careful with myself because I knew how much I had changed. I wasn't living as much for the moment as trying to be *in* the moment. Over time, I had to relearn how much effort to make. I always used to think that if I didn't feel that strain, that edginess of being on the brink with my performance, pushing myself to the limit, then I wasn't doing it correctly. It was hard to erase those old tapes of "if it doesn't hurt, then you're not doing it right." Eventually it became more exciting for me because I learned that I could actually enjoy my performance without killing myself every time and, therefore, it was more enjoyable for the audience.

On that first tour, we played cities like St. Louis, Kansas City, Syracuse, and Schenectady. Bob Young was our enthusiastic and much loved producer. I loved the touring and earning the respect of new friends. Baayork had put together a wonderful company and we had a great crew traveling with us. Even though it was difficult as always living out of suitcases, that tour allowed me to finally get into performance shape and back into the show. All the aspects of my life seemed to be falling into place, as I found myself involved in a new romance. We were in Kansas City and went to see an equestrian show given by the Royal Canadian Mounted Police. Afterward, I went with some of the other dancers back to the stables to look at the horses. One of the riders was a tall, handsome French Canadian named Andre. He was charming, with a kind of wide-eyed joie de vivre, and I soon found myself smitten.

One reason that Andre was refreshing to me was because he wasn't in show business. He was a younger man, not very sophisticated, but very polite, confident without the kind of self-consciousness that many performers have. When we first met, I took the initiative and approached him, inviting him to see our show, which he did. Later, he wrote to me and we kept up a correspondence; the connection between us slowly evolved into a long-distance romance. Fortunately, Andre loved to travel, and we were able to meet regularly over the next few years. So I was working and making a living, I was dancing, I was back on track, and I was in harmony with myself. Or so it seemed.

In retrospect, I realize the relationship with Andre was something that I imposed on myself because it satisfied an important need I still had to be connected. He became my emotional home away from home.

In the spring of the following year, I was excited with the prospect of going to Japan. I figured if this was to be a swan song for me in *A Chorus Line*, what a great way to go out. Japan was a big deal for us, since we were the first English-speaking company of *A Chorus Line* to visit there. We were booked at Tokyo's Koma Theater for about six weeks, to be followed by an engagement in Kobe.

The Japanese were very eager to see us and we were all treated like royalty by our hosts. The souvenir programs were priced at about $70, and they sold out before we had even arrived, as did most of the seats. We stayed at the Akasaka Prince, a beautiful hotel that was all white marble. Actually everything was white, including a man in a white tux playing Cole Porter tunes on a white piano in the lobby. At the time, Princess Diana and Prince Charles were staying across the street. It was their first trip to Japan together, and there was quite an impressive parade, which they led, waving to the crowds from their convertible.

When I first arrived at the theater, which was an enormous stadium, I looked up from the street, and was amazed by what I saw. On a nearby building, there was a gigantic poster, with my image about fifteen stories high. *A Chorus Line* had always been an ensemble, with the cast listed in alphabetical order, but in Japan the producers wanted a star they could promote.

While performing in Tokyo, I enjoyed the Japanese theatrical ceremonies. There was an enclosed shrine above the entrance to the stage that always had to be acknowledged with a bow before walking onto the stage. Being the "star" of the show, it was my duty to honor the custom of an opening ceremony onstage just before the first night. The whole company was gathered there along with our Japanese producers and crew and a Buddhist priest. I confided to my Japanese interpreter that I didn't know the procedure and was nervous about making a mistake. By now I had seen how polite and sensitive the Japanese people were, and I didn't want to bring shame on the company. My interpreter instructed me to just follow the Buddhist priest, who would be doing a series of bows and clapping of the hands, like bow, clap, then bow again. Following his lead, I did my part without a glitch, thankfully. I appreciated their traditions of honoring our profession. After all, being raised in the 1950s in the Midwest, it had been drummed into me that show business was not respectable.

The company soon settled into a daily routine of sightseeing and performing. We were tourists during the day, often traveling by bullet train to see shrines, palaces, and other exotic attractions. We would come back to the hotel in the afternoon in time for a nap and meal, and then went back to the theater. On one of my nights off, I went to the traditional Kabuki theater.

Shortly after we opened, I gave a telephone interview to the *Los Angeles Times* and said, "My *life* is on the stage in this show. I love the richness of bringing it to another country and feeling the power of the piece break through the language barrier and reach people. The Japanese are so quiet, so polite—there's no applause until the end of numbers. . . . It's as if they don't want to disturb you. Outward appearances are very Western, like New York, but underneath, the sensibility is very different. Some of the clichés are true. They love American musicals."

We were well received in both Tokyo and Kobe. I was touched by the many Japanese teenagers who wrote me beautiful fan letters in English. They would wait outside the stage door every night, and these kids were always quaking with emotion when they saw me. I knew that my singing "Give me a chance to come through" must have struck a chord with them, because they would literally scream and throw their bodies at me like I was some kind of rock star.

I had been in Japan long enough to learn how Japanese children are raised to behave one way while feeling another way, not unlike the way I was raised in Michigan. I was starting to feel like I had a lot in common with them. It was beautiful to behold how their passions would surface after they saw the show, as if they were fighting through all of the inhibitions of their upbringing. I saw the purity of their yearning and the desire in their faces and felt humbled and hopeful for this generation.

Playing Japan was for the most part a positive experience, though at one point I came down with laryngitis and couldn't sing. I also broke a metatarsal bone in my foot, which was extremely painful. I took only a couple of nights off, but the Japanese producers were suddenly furious with me. I remember I was having dinner in the hotel and they kept interrupting me with phone calls, demanding that I come to the theater. They were outraged and couldn't accept the fact that I was the one making the decision as to whether or not I was able to perform. The producers then had a blowout with our American stage manager, who was very dear but was caught in the middle. He tried to explain that in our country we allow the artist to decide on matters of health, even women.

I finally did relent and returned to the show. But I went onstage in a kind of obstinate, rebellious way, because I still had the laryngitis and was croaking. I could have done real damage to myself, and I'm sure it must have been painful for people to listen to me. At that point, the Japanese producers suggested to our company management that my standby return to the show.

I soon recovered, and continued my love affair with Japan. When our run came to an end, I was saddened to have to say good-bye to our new friends. One of my most affecting memories was to arrive at the airport in Tokyo with the rest of the American company on our way back to the states, and to be greeted by our Japanese musicians with flowers and tearful hugs. We all cried and said good-bye in our pitifully broken Japanese and their only slightly better English. But we didn't need words to convey how much we all appreciated our artistic exchange. Having come to know the Japanese people more intimately made it such a fantastic experience for all of us.

The tour had been a major triumph for the company that culminated with three weeks in June at the Wilshire Theatre in Los Angeles. All the publicity and my success on the road prompted Joe Papp to invite me to rejoin the production on Broadway that fall. At that point, the dancer playing Cassie was pregnant and planning to take a leave of absence. When asked if I would like to take over for eight weeks, I said, "Would I? Absolutely!"

Years ago when we began the workshops at the Public, I always felt a little discounted by Joe. Michael told me once that Joe referred to me as

"Your Gwen," because he couldn't remember my name. Joe was now more in charge of taking care of the show while Michael was working on other projects. I liked being able to deal with him more directly, and it changed our relationship. Joe became my champion. The Public Theater had a network of apartments in the city that were made available to visiting artists, and he arranged for me to stay in a lovely one-bedroom in a town house on West 88th Street. Joe and his staff at the Public launched a publicity campaign to promote my return, which was something that I hadn't expected. Every weekend in the *New York Times* there was a picture of me dancing with a large title over the picture that said "DONNA'S BACK." In New York, the show, with no stars and the cast listed alphabetically, had never been presented like this before. The publicity helped the show at the box office and also raised the stakes for me.

This was to be one of the most satisfying full circles I would travel in my life. Ten years after I had first performed in *A Chorus Line,* I was returning to the same production, the same theater, the same run, the same role. No actor had ever done that before because up to that time no show had ever run so long. The other irony to me was that this show that had so much of my life in it was now giving it back to me with a new opportunity. I was scheduled to appear for eight weeks starting September 1, 1986, though as it turned out, I would stay with the show for the next eight very happy months.

There was no one else in the production from the original cast, though many of the musicians were still with the show, as was our beloved wardrobe mistress, Alyce Gilbert. At the start of rehearsals, I had a great deal of difficulty adjusting to the conductor's tempos. Of course he was used to playing for someone else, but I thought with rehearsals we would find the right tempos. Cassie's number is so interpretive that the tempos would naturally vary with each actress who played the part.

Larry Blank had been our conductor in Japan, and he was so consistent I never even had to think of tempos being too slow or too fast. It was as if we were breathing together. The original conductor, Donald Pippin, had also been terrific at keeping the tempo every time and if I was dancing with an injury, he would always accommodate. I have always had a great respect for musicians, in particular conductors. Ideally, there is a harmonious musical collaboration between artists and conductors who have the same point of view as they tell the story. But now I was confronted with a conductor whose tempos were all over the place. I had the feeling that he had worked with too many Cassies who kept telling him, "Faster, faster!"

He was so inconsistent that I soon realized I had to say something, at least to take care of my part. I finally called Joe Papp and said that I really didn't want him to conduct me. Jerry Goldberg had been assistant conductor all these years, and I asked Joe to please let Jerry conduct just my number. The next thing I knew the conductor in question was fired and Jerry was conducting the whole show. There was some justice in that since Jerry had been with the show from the beginning and deserved the promotion, but I never intended to have anyone lose a job over this. I found out later that Joe had already been thinking of replacing the conductor and my complaint apparently pushed him into action. I knew how this might appear to others in the company, but hoped it wouldn't affect my relationship with the other dancers.

I probably wouldn't have been as demanding if this had been another production, but I felt territorial about this show. Some of the choreography wasn't being done correctly, and I couldn't bear to see that. The steps were the same but not the intentions being played. Over the years, there had been a number of dance captains, and the show was being taught differently at this point. They were all quite capable, but there really was no precedent for maintaining a show after so many years. I could understand how performers and dance captains could get into a rut, but to allow the standards to decline wasn't professional. I had heard that Michael used to come to see the show on occasion and would fire one or more people, creating fear backstage. Actors Equity put a stop to that, so now it was up to the performers and stage management to keep the show alive and fresh.

There wasn't enough attention being paid to detail, and the piece lacked the dramatic tension that arose from the dancers' audition anxiety. That anxiety is the premise and driving force of the show, and the hardest quality to sustain; it's usually the first thing to go over time. I hoped the other performers understood that I was trying to help when

I reminded them to stay focused on the basic drama of why they were there. I told them, "Remember, Zach has the power to hire you, but at any moment, he could say, 'You, get out! Leave!'"

The cast responded well to my encouragement, and many of them thanked me for giving them new incentive. Most of these dancers had been replacements and therefore never had the thrill of our opening. My return to the show gave them their first opening night in *A Chorus Line* and their first reviews.

Another challenge for me was caused by the way the understudies were divided between the various roles. I had worked before with the actor, Evind Harum, who played Zach. Evind was talented as well as being a good match for me in terms of his age and height. The problem came down to who would replace him when he was out. There were three or four covers for each part, and if the principal was out, they would alternate the understudies night by night. That may have been democratic, taking turns, but it was not very artistic.

I balked at that policy because the age and quality of the third and fourth understudies were wrong for the part and definitely wrong for me. I was just starting to feel the process of change in my own life in terms of entitlement, and I didn't want to defer to other people as much as I had in the past.

It was only a matter of time before I saw Michael again. I had seen him only briefly before I left for Japan. He had known that I was rehearsing with Baayork, Bobby Thomas, and the company in his building at 890 Broadway. Michael had invited me to lunch at the restaurant on the main floor. He was eager to show me around and I was happy to accept his invitation. I assumed back then that my going back into the show, even if it was with a touring company, had to mean something positive to him, because his identification with the show had always been so emotionally powerful. If we weren't exactly the best of friends, to my way of thinking, trying to be friendly was at least an improvement on his part.

I was just guessing about his feelings, because our past was never brought up that day. I was fascinated by what Michael did have to say. He had just come back from London where he was directing a new musical, *Chess,* which he co-produced with his partners, Bernie Jacobs and Gerald Schoenfeld. Michael told me that he had to leave the show prematurely and was under his doctor's orders not to work because of a stress-related heart condition. As I was listening, I found it hard to relate to the casual, offhanded way that he was telling me about this personal crisis. Only many months later was I to learn how catastrophic and painful it had been for him to abandon the show. On the afternoon I visited with him, he seemed excited and proud to show me his new office, with his enormous desk, workout room, and kitchen.

For a few minutes that day Michael let his guard down. Rather than the paranoid theater mogul surrounded by bodyguards, he became the childlike, vulnerable boy from Buffalo. It seemed as if we were hip-to-hip again, metaphorically, like that first night when we went to the tape session and I was there to hold his hand. I felt encouraged to ask him, "Please come to our rehearsal, Michael, and say hello to Baayork and the company."

He was reluctant at first for some reason. I said, "Oh, please just stick your head in the door and let them see you, and wish them well. It would mean so much to them." That really was true. He finally gave in, and made a wonderful surprise appearance that had everyone smiling, including Michael.

The next day he called me at rehearsal, and announced that he was probably going to have an operation. I tried to be reassuring, even knowing as little as I did about what he was going to have to go through. I told him, "Bypass surgery is so successful nowadays. Look at how many people you know who have had it."

"I know," he said, "but the thing I'll really miss is dancing. I'll never be able to dance again."

"Of course you will, Michael," I said. "Look at George Rondo! He had a triple bypass and is back to running three miles a day!"

Our exchange was disturbing because I felt that I had failed to reassure him, and I sensed that he wasn't telling me everything. For him to sound so final about not ever being able to dance again wasn't like him, or rather, like the Michael I knew. But I was still so conditioned not to confront him that I let his comment go, and followed his quick but friendly goodbye with my own.

That was the last time I saw him before coming back into the Broadway company. I wasn't really expecting anything from Michael. I tried to fortify myself by being totally concentrated on my personal challenges, and doing the job. Again, Michael didn't say much to me personally. I only saw him once before we opened. He let me know that he hated the color of my hair. He didn't dwell on it, but made one smirking crack about how bright it was. And he was right; it was too red. Out of insecurity, I was overcompensating with color. Offstage my hair was striking, but onstage it was like neon. Thanks to Michael's comment, I realized this was a look Cassie would never bring to an audition if she wanted a job in the chorus.

Michael's criticism reminded me of a similar incident that had taken place when *A Chorus Line* first opened at the Shubert. Michael had come into my dressing room before the show and asked me, "What are you wearing?" I knew he was referring to my diamond studs.

I said, "My earrings. Aren't they okay?"

Michael had given the studs to me as a Christmas gift. I was proud of them and had started wearing them in the show. In fact, I wore them all the time. He told me that every time the spotlight hit the earrings, they flashed, giving Cassie a look that was too affluent. He told me, "I like you better when you are more simple, unadorned." He had been right then, too, reminding me of the purity of my character's mission in the show. From that point on, I wore little pearl earrings that were perfect for Cassie.

On my return to the show, Michael came to my opening night. Between my nerves and dueling with the conductor, my performance that first night was not what it might have been. Afterward, in the dressing room, I felt I had to apologize. I said, "I'm sorry, Michael. I was a little off tonight. I'm not there yet, but it will get better."

"Oh, I know," he told me, being very kind about it. I thanked him repeatedly for this opportunity and told him how grateful I was to be back. I also felt grateful that at least we had grown past our sense of failure. There would be no personal confrontation between us. We would have only a few private moments that night, and again, nothing personal was ever mentioned. That was how we had communicated in the past, before we were married, on a more professional plane. We had always been able to find intimacy through the work.

So, my being back with the show was a kind of release for me and for him too, I think. We were both embraced again by the community, and I'm sure that mattered to Michael because he lived in his work. At this point, it was more important for me to be focused on being myself rather than being about pleasing Michael. Yet I could tell by his manner that he was pleased. After the opening, I went with Michael in his car to the Algonquin Hotel, where Joe was giving a party for the cast. Only then did I pick up on Michael's inner turmoil.

In a much darker mood, he was saying things like "The business has changed. There is no show business anymore. There's no such thing as having a career anymore. I'm going to retire and do something else." He repeated a version of that lament a couple of times that evening. Looking back, I realize that he was actually saying something more, offering clues by saying that he didn't know what was going to happen with his life. Earlier he had been putting on a brave front, trying to be light-hearted and attentive. He dropped me off that night in front of my sublet on West 88th Street. He hadn't seen the apartment, and after I said "Good night," and got out of the car, he rolled down the back window and asked me, "Is it okay? Do we like it?"

I turned back over my shoulder, smiled and said, "We like it." I had no way of knowing that was to be the last time I would ever see him.

As the run continued and I became more secure, my performances improved. Frank Rich later wrote in the *Times,* "Ms. McKechnie dances as terrifically as ever—and perhaps more urgently. Here is a performer doing her job with complete conviction, for love of working, long after the parade of sold-out houses and fame has passed by. That is the spirit enshrined by *A Chorus Line,* and that's why Ms. McKechnie's 1986 Cassie induces the shiver that comes when performer, role and theatrical history all merge into a poignant one."

My entire time on that run of the show was poignant. The reviews and publicity were inspiring, and it was wonderful to reclaim the role, to be welcomed back that way, to be where I felt I belonged, to be with my friends and to be dancing again. My return was really a vindication for me in this new relationship I was trying to have with myself. I was more compassionate. Compassion was a big issue for me, to be able to forgive myself, when I had so much shame after so many years of feeling that I wasn't good enough. Coming to terms with that inner conflict allowed me to see myself and to see other people more clearly, to work more effectively and bring better people into my life.

There was a beautiful article with backstage photos in the *Times* in which I was given the opportunity to talk about my battle with arthritis. I was now able to take the risk of talking openly about the condition and about starting over because I was performing and no longer paralyzed by the stigma. After the interview appeared, I received hundreds of letters asking for advice. I tracked down Dr. Getlen and sent him a letter with a copy of the article. I thanked him for his help and asked him what advice I could safely offer people. He was about 105 years old by this time. He wrote back a lovely letter that began "Dear Miss Chorus Line," and gave me his cleansing diet to pass on to anyone who needed it. These were general guidelines, like the yes and no list that he had first given to me. I included the guidelines in a newsletter that I sent to people who wrote to me. The letters that I received inspired me to want to share my experience, to help others in any way I could.

On my forty-fifth birthday that November, the cast gave me a party. There was a reception after the show and then we went out to a Mexican place in the West Village and sang and danced and drank margaritas. All that attention and affection made me happy and proud. The following month my mother and grandmother came to New York to have a family Christmas with me and my brother and sister. My grandmother had a heart condition and I was worried about her. She seemed more fragile than the last time I had seen her, and my mother still had a lot of sadness and loneliness in her life, though she never complained about it. I didn't have much time to spend with them or to take them out sightseeing because I was working, but we managed to have a lovely holiday. I was grateful for their visit because that was the last time I saw my grandmother before she passed away the following summer.

While performing in *A Chorus Line,* I also put together a nightclub act for a short series of engagements at Freddy's Supper Club. I would do the act on the weekends after I did the *Chorus Line* performances. I had a great musical director, Michael Wolff, who later became the musical director of Arsenio Hall's TV show. Michael helped me put together a revue using some of the same material that I had been using all along. Unfortunately, I had overextended myself again and was ill when I opened. The reviews were fine for the show, but not for me. I was crushed. I heard Dr. De la Vega's voice in my ear, saying, "Your feelings will always have the last word. You can throw them out the window, but they will come through the back door and kick you in the ass."

It was time for me to be honest with myself and to face some difficult questions. What was I trying to prove? Weren't eight shows a week enough? Why was it so hard for me to enjoy this success? Why am I acting like I'm not enough? Aren't *I* enough? I remembered my good doctor's counsel: "Change doesn't happen overnight." I decided I had to pay more attention to what I needed, and not try to live up to unrealistic expectations. My cabaret act may have been a disappointment, but I wasn't about to give up on it and continued to make plans for the future.

Near the end of my *Chorus Line* run, a man and his wife who were neighbors of Michael's in East Hampton came to see the show. They introduced themselves, and after the social exchanges the man looked at me and said very seriously, "You should call Michael and go visit him." He implied that Michael was very ill, but didn't tell me what was wrong. I asked Baayork about him, and she also told me that Michael was ill, but said that he didn't want to see anybody. We assumed it was the heart condition he had talked about. I sent him a card wishing him a speedy recovery and told him to know that he was loved. Months later, in an airport, I would read in a newspaper that Michael's "heart condition" was actually AIDS.

At that time, Michael sold his building and everything he had in New

York and moved to Tucson, Arizona. Later I heard that Bob Avian went to visit him, and so did his mother, although I was told that Michael sent her home after two days. Baayork and I seriously considered going to Tucson at this point. We were going to just show up at Michael's door, but we finally decided against visiting, respecting his wishes to be left alone. It saddened me that he had such difficulty accepting support from the people who were his friends, the people who cared about him, but the last thing I wanted to do was upset him. Looking back now, I regret that I didn't make that trip.

One afternoon while I was still doing the show, I answered the phone and was surprised to hear Bob Fosse's voice. I hadn't spoken to him in about fifteen years, not since a time when by chance we got off the M104 bus together. He had walked with me to 69th Street where we had our respective apartments, my one-bedroom walk-up and his Tudor penthouse that he shared with Gwen. Before we parted, he told me that he had seen a Milliken show in which I was featured. This show was an annual musical extravaganza performed by Broadway performers and choreographers at the Waldorf—a highly coveted trade show. Fosse said he was pleased to see that I had developed my own style. That was high praise coming from him. I think I handled it well, by not fainting at his feet.

When I received his phone call all these years later, I immediately said to myself, *No matter what he says, this time the answer is* yes! In his soft-spoken voice he told me that he was putting together a national company of *Sweet Charity*, now that the Broadway revival had closed. He said that he was interested in having me do the role of Charity. I managed to ask a few sensible questions about dates, trying to sound professional even as I felt a flurry of butterflies rising in my stomach. I told him, "Oh yes, I'd love to!"

After hanging up, I quickly called my agent, Ed Robbins, with my excitement fully blown. "You'll never guess what just happened! Bob Fosse just asked me to audition for *Sweet Charity*. Yeaah!"

"Donna, Donna," my agent interrupted. "There is no audition! He wasn't asking you to audition. He was asking you if you wanted to do the role!"

"What! Oh, my God." Fosse had actually come to see me in *A Chorus Line* six times, trying to decide if he should offer me the part in *Sweet Charity*. That was the same way that he directed. He wouldn't ever just do a scene once. It had to be six or a dozen times. He left nothing to chance, and he wanted to be sure that my performances would be consistent. He apparently harbored no bad feelings after losing the 1976 Tony competition between his *Chicago* and *A Chorus Line*. I was aware only after the fact that the political warring between Michael and Bob had been intense during that time. So in retrospect, it was something of a surprise that Bob hired me out of *A Chorus Line* to be in *Charity*.

I knew that I was in for some very demanding but exceptional work with *Sweet Charity*. I was thrilled in part because this was yet another important circle in my life being completed. Twenty-five years earlier, Bob Fosse had been my first choreographer on Broadway and I was one of his dancers. Now, he was the director and I was the actress.

I loved Charity. The sweetheart taxi dancer in the Fan-Dango Ballroom was written as a star vehicle for Gwen Verdon, but every actress who has done this role feels as if it was written for her, and I certainly was no exception. Chita Rivera came backstage to see me at the Shubert when I was in *A Chorus Line* and offered her congratulations. That meant a great deal to me because along with her Broadway shows, Chita had starred in the first national touring company of *Sweet Charity* and she was brilliant. I was basking in her praise, but I completely understood her when she said, "There's only a few of us, the leading lady triple threats. You can count us on one hand, but Gwen stands alone."

The 1966 musical was written by Neil Simon and had been loosely based on Federico Fellini's movie. *Nights of Cabiria*. I gave my last performance of *Chorus Line* on May 16, 1987, and then we had a month of *Charity* rehearsals in New York before heading out of town to start our tour in Toronto at the Alexandria Theatre.

Before the company rehearsals began, I rehearsed at the Minskoff rehearsal studios and was put through the paces by Gwen and her assistant, Mimi Quillin. Mimi was a tall, stunning woman who was going to be in the show as well as serve as our dance captain. Whenever Bob came to rehearsals, I felt some tension and suspected that something was going on between him and Gwen. It was like being with my dysfunctional family again, caught in a tug-of-war between my mother and father. Bob would say to me, "Which version do you want to do—hers or mine?" Gwen would be behind him pantomiming gestures, saying, "Do mine! Do mine!" They would make fun of each other, but there was always an edge.

Sometimes the edge could be amusing. One day Bob came into the rehearsal room as I was beginning to work on the music. He walked over to the piano where I was standing with a new vocal selection book. It had Debbie Allen's picture on the cover under the title *Sweet Charity*, with her name over the title magnified 100 percent, as the show was always advertised. He took the book from my hands, put it on the piano, and without saying a word took a magic marker from his jacket. Then he spelled out in gigantic letters, magnified at least 200 percent, Directed by BOB FOSSE!!!

I was surprised, and laughed out loud, thinking what a cute and charming way he had to deal with what had obviously been a contractual thorn in his side. I hadn't even realized when I bought the book that his name was nowhere on the cover. I still have that songbook with his markings intact, and I keep it as a sweet remembrance of him.

Even though Bob said he was having the best summer of his life, he seemed frustrated and moody at times. Gwen always believed that his depression was a result of the Shubert Organization pulling the rug out from under him the year before on his show *Big Deal*. She blamed Bernie Jacobs for withdrawing support and causing the emotional tailspin that eventually led to Bob's death. She even refused to allow him to come to Bob's memorial service. That was one obvious difference between Michael Bennett and Bob Fosse. Michael knew how to deal with politics. He would manipulate and wine and dine people, while Bob stubbornly chose to hang on to his integrity.

Naturally, I felt I had to prove to Gwen and Bob that they were right in choosing me to play Charity. While Gwen rehearsed me, Bob was often in the rehearsal room next door working on a ballet, something brand-new for him. When he would take a break from his work, sometimes he would sneak into my rehearsals and watch from a folding chair at the side. At first, I was a little self-conscious when I saw him walk in. Officially, he wasn't scheduled to work with me until the following week. He would say, "Oh, don't mind me, I'm just sitting here." Then he would change chairs, as if to see better, proceeding chair to chair, little by little until, eventually, he was sitting front and center, by the mirrors.

Well, I thought that was one of the most adorable things I ever saw. Gwen was still conducting the rehearsal, but every once in a while Bob would jump up and offer some direction. I loved seeing him being pulled in by what we were doing. That's one way that Michael and Bob were exactly the same. Their work in progress captured their complete attention and devotion.

As our rehearsals progressed, I was losing weight quickly because I was too tired to eat at the end of the day. I worked full-out with Gwen, never marked the steps, and we never took breaks. If I had told her that I needed to go to the bathroom, I suppose she would have let me go. She was usually a lovely, generous person, but the part of her that was all about work was a demon.

We soon started rehearsing the book scenes and were joined by the rest of the company. I didn't know all of the text yet. My fear often shows in that way. I'm a procrastinator and try to learn the words slowly, as I rehearse them, in order to find my way into the part. That was the defense I offered to Bob, but he wasn't buying it. He wanted those words put to memory, and he was right. I wasn't terrible, but it made me hesitant at times. He wanted everything memorized so when we staged it, we could just do it and do it and do it, as he loved to do. Then we could get to that freeing place where you don't have to think about what you're doing. He put it across to me that I had to learn the lines straight-away, and I felt the pressure, because there was very little margin for error with Bob Fosse.

He could be rough, and I had to learn how to take his criticism and find my way. Gwen threw herself into the work with intensity and I followed her lead. Through the work, she found her empathy with me. I remember she told me, "If you can just get through the first act, that's your barometer and you'll know you can do the whole show, because that first act is a bitch!" The last twenty minutes of the first act was a scene in Vittorio Vidal's apartment with the text interpolated into four choruses and dance sections for Cy Coleman's song "If My Friends Could See Me Now." It was a great deal of work to learn it all. Once I got it, I knew I would have to infuse the part with my own personality.

All of the business for this number was choreographed. It was all very specific, technically precise and to the beat, including hat and cane tricks. Gwen knew the staging backwards and forwards. During one rehearsal, she said, "Do you want me to show you the way that Debbie did it, or the way that Annie did it, or Chita, or the way that I did it?"

I said, "I think I would like to learn your version, Gwen." I wasn't trying to win favor; why would I want to learn anyone else's version if I could learn hers? I wondered why she was offering me those alternatives, but I believe she was just being generous. It was an honor and the gift of a lifetime to be taught this role by her, and when I learned her version, I hoped it made her as happy as it did me.

I soon had to face the test of the first-act run-through, which was to be both my moment of truth and my rite of passage into the show. There were the usual four of us in the room: Gwen, Mimi, the rehearsal pianist, and me. I did manage to get through that whole first act, and when we finished, I was on the prop bed and out of breath. I looked over at Gwen and saw tears in her eyes. Her big beautiful blue eyes were filled and overflowing with her feelings. I just looked at her and knew that something powerful had happened.

As I climbed off the bed, Gwen walked over to me with her irresistible smile, took my hands and said, "You did it." That may have been one of the most wonderful moments of my life. I understood again how we pass along knowledge in the theater in an authentic way, and that it's not just the steps. Teaching all of these Charitys wasn't her job; any number of dance captains could have done it. But Gwen made it her duty to pass the role on with all of its textures, layers, and nuance, and she did it with love. How many times had she taught that same role? Each time she gave part of her soul as well. And I could imagine how painful it must have been for her at times. But she couldn't be any other way, and after all this show was hers. The role had originally been given to her as a Valentine from Bob.

After we arrived in Toronto, someone overheard Bob and Gwen when they were backstage watching me in one of my first performances. He said, "We didn't make a mistake picking her, did we?" Gwen said, "No, we didn't." When asked why I was still a good dancer when moving into my fifties, Gwen told the New York Times, "She's an actor-dancer. She knows it's not just steps. There's an emotional quality to every dance."

The company was made up of great dancers who could all sing and act. Each one had been handpicked by Bob. My two sidekicks in the show were Stephanie Pope and Lenore Nemitz. Bob loved them both, Stephanie with her long gorgeous legs and classy elegance, and Lenore with her hilarious, rough-and-tumble style and Clara Bow face. I felt a special sort of confidence being onstage with them. We were each very different and made a great unit together, especially when we sang and danced in "There's Gotta Be Something Better Than This."

Ken Lande was a wonderful Oscar. He reminded me of a young Spencer Tracy with his ruggedly handsome features, and there was such honesty in his acting. Graduating into rehearsals with the whole company pushed everything up a notch for me. I was now as close as I had been to performance level in rehearsal. My stamina was starting to take hold. My barometer was the "I'm a Brass Band" song and dance with the male dancers. Seeing the reflection of this number in the mirrors was a thrill for me, to see how the choreography moved the dancers on and off the stage and moving toward the front with these isolated, eccentric, Fosse moves imitating the different musical instruments. First came a piccolo, then a clarinet. The number built to a point where all the men come on from the back of the stage in a diagonal group and joined me. Then we traveled together with this kind of leaping strut across the stage. That made for a terrific moment.

When we toured, the company was so large that it took seven trucks to move us. Joseph Harris was a very capable producer, Craig Jacobs was our very capable stage manager, and Bob took the time to go on the road with us. Gwen told me that he had never done that before. She said that once a show opened and went on tour, he would never revisit it. He would ordinarily come only for the opening and then move on to the next show. He always had great stage managers and dance captains who would take care of the touring show after it left New York. But this time he followed us to each city and rehearsed us before each opening night. As always, he wanted to make sure his show was being done right, though there may have been something more that was driving him.

On July 2, 1987, I was dressing and getting ready to go to the Alexandria Theatre in Toronto, to do our first dress rehearsal of *Sweet Charity*. I was keyed up, because this was an important day for me. The new environment of a theater stage with the sets and lights and orchestra together for the first time is powerful, and the opening was already upon us. As I was rushing about checking everything on the list that I needed to put in my dance bag, I happened to hear something on the radio about the death of choreographer Michael Bennett. I thought my ears were deceiving me and quickly sat on the edge of the bed next to the radio.

The announcement was repeated, confirming that Michael had died of AIDS that morning. I could barely breathe as I listened to the rest of the report. Actress Swoosie Kurtz had recently worked with Michael, and as a close friend, she was being interviewed for her reaction. Swoosie quoted Michael, saying she had talked to him on the phone shortly before he died. She recalled that he told her something along the lines that he had had a "good life." Those words pushed a button in me, because it sounded like Michael making nice, trying to sound like everything was fine. That really set me off, and only then did I allow myself to breathe and scream, "Noooo!"

It was a sound I hadn't heard since my father died ten years earlier. I couldn't quite grasp it and I couldn't push it away. Michael gone! How could that be? I lost all sense of the world around me and I felt so alone. And perhaps a little scared to be so out of touch, and not having known about Michael's actual condition. I called my friend Toni Parisi and he let me cry and carry on. I then impulsively called Kelly Bishop, who had been such an important part of the whole *Chorus Line* experience. I was feeling desperate to talk to someone I could trust, someone who knew Michael well. I was hoping she might understand my agony and rage.

While feeling her own sense of loss, Kelly listened to my screaming and crying. At one point, I remember yelling, "He would have given everything to be alive! That wasn't Michael to be resigned that way. He would have given everything, all his money and success, to have his life back." Acknowledging that truth would never bring him back and I felt totally bereft, knowing he was gone forever.

I shed more tears until I realized that I had to go to work. I pulled myself together as much as I could. Then I went to the theater and hurried straight into my dressing room. Gwen and Bob came in the room together, and they had such looks of concern on their faces. I was doing all that I could to get organized to go on by putting on more eye shadow to hide my swollen eyes. Bob said quietly, "I'll understand if you have to take tonight off, Donna. I don't expect you to do the show."

I said, "Thank you, but I can't *not* do it. I have to go to work. That's the only way I can cope." Once again it was the discipline of dancing taking over and pushing the feelings away, but the difference this time was that I knew eventually I had to allow myself time to grieve, or risk getting sick again. Gwen went to the theater to work in *Sweet Charity* on the day her mother died; I knew she would understand why I chose to be onstage that night.

Even though reviews weren't foremost in my mind, we were received well and I was grateful to be working, putting into practice everything I had learned about keeping myself alive in my feelings. I had to respect and honor what was going on in my private life in order to work artistically with full commitment. It was an emotional juggling act, but thanks to the support I received from the rest of the company, I knew I would be able to work through this loss, even if the joy in my work might be on hold for a while.

On our next stop, in Philadelphia, Bob came into my dressing room with a copy of *Newsweek* that had a rave review. It was rare to see him that buoyantly happy. He paid me a great compliment by telling me, "Not since Gwen have I seen an actress take this role and keep growing and improving." I told him how much hearing that meant to me. I thought it was the highest praise I could ever receive, and was on a cloud for the rest of the run. How could I let any review intimidate me after receiving that kind of validation? It made all that intense work worth it.

I wanted to get Gwen a thank-you gift, something personal as a token of my gratitude. It had to be just right, and I wracked my brain. *What do I get someone who has given me so much, a part of her soul really?* One day in Philadelphia as I walked past an art gallery, an exhibit in the window of one-of-a-kind glass objects caught my eye. I particularly liked a beautiful pink perfume bottle with a little black top. It reminded me of Gwen because she loved those colors. When I gave it to her, she looked surprised and delighted. She asked, "Did you know that I collect glass perfume bottles?"

"No," I told her, "honestly, I didn't know."

She beamed as she said, "It's beautiful! I'm going to put it on my shelf right next to Colette's."

Later, just before we opened at the National Theatre in Washington, D.C., Bob was directing scenes with the whole company in the upstairs lobby. Again, he was pushing through each scene a minimum of six or seven times. We were all exhausted, and I remember thinking, *Doesn't he realize we have to open tonight?* I thought the show had been going well, but I had heard that the ticket sales were slow, so I figured that's why he was being so fastidious about these last-minute details.

I was able to pull him aside during a break and confide in him how worried I was about an interview I had just done. From the nature of the questions, asking me to compare Bob's work with Michael's work, I sensed that the writer might be taking a negative slant for the article. I wanted to prepare him for that and to apologize in advance. He listened and then smiled at me and said, "Don't worry about it. I just won't read it." He gave me a warm, friendly hug and then we went back to work.

We moved downstairs to the stage at one point, and that was when I suspected that something else was going on. He sat us all down in the orchestra chairs while he sat perched on the back of a seat in front of us. He then talked to us more like a father than a director, telling us to save our money on the tour and not to worry about the ticket sales. He said that wasn't our job. Our responsibility was to do the best performance we could do every single time. He went on, "If you think you can do better, then do better. Don't compete with anyone, just yourself. When you are in trouble or have a dilemma, ask yourself, 'What's the important thing?' And when you wake up in the morning, ask yourself how you can be a better person, not just a better performer."

A short while later as we started the rehearsal onstage, I saw Bob run up the aisle to the back of the theater. Then Gwen followed him. It was time to get ready for the opening so everyone scattered to their respective dressing rooms. During the show, I kept trying to get the little changes right, thinking that he would be watching from the back. It wasn't my most inspired performance, having to think about the new directions as I performed, but it was more important for me to show him what he wanted.

After the performance I went to my dressing room and found Cy Coleman, the show's composer, and Joe Harris, the producer, waiting for me. I was alarmed by the serious look on their faces. I thought to myself as I walked in the room, *Oh no, we're going to close.* Then Cy said, "I think you should sit down, Donna. We have some bad news."

I said, "I'm okay, Cy," as I stood and prepared myself for the bad news that we would be getting our two weeks' notice.

But I could never have been prepared for what he said next. "Bob died."

"What?" I said, frantically trying to think of a Bob. Did he mean our assistant stage manager? Then I asked, "Bob who?"

"Fosse," came the reply. "He died soon after he left the theater."

Now I sat, unbelieving. "Where's Gwen?" I asked.

"She flew back to New York."

I told them, "I'm okay. Thank you both for telling me this way."

There were silent embraces and then they left the room. It was only then that I heard the cries of sorrow coming from the hallway where his family of dancers were consoling each other. It was all the more unbelievable because he had been with us in rehearsal that very afternoon. Gwen knew that Bob would never leave a rehearsal, and that was how she knew something was wrong that day. He and Gwen had been walking back to the hotel when his heart failed and he collapsed in the street. To lose both Michael and Bob in such a short period of time was devastating; the two brightest Broadway lights in my life were now gone.

Gwen returned to New York for the funeral, and we continued with the run. While still in Washington, I received an unexpected visitor. A young woman called me at my hotel and identified herself as Michael Bennett's nurse and asked if she might see me. She told me she was just passing through and didn't even know I was here, but she saw my name in the paper. She had heard Michael speak of me, and thought I might want to talk to her. Her name was Victoria Allen, and she had been with Michael throughout the last months of his life. Vicky had been very close to him, and it was a great consolation for me to hear her talk about him. When I asked how he had been emotionally, she told me she thought Michael had come to terms with dying. She told me how courageous he had been at the end. She said she never saw him cry except on his forty-fourth birthday. On that day, she saw tears in his eyes as he said, simply, "I made it."

Vicky enabled me to understand what he had been through. She shared with me her own discovery about Michael's independence and his resistance to asking for help. Even when he was in such a debilitated state, they would watch TV together, and when she would say good night and start to leave his room, he would quickly ask for a glass of water or something, wanting her to stay but unable to ask her not to leave.

This was a time when the stigma attached to AIDS made it a difficult subject to discuss, and I appreciated her candor and sensitivity. She told me that Michael had arranged his bedroom so there was a wall of photographs and memorabilia covering his entire life and all his shows. And at the center of the wall, in front of his bed, he had placed our wedding portrait. She was so very thoughtful to tell me that, and naturally, I was touched beyond words. Michael showed his appreciation to this caring woman by leaving her money in his will for her to go to medical school to finish her studies and become a doctor.

The few times that uninformed people asked if I had reason to be concerned about my health, I was surprised. I lost track of Michael's love life after Sabine, and I really didn't want to know about it. When I got back to New York, Michael's longtime agent Jack Lenny told me that

Michael contracted AIDS from a man in San Francisco. He let me know that this affair began long after I had been out of his life. I never felt concern for my own health, because I hadn't been intimate with Michael in ten years, but it did help to have my feelings confirmed with this knowledge, because then I could understand why Michael kept the truth from me. Bernie Jacobs was kind enough to share with me that it was one of the worst days in his life when Michael told him he was ill. Bernie was his friend and like a father he wanted to help and protect him. He did, for as long as he could.

Some months later, I took time off from *Charity* to attend a memorial service for Michael in New York. After the service, a group of friends and I met at a restaurant on the Upper West Side to mourn and celebrate him. Later that night when I went out onto 69th Street, I literally bumped into Gwen as she came rushing around the corner. I hadn't seen her since before Bob died, when she was running up the aisle, following him out of the theater. We embraced and I quickly asked her, "Are you okay, Gwen? We've all been worried about you."

She said, "I'm okay. I'm fine." Then she looked at me with those eyes of hers and added, "Just remember, Donna, we keep them alive inside."

Since that time I've come to believe that it's an obligation for us to do what we can to pass on the legacies of those great choreographers. We survivors carry the knowledge they gave us and we provide an example, whether in class or in a show. If not for Gwen, I might not have had a career. She was that much of an inspiration for me and I still revere the things she taught me. Now that Gwen is gone, I keep that part of her with me. She will always be my beacon. I have kept Michael with me too, and sometimes when in a dilemma about work, I find myself asking, "Michael, what would you do now?"

That question arose under difficult circumstances when I traveled to Paris in the winter of 1988 for a seven-week run of *A Chorus Line*. I found a beautiful apartment on the Île de la Cité, and the show promised to be another magical experience.

It took us thirteen years to get to Paris because the French reputation for not appreciating American musical theater was well deserved. Important French theaters usually turn their noses way up unless the music is jazz, opera, or classical. I had heard that the American musical was not considered an art form in France but rather an entertainment. But despite the French high-brow chauvinism, here we were at the Théâtre Châtelet with an American musical that we would perform in English. Because of the social-democratic atmosphere and theater politics that limited any run of a show, it was as if capitalism was something foreign in Paris and no show could be a hit like we have in New York or London. After thirteen years of advance publicity, plus the release of Richard Attenborough's film of *A Chorus Line,* we could have run for at least a year. There were huge lines to get tickets.

The difficulty began when some of the set didn't arrive in time for the first preview; unfortunately it was the five mirrors that were featured in my dance. I soon found myself embroiled in a confrontation with the European producers and Jack Lenny. All of a sudden I was put in the position of having to defend myself as well as Michael. They wanted me to dance without the mirrors, and I was refusing to do that. I said, "How can we possibly do it that way! They are an important part of the number. They justify the change in the tempo and in the choreography. Michael would never have allowed this to happen. It took us thirteen years to get here, and out of respect for Michael, he would want the show with the mirrors!"

Everything else had been so wonderful, so I tried to see the full picture. Was I being too much of a purist? Was it in the realm of possibility that I could make it work? I heard Michael's voice in my ear say, "Do it, and make it work." Baayork looked at me sympathetically, bearing up under the pressure they already had put on her. She said, "Donna, it's up to you, to do the number or not." My option was to let the understudy go on for the preview and I would go on tomorrow with the full set. "Okay, I'll do it." The purist in me was going to have to be more flexible. Even though it wasn't the most fun I've ever had onstage, I met the challenge and did the best I could. The audience received us well that night, but I really missed those mirrors.

Thank God the rest of the run—with the mirrors—was successful, and it was glorious being in that theater, across from the Sarah Bernhardt. The Châtelet was one of those beautiful pre-belle époque buildings that had been kept up immaculately, and I felt like I was stepping back in time. My dressing room on the third floor was magnificent. I had a gorgeous piano, a bed, a newly tiled marble bathroom, and a beautiful old-fashioned dressing table sitting between two full-length windows that opened onto the Seine. On my left, when the window was open, it framed Notre Dame, and the window on my right framed the Eiffel Tower. I remember sitting there in my dressing room each night, looking out those windows and thinking that I had died and gone to heaven in Paris.

Chapter 9

---❧---

INSIDE THE MUSIC

At the end of 1988, I was invited to London to perform in a revival of the Cole Porter hit *Can-Can*. This was the 1953 musical in which Gwen Verdon first emerged from the chorus and won overnight recognition and her first Tony Award. According to what I was told by my agent before I arrived, this revival was to be a big elaborate production. I was elated with the prospect of the work ahead, and to be returning to London to see friends, like Alix Kirsta with whom I had stayed in touch over the years, ever since the West End production of *Promises, Promises*.

The cast included the wonderful Irish actor Milo O'Shea, the delightful and talented Janie Dee, and a beautiful actor from the Comédie-Française, Bernard Alane. It was to be my first British show that wasn't an altogether terrific experience for me, and yet there would be memorable moments. I immediately liked the choreographer, Ken Oldfield, who created a very exciting can-can that would be our finale, as well as a dance for me and three men.

After rehearsals began, I quickly found myself again in that familiar territory of being out of town with a musical in trouble. However, this was not the U.S., and we weren't in London, but in the city of Bradford in West Yorkshire. We were having monstrous technical problems, with one of those sets that ate the stage. I thought the design was impressive-looking, but it involved an enormous steel contraption that was heavy and unwieldy. Stagehands moved it on rollers and it dug right into the stage floor. The theater in Bradford could handle the weight, but no one could anticipate how it would work in London's beautiful old Strand Theatre, which was where we were scheduled to open.

It was unfortunate because the lavish designs were beautiful and perfect for the piece. *Can-Can* is set in the colorful bohemian world of Paris of the 1890s and focuses on the wild dancing showgirls of Montmartre, who perform the banned dance known as the can-can at the Bal du Paradis nightclub. I believe that some of the English critics had a chauvinistic attitude about the show, which featured an American, an Irishman, and two Frenchmen. Perhaps they were further irritated by the fact that we all spoke with different accents. The director left it to each of us to decide which to use, saying, "Just do whatever you do." I was caught in the middle, so I used my stage English, because we had two very thick French accents and I didn't want to compete with them.

Like the set, one of my dance costumes was also an unwieldy contraption, with a bodice of heavy brocade and many layers of material. The ruffled skirt was covered with elaborate beadwork, and felt like it weighed more than I did. The design was gorgeous, but a terrible mistake for a dancer. Our producer was British, and this was his first show. Whenever problems came up, the cast had meetings with him, the director, and the designers. I remember a meeting during which I finally had to say, "Listen, guys, this isn't my department, but it's not humanly possible to manipulate this skirt when I'm turning. It turns with its own weight and it's never going to work. There must be another way to do this. Can't we just replace the costume?"

My pleading was a lost cause. They couldn't afford to create another costume, so they tried to take off some of the weight, which wasn't a solution. There was no one on hand like a Bob Fosse or a Michael Bennett to say, "Get rid of the costume." I thought I had no choice but to wear it and do my best, but that steel set from hell soon made life even more difficult.

The set machinery kept malfunctioning, even more so when we

returned to London and started our preview performances at the Strand. The softer wood floor of the stage floor could not withstand that heavy set moving from one side to the other. I depended on that moving set. It was the only way I could get down from near the top of the proscenium, because the staircase to leave the set was in the wings on the other side of the stage. During one preview, we started our journey for the change, the set and me, and we got as far as center stage and stopped with a jerk. I held on tightly, expecting it to continue moving, but it didn't budge.

After a minute, the set didn't move, and after another minute it didn't move. Sixty seconds can seem like a very long time onstage when nothing is happening and no one is saying anything. The audience was quiet, patiently watching an actress who was patiently watching the wings for help or some kind of announcement. But there was no announcement and no help. I thought, *Have they forgotten that I'm up here? Is that possible?* The answer to both questions was *yes!*

I expected the curtain to be lowered, but no such luck. I heard a lot of commotion backstage, a lot of running around. I looked at the audience looking at me, and I didn't see any way out of this, unless someone lowered the curtain or brought me a ladder. I knew we were out of the play now, so with a performer's instinct, I went into a desperate Fanny Brice routine from *Funny Girl*. "Mr. Ziegfeld, Mr. Ziegfeld!" I yelled to the front of the house. "Hello, are you there?" There were a couple of nervous titters. I then turned my attention to the empty wings and began to yell, "Curtain! Curtain!" But nothing happened.

I looked again at the audience and made one more pathetic attempt to put them at ease by saying, "Well, it ain't television. You were there!" There were some more nervous laughs and then the house lights went on. At that point, mortification set in, with not even a glimmer of hope now for anything magical. A stagehand finally came with a ladder, and I climbed down in full view of the audience, to pitiful applause.

That scene was typical of the chaos that had beset this production from the outset. My body was trembling with anger as I walked back to my dressing room, but I didn't know who to be angry with. "These things happen," I said to myself, trying to calm my system, but I had felt so abandoned. I knew I wasn't going to be able to work through this show if I was passive and behaved as if I had no options. It was at times like this that Hal David's lyrics from *Promises, Promises* would sing in my brain: "Knowing when to leave may be the smartest thing that anyone can learn."

I was back with the William Morris Agency in New York at this point, mainly because of the experience and integrity of my agent, Ed Robbins. He came over early on to attend the opening. I remember telling him, "You've got to come to rehearsal, Ed. I make my first entrance in this outrageous green satin costume covered with beads. I have to climb in the wings up an enormous staircase—it's like three stories high on scaffolding, and it's wobbly and very scary! I walk down these circular metal stairs singing my first number, and on the way down, I'm turning my back to the audience, which is never good, of course. But the worst part is that my beads keep hitting the metal staircase. I'm making such a racket it sounds like I'm the Ghost from Christmas Past. I mean, I'm clanging out there! Please, you've got to help me."

He watched the rehearsal, and afterward said, "You're right, Donna, it's terrible for you. You can't make the entrance that way." Ed later spoke with the director, who insisted that was how he wanted me to play the scene. I respected his wishes for a while, very unhappily. But eventually, I asserted myself and simply refused to enter from the staircase. It was a situation where I had to pretend that I was one of those diva movie stars. I told the director, "Okay, now this is how I'm going to do the scene! I'm making my entrance from the center door, and I'm coming in and I'm going to start my song. I look to the right and look to the left, and then come down to center stage to finish the number." He was nonplussed, but I prevailed and that was how I finally made my entrance, which was ultimately much better for me and for the audience.

When the show was well attended, the audience had a good time. The music was beautiful and there were some effective production numbers. The show was colorful and fun and romantic. Despite poor notices, there were some delightful moments that charmed people, and they always came back afterward to collect autographs.

16

With Ken Howard at the Tonys, 1976.

17

With Michael Bennett at the 1976 Tonys, on our way to the after-party.

Michael and I were married in Paris, 1976. Jean-Pierre Cassel (center) was the best man.

With or without the mirrors, the show goes on. Performing *A Chorus Line* in Paris, 1988.

Michael and me at the *Chorus Line* gala, 1983. What looks like a tender moment was actually a business proposition.

20

21

With Joe Papp and LuEsther Mertz, our angel, who wrote the check that moved us to the Shubert, at the Algonquin after-party to celebrate *A Chorus Line* as the longest-running musical.

The "Tick-Tock" dance from *Company*, choreographed by Michael, 1970.

22

Annie Get Your Gun tour, 1989.

24

Performing "Losing My Mind" in *Follies*, 1998

As Charity in Bob Fosse's last production, a national tour of *Sweet Charity*, 1987.

As I grew up, I learned to appreciate my mom; here we are in Capri.

26

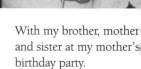

With my brother, mother and sister at my mother's birthday party.

With Fred Astaire and Michael after dinner at Fred's house, 1976. Cole Porter's painting hangs on the wall.

28

Christopher Durang, Thommie Walsh, and me, on opening night of *Inside the Music* at the Cincinnati Playhouse, 1997.

With Gwen Verdon, rehearsing at Avery Fisher Hall for a charity performance of *Sweet Charity*, 1998.

With Stephen Sondheim after the opening of *Follies* at the Paper Mill Playhouse, 1998.

When Bob Fosse died, Gwen Verdon gave me this photo. 1987.

Me, today.

After the show came to London, my mother visited me. I was staying in Little Venice, having sublet a place from one of my English friends, Nadia, who was living in New York at the time. I gave a big Christmas party for the cast, and on one of my nights off, I took my mother and Elaine Stritch to see a play in the West End. Like many of the London theaters, this one had a Queen's Box and a manager's office that doubled as a reception room for Her Majesty, whenever she might deign to visit. That night, while the Queen wasn't in attendance, we were served tea in her reception room during the interval. I remember how impressed my mother was by this royal treatment, sitting in a high-back chair, holding her china teacup. It was one of those moments I still cherish, as her happiness that night once again confirmed my own.

Before *Can-Can* closed its brief run, we recorded a cast album, and when we arrived in the studio, I saw that everyone was getting paid in cash except the actors; the musicians got their money up front before they had even played a note. This should have been a big clue, but it was lost on me. None of us were paid because the recording company went bankrupt the next morning. I lost about $5,000 when all was said and done. Even though the show wasn't a hit, I left London feeling like I had nonetheless managed to work through the obstacles on my own terms. I reminded myself that even though I might fall into quagmires like this, I was still doing something that I never thought I would be able to do again. I counted that blessing every day.

Back in the U.S., I was homeless again. I was still holding on to my place in Los Angeles, but I couldn't afford to live there and not work. I was determined to continue working even though it meant staying on the road for long periods of time. I sublet my house and occasionally spent some time in Toronto visiting with Andre. Then I would take off again to wherever my unpredictable gypsy life led me.

In the spring of 1989, I went on a tour of Irving Berlin's *Annie Get Your Gun* in Florida, performing the role of Annie Oakley, the famous trick shot artist of Buffalo Bill's Wild West Show. I was happily working again and my friend Harvey Evans was playing the role of Charlie. Lawrence Guittard played Frank. Ethel Merman had played the original Annie, and that production was like the meeting of two legends. Annie

is the larger-than-life sharpshooter who finds out in the course of the
show that "You cain't get a man with a gun." I enjoyed taking on the role
as another departure and stretch for me. Interviewed by a journalist in
Palm Beach after opening there, I said, "Annie's bold. She says what she
thinks, sometimes too much. She's not shy. By nature, I'm more intro-
spective and shy. She just does it. Annie is not like me at all, but I'm trying to be more like her."

That was my attitude at the time, trying to be more outspoken about
my needs and recommitting myself to the independence and self-
possession that I had won in analysis.

In the summer of that year I was thrilled to take off on yet another
national tour of *A Chorus Line,* playing twenty-six cities, again directed
by Baayork. I was now forty-six years old. Interviewed in Omaha, I
explained my feelings about the show's longevity and my own, "Michael
once said, 'Look, this show will have a life of its own.' He was right.
Another whole generation is seeing it. That's why it still runs after fourteen years on Broadway. I feel like Lena Horne when she told her age,
and said, 'I've earned every year of it.' I love the fact that I'm my age and
I put no boundaries on myself. If I can be inspirational to people who
think they're too old to do things, I'd like to be that kind of person. I'm
dancing better and I'm emotionally more integrated as a whole person.
I don't know how you can gain that without your mature years."

I wasn't about to let up. In May 1991, I did a production of Cole
Porter's *You Never Know* at the Pasadena Playhouse. I played Madame
Baltin, and the ensemble cast included David Garrison, Megan Mullally,
and Harry Groener. I also performed in another revival of *Sweet Charity*
for several months at Harrah's in Lake Tahoe. While I was there I gave
another newspaper interview about my having overcome arthritis, as the
subject seemed to have such wide interest. I was—and still am—very
emotional about it. While admitting that I didn't have an answer for
arthritis for everyone, I hoped that I could offer inspiration and hope to
some of those who were suffering and unable to find relief from doctors
and drugs. I concluded with words that I was still trying to apply in my
own life: "Don't abandon yourself. Don't let anyone tell you what your
destiny is."

Later that year, again under Baayork's direction I did my last tour of *A Chorus Line*, knowing it was to be my swan song. I poured my heart into filling the role of Cassie. The end came as something of a challenge, as we had to perform the show in a theater-in-the-round in Valley Forge, Pennsylvania. Without any mirrors this time. We did all we could to re-create Michael's staging under the circumstances, creating the illusion of mirrors, sometimes reflecting each other. I was deeply moved again by what this show gave the audience and by what it had given to me. The poignancy of this last tour also reminded me of my priorities as a performer. I said at the time, "It has made me realize again how passionate I feel about theater. There is nothing more exciting than being on the stage, doing something meaningful, and affecting people at that moment."

I wouldn't allow myself to be distracted by Hollywood again. What I really loved was the theater, and I knew that's what I should be doing, not just dancing, but everything I believed theater could be. In a way, that growing awareness had an indirect impact on my personal life. I broke off my relationship with Andre while I was on tour in St. Paul. It was one of those moments when I had to ask myself, *Where is this going and where am I going?* I decided it was time to move on.

Though the relationship had helped me get through my touring for nearly six years, I realized that I had continued seeing Andre only because I was afraid of being alone. I didn't have a real home yet, and I had inadvertently made Andre my emotional home. After finishing the *Chorus Line* tour, I went to Toronto, collected my belongings, and said goodbye. As it turned out, I learned that Andre hadn't been entirely honest with me. He had been unfaithful while I was touring, and though our parting of ways was rather sad, I left without regret or rancor.

A short time later, I was given another chance to develop my cabaret show, thanks to my friend Joel Vig who introduced me to the Theatre Guild and its distinguished director, Philip Langner. (Philip's father was Lawrence Langner, who, in 1919, created the Theatre Guild, which produced some of the most important plays and musicals in the twentieth century, from *The Iceman Cometh* to *Oklahoma!* and *The Unsinkable Molly*

Brown.) I didn't take my act on the road this time, but out to sea, with three tours on a cruise ship, each lasting about two weeks. We went to the Mediterranean twice and also to South America, up the Amazon in Brazil. These cruises brought together marvelous musicians and entertainers like Joel Vig, Brian Bedford, Leroy Reams, Gena Rowlands, Patricia Neal, Cliff Robertson, Richard Kiley, Zoe Caldwell, and Kitty Carlisle Hart.

I brought my mother with me on the ship for two of these engagements, and my sister for one. There were a group of regulars who were a mainstay of the Theatre Guild audience, and my mother made a number of friends. It was a special delight for me to see how people responded to her, and how important it was for her to have this experience socially in her life. I was happy to be able to provide that after being so distant from her during those years when I had to find my own way. Between my work in New York and being on the road, I couldn't spend the time that I wanted with her and it had been a painful separation especially since my father's death.

I was in yet another phase of transition, needing to pick myself up without knowing exactly how I was going to do it. I remember one day sitting in my enchanted cottage in Laguna Beach and looking around and saying to myself, "Have I retired? Well, if I have, this is the perfect place to be. But if I haven't retired, then I have to get the hell out of here!" I wasn't ready to quit. I couldn't afford to retire anyway. But I knew I was going to need all the determination I could muster to do what I most wanted to do, which was to continue performing.

The very next day the phone rang and it was a director friend, Sue Lawless, who was about to do a new musical called *Cut the Ribbons* with a lovely score by Mildred Kayden, Mae Richard, and Cheryl Hardwick, set to open off-Broadway at the West Side Theatre. This was a three-women show, and I was cast along with Barbara Feldon and Georgia Engel. For me, getting back to New York was always a metaphor for getting back to me and starting over. It wasn't Broadway, and it wasn't a lot of money, but I hoped it might be another beginning.

Dr. Saperstein was disappointed that I had to leave therapy, but he was supportive in his acceptance of my new plan. During one of the last sessions, he said, "You're like a book half-read." I appealed to him that I needed to take the work we'd done and the progress we'd made into the world, because I live in a world with other people. The following session was our last, and he began by thanking me for teaching him something, for reminding him of the value of the practical application of our work, and for telling him what I needed. It was important to me that I receive his support and blessing. He knew that I had to leave with love and not in the tortured, rebellious way that had separated me from my parents so many years ago. He helped me to rewrite my history that day when he said good-bye. It still reverberates with me today. He lovingly opened the door for me, wished me well, and sent me on the rest of my journey.

Cut the Ribbons was about three generations—a mother, a daughter, and a grandmother—and the life passages that they go through with each other in their complex and emotionally powerful relationships. As written, each of us would trade roles from song to song. Sometimes I was the daughter singing a solo about my relationship with my mother and sometimes I was the grandmother singing a song to my granddaughter. It was very engaging to work on this piece with such smart and talented women, and we had many insightful conversations. I related to each character's point of view, and couldn't help but think of my own mother and grandmother with admiration.

Cut the Ribbons opened September 8, 1992, and, unfortunately, ran only about a month. At this point, I was no longer moving steadily from Broadway show to Broadway show and progressing from one step in my career to the next. The business was changing, and I had changed as well. I was in another kind of transition. Because I had been around for quite a while, most people knew my age range, but I still had a youthful appearance and at times that worked against me. I felt that I could go up for a role for which I had the right look for a woman in her thirties but when my age was revealed, I wasn't invited to audition.

I wasn't quite a character-type leading lady either. This business is all about perceptions, and I was as confused as anybody as far as where I belonged. I wasn't alone. Many of my actress friends complained as well, about what they called "the age of being neither here nor there." But happily, at the beginning of the next year, I found myself traveling to another one of those charmed circles in which my past came back to rescue me from the present.

At the center of this circle was Dean Jones, who had briefly played the role of Bobby in *Company,* before withdrawing from the show under much personal duress. Now Barry Brown was producing a reunion concert with the entire original cast of *Company* in Long Beach. It was to take place on the night of January 23, 1993. All of us in that original show had an unresolved history with Dean because of his early departure, which took quite a toll on him. He was a sweet man who had a lot of dignity and pride. He took on that incredible role, and he was perfect for it. But he was going through a messy divorce at the same time, and taking care of his daughter.

The hellish phase of that show out of town was especially hard on Dean. I don't remember if we were told or someone suggested that we stay away and leave him alone. He thought we didn't like him, but we were really just trying to protect him. Everyone in the show adored Dean. We all saw how hard he worked, how professional he was. Dean was put in the position of grappling with his troubled personal life, as well as whatever was transpiring between him and Hal Prince and Stephen Sondheim. I can't imagine how difficult it must have been for him to be in the middle of a divorce and do a show about marriage.

The night of the reunion was glorious for us all, and any misunderstandings of twenty years earlier were put to rest. When we came together onstage, it was heartening to see Dean make the first move. His being there was a gesture in itself, and his joy at being with us was like spontaneous combustion. The evening was like a big group hug for us, reliving that experience through the music. The event was so successful that Barry soon found a way to bring us to New York to do a benefit for Broadway Cares/Equity Fights AIDS.

We were to perform the concert at Lincoln Center's Avery Fisher Hall on two nights in April, and it was going to be filmed for the New York Public Library. Hal Prince would direct us again. John McDaniel was the conductor, and the orchestra would be onstage with us. The idea was that we would each come out individually to start the evening and formally stand in front of our chairs. Then we would sit down and the concert would begin. But the piece turned out to be something more than just a concert rendition of the show.

In Long Beach we didn't have much room onstage, so when the dance music started, no one ever expected me to do any part of my "Tick Tock" dance. But there was more space at Avery Fisher Hall, and I thought what fun if I could resurrect some of the choreography. I didn't remember all of it, and had to look at a film to learn it again. Of course, we didn't have Boris Aronson's fabulous set. In the original, the first part of the number, with me coming up in the elevator and then leaping onto the stage, was all done beautifully as the orchestration built. I knew the athleticism of my bursting onto the stage and leaping across those platforms wasn't going to be possible this time.

But I rechoreographed myself for the concert setting. I took the "Tick Tock" dance proper, when I was first on the stage floor, and edited the music so it would be a three-minute dance piece with the same ending instead of the full seven minutes. I knew it was risky. I was in good shape, but I wasn't doing eight shows a week and didn't have that performance confidence with this dance. Still, it was a one-time-only opportunity, and I thought, *I'm here to be brave. I've come through a lot and I'm here to do this. If I fall, I fall.* Whatever might happen, I knew it would be fun for everybody, and unexpected as well. When I started working on the number, I had more strength than I realized. People loved the dancing, and for me, the piece became a confidence builder and private celebration.

In rehearsals, we were given blocking and worked through our scenes. George Martin coordinated the musical staging. Elaine Stritch drove everybody crazy with her endearing madness for detail and endless questions for our director. Hal adored her and knew she would deliver, but Elaine needed a lot of attention. She drove fellow actor George Coe to hilarious distraction just as she had when we first did the show.

George and I had always been friendly, but sort of antagonistic toward each other in the past. He was fond of sparring, but this time around he became a support system for me, and we started dating. I adored George and we had a history with the show, so I was pleased that we were able to be intimate friends. As it happened, George would be undergoing treatments for cancer soon, and I gave him as much support as I could. There were times over the next few years when we were both in need, and we were constantly there for each other.

The two nights of the *Company* reunion became one of those magical New York theatrical experiences that live in the memory of all who attended. As one critic put it, "This was one of those rare conjunctions of tear-flooded nostalgia, high art and supreme artistry in which every ovation outlasted—and outblasted—the one before." Frank Rich aptly noted that all of this nostalgia was for "the least sentimental Broadway musical ever written." But that show and those characters proved they had enough heart and substance to touch people all over again.

The reunion gave me the opportunity to stay in town, and with the help of friends, I found a sublet on 81st Street off Columbus, overlooking the planetarium and Museum of Natural History. That spring I was cast in an off-Broadway production of *Annie Warbucks*. The score was by Charles Strouse and the show was to be directed by Martin Charnin and choreographed by Peter Gennaro. Marty and Peter had teamed up on the 1977 Broadway hit, *Annie,* based on the *Little Orphan Annie* comic strip, and this off-Broadway venture was to be a sequel.

The book, by Thomas Meehan, was a charming story about keeping Daddy Warbucks and Annie together and making them a happy family. I played Mrs. Kelly, a deceitful villainess. The cast included the marvelous actress-comedian Alene Robertson, who played my mother, Commissioner Doyle. I was looking forward to working with Harvey Evans again. Marguerite MacIntyce sang beautifully and played Grace, the love interest of Daddy Warbucks, who was wonderfully played by Harve Presnell. My character was the other potential love interest. I was an Irish woman with a certain allure and vulnerability, but later I was unmasked as a would-be killer. My mother's evil plan was to trick Daddy Warbucks into marrying me, and then we would murder him and Annie and inherit his money. I thought the show had a lot of heart and

integrity because it so well captured the spirit of the era and those original comic strip characters.

I loved the score with its lovely theater songs and ballads. Charles
Strouse once told me that this was one of his favorite scores. When it
was later recorded as a CD, I thought Tom Shepard did a great job by
presenting it in the format of a 1930s radio show. That was a wonderful
way to offer the soundtrack of a Broadway musical, with the cue lines
and connecting transitions that usually aren't included with the songs.

One of the delights for me on this show was working with Peter Gennaro. Many years before, I had been a Peter Gennaro dancer on *The Ed
Sullivan Show,* and we frequently bumped into each other on the Upper
West Side. Peter had done some of the choreography on *West Side Story,*
so I revered him. He always took the road of good taste, and was ever
faithful to the wise rule of thumb that *less is more.*

I had a showy number with Alene that was a bit over the top, but we
were both actresses and so it had to be grounded in the emotional lives
of the characters, in that sense of realism. Maybe it was my insecurity,
but whenever I was doing an acting or singing role, I always wanted to
dance and embellish. In this number, Peter had us doing a kind of
vaudeville step, kick, step, kick routine, and I wanted to do more of a
trick, adding a double turn into a high kick or jump kick.

After I showed Peter what I had in mind, he said, referring to my character, "You know, you weren't in *Follies.* It looks great, Donna, and
would probably stop the show, but it's too much. You have to stay with
what's real." He was right to have me tone it down for the good of the
show, because it would have been overdone and taken the audience out
of the story.

Annie Warbucks opened August 9, 1993, at the newly renovated Variety Arts Theatre in the East Village. We ran two hundred performances
before closing the following year. The *New York Times* described it as
"Full of peppy melodies, plenty of laughs, marvelous choreography,
smart sets, bright lights and snappy costumes." And *New York* magazine
called it "Surefire family fun!" I thought the performances were fabulous, though unfortunately that renovated theater was not ideal. Little
Kathryn Zaremba was a charmer as Annie, and Harve Presnell as Daddy

Warbucks had great stature, although when he stood up, his head almost hit the top of the proscenium.

We were all cramped on that stage and deserved a larger space. To make matters worse, there was terrible ventilation in the theater, and during the winter we all came down with bronchitis. We dressed in a hallway that had mirrors and a long shelf that served as a dressing table, sitting together on folding chairs. The men were on the next floor against the wall with the same setup. There was no class system, which was fine, but it was close quarters and we had to keep our elbows in when we applied our makeup. Still, we were in it together, and we bonded as a troupe and laughed constantly.

This was another one of those times when I was pleased to be able to invite my mother to come to New York to see the show. She was living in San Diego and she stayed with me at my apartment. She was a big fan of Harve Presnell. When I used to visit her in the 1960s, I would hear his album played over and over again. I guess to some extent I was still trying to make up for those years of guilt over how I had affected her and the rest of my family, but it gave me a big thrill to introduce her to Harve. He gave her a hug and a kiss. They took a picture together, which she framed when she returned home.

Because *Annie Warbucks* was such a family show, it was picked for the Christmas Day entertainment at the White House. We received a lot of attention from our hosts, though we had to dress in a little room in the basement. The White House staff gave us a dish of cookies and we all had a giggle. We were later greeted by President Clinton and the First Lady, and they were stunning. They had their Christmas tree in the Blue Room, and off of that was another room where a small stage had been constructed. It was all very quaint, with a Christmas party for needy children.

Our run continued into 1994, and I figured I was back on the boards even if it was downtown. I was doing a part that was interesting for me, certainly different from any role that I had done before, and I was singing more. I was more stable and was still seeing George. I had a better outlook on life, and a better relationship with my friends and family. I was finding new significance in my day-to-day routine and felt like

I was leading my life rather than having it lead me. I had that heart-to-heart with myself and knew more clearly what I wanted, which had less to do with fulfilling the expectations of others, so there was less pressure on me.

A lot of my growth was about being less symbiotic with my mother. I realized how we were living through each other over the years, and it wasn't just her problem, it was mine as well. The power of that maternal bond can't be underestimated, and I began to appreciate that much more. I started taking responsibility for being my own separate person, which made me feel good about myself.

I also had come to respect the fact that my mother had her own life now, even if at times she seemed a bit narcissistic about it. I remember a call I made to her in desperation at one of my low points after my divorce, something I rarely did. I needed to talk to her, and she said, "Oh, I can't talk now, I've got a date." Of course, that remark was totally innocent on her part, but it would take me a while to come to terms with the changes both of us were making in our lives. All of that was behind us now, and we were closer than we ever had been. It was inspiring for both my sister and me to see how our mother blossomed with her new life at her age.

Meanwhile, an unpleasant situation had developed with my house back in L.A. The tenants were no longer paying rent, but were simply squatting. After *Annie Warbucks* closed in 1994, I knew I had to go out there to straighten out my affairs. Eventually, I would have to give up the property. George helped me make the trip by giving me some of his frequent flier miles. After I took care of business and came back to New York, I wasn't getting any job offers and couldn't really afford a place to stay. But George had an apartment in Manhattan that he kept for his daughters who had gone to school there and that was where I settled for a while. Thanks to George's generous support, I was able to turn down a lot of money for a tour of *Show Boat* that same year and instead devoted myself once more to developing my own show.

I had been working on my cabaret material so long that I knew I couldn't be objective about it anymore. I needed help to develop a more theatrical show. I brought in Christopher Chadman to help me with the staging, and he brought Mark Hummel to help with the music. Bob Fosse adored Chris and had given him the "Yankee Doodle Dandy" number in *Dancin'* to choreograph; Chris then went on to do the revival of *Guys and Dolls* in 1992. Mark had worked on that show, and later he did the dance arrangements for *The Boy from Oz*. Chris was instrumental as director in helping me to focus. He was generous during our collaboration, allowing me to be the artist and to bring my own creative ideas to bear. He also helped me to eventually promote the project to various producers, as it was always difficult for me to sell myself.

That spring, Marvin Hamlisch invited me to perform for a week with the Pittsburgh Philharmonic, and I had a chance to talk to him about my show. I told him that I was using his song "Inside the Music" as the centerpiece and title song for a one-woman show that I was developing. He gave me his blessing and said, "It's a shame Michael never figured out how to fix that number." I told him that in the context of my show, it always seemed to work. I was pleased to come away with Marvin's enthusiastic support.

After I returned to New York, the Bay Street Theatre in Sag Harbor gave me an opportunity to stage *Inside the Music,* as I was now calling my show. I met the Bay Street producer, Sybil Burton Christopher, through one of my dance teachers, Michael Owens, who happened to have a house in Sag Harbor. Michael took me to see the theater, and I loved it. Bay Street did something they had never done before, which was to create a spring season with musical weekends. I was going to be the first, with two nights. It was a lovely three-hundred-seat theater with a built-in audience, and at last I had space to dance.

There was a full house for both shows. The audience reaction was warm, and overall the piece started to gel, but I could tell it still lacked continuity, and the opening number wasn't working.

After Bay Street, I was offered another engagement at the historic White Barn Theatre in Westport, Connecticut. That theater was soon to close, but the owner, Lucille Lortel, in her supportive way, kept it open for me. I was given two nights, and it was great to see that the show could work, that the audience really connected with some parts. Chris had encouraged me to bring in a writer, and I gave him a list that included Christopher Durang, one of our important American play-wrights, who had his own cabaret act, "Christopher Durang and Dawne."

Christopher saw the show at the White Barn and agreed to help me take it further. There wasn't a great deal of writing, though over the years I had continued to add bits and pieces of storytelling to refer to the songs with my stage career. I said in an interview at the time, "The trick is to create human interest with a character called 'Donna McKechnie.'"

I included moments that I thought were telling and amusing and sometimes self-effacing, like the story of one of those down times when I thought I had been completely forgotten and felt invisible. I told the audience, "So what do I do? I go home and clean the apartment. I turn on the TV to some game show, and I am polishing the coffee table, and polishing the coffee table, and crying, and then all of a sudden, I hear my name. I look up and there I am on television—I'm an answer on *Jeopardy!* Well, I had to stop crying so I could listen and find out what the question was! And the question turned out to be: Who are dancers and choreographers? I was in the category along with Gower Champion and Peter Gennaro." I then went on to tell the audience that I was the trick part of the answer. I hoped that relating private moments like that would make me more accessible as a character with feelings the audience could relate to.

This incarnation of *Inside the Music* was still loose when we had a showing at the Dance Center on Broadway at 56th Street. I rented the studio, hired three musicians, and invited some friends. I was to perform with the first draft of a script Christopher put together with new music. It was like a backers audition, and producer-director George Wolfe from the Public Theater came, as did Richard J. Alexander, who was working as Cameron Macintosh's assistant and was in charge of maintaining *Les Misérables* on Broadway. Richard gave me a great deal of encouragement. We also called the Shuberts and others. Our goal was to get a producing team together or to have a theater take it on, so I was hoping to put my best foot forward.

But the run-through at the Dance Center proved to be tense and difficult. The piece still lacked cohesion, and showing it didn't lead anywhere right away, though there was some interest expressed. Nobody seemed to have money for it, but they had suggestions about how to get it to the right theater. At the time of the run-through, Chris Chadman had just come out of the hospital, though none of us knew that, and I hadn't realized that he too had AIDS. Chris later told me that he was unable to work anymore. I remember asking him why he hadn't let me know that he was ill, and he replied, "I was afraid that you would fire me." I was shocked by his admission, and thought what a heartrending commentary it was on the way this disease impacted all of us. I was deeply saddened the following year when Chris died, at the age of forty-seven.

Without money or a theater, my show was once again back on the shelf. Later in 1995, I had a meeting at the Public Theater with George Wolfe, who was now the artistic director. Richard set up a meeting for me with George, and it was to be the first time I had been back to the Public since doing A *Chorus Line* there. Richard suggested, "Can you imagine doing your show on the same stage where you did *Chorus Line?*"

I thought that was a great idea, since so much of *Chorus Line* was in my show. When I met with George, he reminded me that we had first met when he was an apprentice on *Threepenny Opera* in Williamstown. He had come a long way since then, and I admired him. He was supportive up to a point, but it was his first year and he had specific ideas he wanted to pursue, so there was no place for me. Naturally, I was disappointed, but I appreciated his honesty and directness.

Ironically, it was my history with the cabaret show that brought me back to Broadway, because of my relationship with Philip Langner and the Theatre Guild. Philip was planning a production of *State Fair*, which was to be a musical adaptation of Richard Rodgers and Oscar Hammerstein's much loved film of the same name. I was cast in the role of Emily Arden, a big band singer and dancer who is intent on making her way from the Iowa State Fair to New York City during the 1940s. Ann-Margret had played Emily Arden in the 1962 movie version.

John Davidson, Andrea (*Annie*) McArdle, and Kathryn Crosby were also in the cast, and we were scheduled for a seven-month national tour prior to opening on Broadway in March of 1996. I was delighted to be in a singing and dancing show with a wonderful acting part as well. Randy Skinner, our director-choreographer, created two wonderful dances for me. One was a rousing tap number with the other dancers. The other one enabled me to realize one of my longtime fantasies: to be Ann-Margret with my "boys" backing me up. Scott Willis, Ian Knauer, James Patterson, and Michael Scott—these wonderful men were called "The Fairtones" and they were all triple threats. The children of the composers were represented, as Jimmy Hammerstein was Randy's co-director, and Mary Rodgers was also with us each step of the way. Bruce Pomahac orchestrated it, and most of the songs had never before been performed on the stage.

The seven-month tour before Broadway was a joy, and helped me to bounce back financially. The cast of this show was like love personified. Kathryn, John, and Andrea were the salt of my earth, and we had great respect for each other. On the road, we had a fabulous time. Andrea wasn't your typical ingénue; she brought a tougher edge to the role, and I loved that about her. She traveled mostly with her daughter and her husband, and John traveled with his wife and daughter. It was truly a happy family show. We were in Des Moines for the Iowa State Fair and played in an enormous civic center. During January of 1996, we played the Kennedy Center, and during that run I had the opportunity to teach musical theater master classes. I also enjoyed teaching Bikram yoga to Kathryn and others in the cast.

When we came into Philadelphia, Philip Langner needed to bring in some additional financial support to the production team, so David Merrick was invited to see the show. He was in such bad health that he came to the theater in a wheelchair, and couldn't speak. Philip needed another half-million to bring the show into New York. I later heard the story that David Merrick visited the production offices and handed over a paper bag with $500,000 in it. He then became so worked up about the project that he started speaking again.

So coming into New York, I thought this show was the perfect vehicle. Before we opened, the New York Times published an article entitled, "A Long and Twisting Road Back to Broadway," for which I was interviewed by Alex Witchel. To share a moment of my life on the road, I showed her a framed photograph that I carried with me as a keepsake when I was on tour. There was an anecdote that went with this memento that I had embellished and incorporated into my one woman show. The photo had been taken almost twenty years earlier, and showed me standing between Michael Bennett and Fred Astaire.

Telling the full version of the story for the *Times*, I explained that Fred Astaire had come to see *A Chorus Line* in Los Angeles, and afterward he had taken Michael and me, along with our mutual friend, Leonard Gershe, to dinner at Trader Vic's in Beverly Hills. I was so in awe of Fred Astaire that I could hardly speak the whole night. As I say in my show, I felt like Jane Wyman in *Johnny Belinda*. After dinner we went back to his Bel-Air mansion for aperitifs and he entertained us with wonderful stories about dancing with his sister Adele and how much he was in love with Barrie Chase, and how Rita Hayworth was his favorite dance partner. When there was a lull, I asked, about the painting of a horse behind the bar. He said, "Oh, Cole Porter painted that many years ago."

I said, "Cole Porter?"

He nodded, and I couldn't speak again.

When I went into the powder room, I saw that the initial P was embroidered on the hand towels, for Phyllis, his wife, who had passed away many years before. He hadn't remarried, and I remember thinking, *He's lonely and living in a time warp.* Later, he told me, "I don't go out much anymore because of all the devoted husbands tapping me on the shoulder and asking, 'Will you dance with my wife?'"

When we were leaving, I thought, *He must think I'm just a stupid dancer who can't speak.* There was a porch with a light over it and a circular driveway. As we were heading off in the car, I looked back at him standing there and I waved. Then he suddenly struck that classic Fred Astaire pose, lunging with his arm extended. I punched Michael with my elbow and said, "Look!" I was so touched because I thought that was his way of telling me that he understood how intimidating his image could be. It was like a gift of affirmation that only he could give. That last image is a special autograph.

When we came into New York with *State Fair,* my spirits couldn't have been higher. The Music Box was the perfect Broadway theater for that show, even though it was somewhat run-down and in need of renovation. The theater's history dated back to Irving Berlin's *Music Box Revues* that were staged in the early 1920s. The composer's estate now owned the theater in partnership with the Shubert Organization, and there was apparently a standoff between them over maintaining the building.

When we started rehearsals, Kathryn and I had adjoining dressing rooms, and we decorated them ourselves with yards of fabric that we put up with a staple gun, which much improved the atmosphere, making it soft and pretty. There was so much romance there for me, to know that so many actors had hurried down those stairs to make their cues. Now it was my turn to follow them, and at least for a short time I was where I belonged, and life was heavenly again.

Chapter 10

———————— ❧ ————————

MY MUSICAL COMEDY LIFE

Before *State Fair* opened in New York, I moved out of George's apartment and into a West Side penthouse that my dear friend Harvey Evans, one of the most loved and well-known gypsies in New York, sublet to me. I had wanted to find a more permanent home for myself, but Harvey was going away on tour with *Sunset Boulevard* for two years, and his place was terrific. How could I say no? It had two bedrooms, lots of light, and an enormous rooftop deck that overlooked the Hudson River. The rent was under market value and very affordable, so I could continue to save my money for an apartment I might one day be able to call home.

George, who had prostate cancer that had gone into remission, now wanted to return to Los Angeles because he felt more at home there. Our relationship had for some time been pushed to the side to make room to accommodate some of the more immediate problems of our individual daily lives. I was very proud of him; to witness him day in and day out, diligently taking care of himself, educating himself about diet and the technique known as "imaging." He would meditate on the image of little men with hardhats and lights, like miners with their pick-axes, inside his prostate gland, going to town on the cancer. I loved his actor's imagination, and he would break us both up when he described their behavior and how they all spoke with a Yiddish accent. "Oy vey, dis is a tough von!"

He always regarded my recovery as something short of miraculous, so now I could say, "It can be done. If I can do it, you can do it." He chose to do limited treatments of chemotherapy, instead of full treatments with radiation. With all the things on which we seemed to disagree, his holistic approach to good health was one subject on which we could easily agree. So it was a happy day when his doctor called to tell him that his cancer was gone. Now, we had our relationship to deal with. There was very little romance in our lives at this point. I loved George dearly, but I wasn't in love with him. He had been such a good friend when I needed a friend, but my friendship wasn't what he needed. Thankfully, we were able to speak honestly with one another, despite the painful feelings of failure and rejection that accompanied our carefully chosen words. Finally he said, "I've got to get the hell out of New York!" And I said, "I know you do, and I've got to stay here."

Although George and I decided to go our separate ways, we did so amicably and remained on friendly terms. It gave me great pleasure to see him looking fit a year later, when I was performing in Jerry Herman's *Mack and Mabel* in Los Angeles. He came backstage to congratulate me and to introduce me to his new bride. He looked so happy and I was happy for him, though I had a little twinge of jealousy that I quickly put in check. It was somewhat unsettling at first to be on my own again. I thought, *My God, I've never had a time in my life when I was really alone. I've always been either getting into a relationship or out of one.* But over time, not being involved in a relationship gave me another opportunity to redefine myself. I was no longer thinking of my identity in terms of the man I was with, which led to a kind of prolonged epiphany, if there is such a thing. Without returning to analysis and despite having to face some new and unexpected challenges, I was determined to find fulfillment on my own terms.

State Fair opened on Broadway on March 27, 1996, and I was happily snug in my new "home." The reviews were disappointingly mixed. We really needed that "money" review to insure a success. The producers didn't quite know how to market such a traditional musical, one that celebrated the family values of mid-1940s Iowa. They were short of funds, I imagined, when there wasn't a clear marketing blitz after the reviews. Still, it was the kind of show that I took great pleasure in performing night after night, and I was later honored to be recognized for my work, along with Savion Glover, with a Fred Astaire Award, for best female and male dancer in the 1995–96 Broadway season. The bad news came a few months after we opened in the form of a two-week closing notice.

One day while I was home, before I had to leave for the matinee, I had a moment of enlightenment, a spiritual experience, I think. I received a message. It was my voice, the way I usually hear it inside my head, but I instinctively felt it was a voice from my heart, a voice that I wasn't always able to hear clearly because I was always running in one direction or another, usually preoccupied with immediate survival. This voice needed an atmosphere of stillness to be heard. It comes to some people when they meditate, others when they pray, and to some when they are just looking out a window daydreaming. I was in a contemplative mood, thinking about the inevitability of the show closing soon, and "what do I do now?" That was when the message arrived. The voice said, "Your mother just celebrated her seventy-fifth birthday. The roses you sent were lovely and she wouldn't expect more, but she just turned seventy-five! This is a landmark year for her, and you don't know how many more she has left. Throw her a party with the people she loves."

Of course! I continued to put it together in my mind, my imagination now at work: "We'll have a grand party on the deck, with a band, music, drinks and hors d'oeuvres . . . at sunset, on a beautiful summer evening. A catered affair with surprise guests and a big cake, and lights hanging from the trees. But there are no trees. So I'll get trees, and shrubs and flowers!" I immediately called my mother and told her I was throwing her a belated birthday party with surprise guests. I could hear the excitement in her voice when I asked her to pick a date when she could fly to New York. She would bring her companion, Jack, with whom she lived in San Diego.

After I told George, his reaction was normal for him. He said, "Are you crazy? You just lost your job!"

I told him, "I know, but this is something I must do." My brother and sister helped me organize it. I loved the fact that it was a family affair, bringing us all together. My brother, Ron, knew a Brazilian band that would be perfect for this kind of event, and he had a graphic-artist friend design beer labels that said, "Mother McKechnie's Brew," with a beautiful picture of our mother in her twenties. My sister called our Aunt Carlie and arranged for a surprise by having her bring our cousins Eileen and Carol with her new baby, Allison, whom my mother had yet to meet. They would be the surprise guests.

Barbara helped me with choosing the special printed invitations. I invited some of my friends from *State Fair* along with Kathryn Crosby and our distinguished producer, Philip Langner, and his charming wife, Marilyn. Some of my mother's Theatre Guild tour friends came to the party, and the actress Pat Neal, who had traveled with her on one of the cruises, sent her a beautiful bouquet of fragrant white flowers. I had a ball before the party when I went down to the Flower District and acted out one of my favorite fantasies. I stood in the middle of all these plants and juniper trees and said, "I'll take that and that and that and that and three of those!"

Seeing the trees and bushes lined up on the terrace with all their beautiful pottery, I felt like a designer on a movie set giving strategic direction. The caterer came with five waiters in black tie. Ten round tables with pink linen tablecloths were set all around. Champagne would be served on silver trays as the sun was setting. My sister kept my mother and Jack away from the apartment after she picked them up from the airport by taking them to Central Park. They parked the car and started walking to a prearranged spot where my Aunt Carlie appeared with Eileen, Carol, and baby Allison. It was such a surprise that at first my mother didn't comprehend who was there and why. Then there were shrieks of delight and laughter.

By the time they arrived at the apartment, we were ready for them. The gentle strains of a bossa nova melody played in the background as my mother walked in, looking lovely in white. When she saw everyone on the terrace smiling in her direction, the expression on her face was priceless. She looked radiant. Among the mementos that I still carry with me on my travels are treasured pictures of us together that night.

Jack and I had never been close, but on that night we made an effort to be friendly for my mother's sake. At this point, I was more accepting of his being part of my mother's life. I could see that Jack made her happy, and that was all that mattered.

Although my mother seemed to be enjoying herself, unbeknownst to us she was actually in pain that evening. She didn't want anyone to know that she wasn't feeling well, and she was stoic as always. The following day we sat together outside on the terrace and had coffee, just before she had to leave for the airport. She was by nature shy about relating her feelings, and, as usual, I had to ask questions to draw her out. After all the excitement of the party, I hoped that she would share her happiness with me. I asked her, "Well, did you enjoy your birthday party? Wasn't last night fun?"

The look my mother gave me was the best thank-you that I could ever have received. Her eyes welled up, and she was unable to even look at me when she said, "It was the best birthday party I ever had." Then she added, "I never had one before."

That surprised me. I said, "Really, Mom? Even when you were a child, you never had a birthday party?"

She said, "No, never."

I made a comment like, "Well, it's about time you had one!" After thinking about it for a moment, I realized that I couldn't remember any birthday parties. We always celebrated her birthday, one-to-one, with a card or a present, but not with any sort of family gathering or celebration with invited guests. My brother and sister and I didn't have birthday parties either. That wasn't the way with my family. We never really had the money to throw parties, so I was especially pleased to have been able to give her this experience. I am grateful I listened to my inner voice, because of the fateful timing of her visit. None of us realized that this was to be her last birthday.

About four weeks after my mother went back to California, I was set to go to London to do my show, *Inside the Music,* and also to perform in a full-length concert version of *A Chorus Line* for BBC Radio. I was thrilled with the prospect of having a London premiere for my show, not to mention that I had a job again, so soon after the closing of *State Fair.* While working out the production details in New York, I learned that my mother was ill, although I didn't realize at first how serious her condition was.

She had been in and out of the hospital for operations on her colon. They had been successful and she seemed to be in good health these past few years, even though she knew she had emphysema from all her years of smoking. One morning a few weeks after she returned from New York, she went to her doctor with extreme pain in her abdomen, and he sent her home without discovering that she was bleeding internally. It wasn't long before she was rushed to the emergency room and prepared for an operation that would stop the bleeding. For some unknown reason, Jack didn't want us to know. Their next-door neighbor, Charlotte, was very concerned and said she was going to call us. This enraged Jack and he threatened her. She was used to his rantings so, of course, she called us right away, and that's when I dropped everything and flew to San Diego.

The operation was successful, but the surgeon discovered lung cancer. Her condition was grave, and our family gathered at her bedside. The cancer was spreading quickly through her body and it wasn't long before it was everywhere. One of her doctors was suggesting experimental chemotherapy and radiation. There were several doctors working on her, with each one pushing a different agenda based on their specialties.

Confronted by this medical nightmare, my family was at a loss what to do and couldn't agree about the best course to take. My sister and I were at odds for a few days, and the hospital had counselors speak with us, but I don't remember anyone really doing so, because they were just as confused as we were.

Our mother was in a medically-induced coma and couldn't speak for herself. I felt that Barbara was living under the delusion that our mother was somehow going to come out of this. My sister, ever hopeful, felt that we should try to give her any possible treatment, even if it gave her only a few more months. I did appreciate her being grounded in the idea of the decision being our mother's. Meanwhile, Jack wanted to bring in someone he had just met to pray over our mother, an outlandish suggestion that made me want to have him removed from the premises.

Her surgeon and her nurse made it clear to me that the chemotherapy would be more helpful to the other doctor than to our mother. My feeling was that we should just make it as painless as possible for her and let her go peacefully. The last thing I thought she needed was more poison in her system. During one of our family meetings, I remember saying to my sister, my brother, and Jack, "She's dying! Don't you get it? She's dying." It was shocking for me to say those words out loud, even though I knew they were true. I could have never imagined the emotional pain of being in such disagreement with my family in that waiting room.

At times, my brother, Ron, even with his own grief, was able to support me. When I needed to tearfully confide in him, he was there, strong and reasonable, which was reassuring. I had never seen him that way before. He had been a grown-up for many years. He was quite accomplished academically, with a teaching degree in science, but I always saw him as my little brother. I tended to want to take care of him, like I did when we were children, which probably wasn't the most helpful thing for him. Eventually, my brother and sister and I worked through our differences in order to give our mother the loving support she needed as well as ourselves.

My mother's body had deteriorated rapidly, but her heart was strong. She was unconscious from the morphine they were giving her, but she was still fighting for her life. I was learning something important from her about living and dying with courage and integrity. She made me more keenly aware of how death is a natural part of life, and how precious life is. Her human struggle illuminated her spirit to me and I had the utmost respect and love for her. She was teaching me this lesson at the end of her life, and I was so grateful to be there holding her hand.

Just after they moved her to a wing in the hospital where they could do more pain management, we were told that she had slipped away. The sudden reality of her death brought up feelings of anger and impotence for all of us. I didn't know how to deal with all the feelings. I kept asking myself what I could have done differently had I known earlier about her condition, and I was left with many resentments and regrets.

Anticipating the funeral and knowing that arrangements had to be made, I was utterly distraught. In the midst of my bereavement, I was trying to be practical. My London opening was only a few weeks away, and I had already booked a flight out of New York that I was going to postpone. At that point, I also had to consider canceling the production altogether. We had another family meeting, during which my Aunt Carlie suggested that I leave right away. I said, "I can't leave now! How can I leave?" But she insisted, "You've got to go, Donna. Your mother would want you to go and do your show. You've made a commitment, and your show is important, because it's about her too."

Despite my resistance, I knew my aunt was right. The show was like a cause that we shared as mother and daughter. My sister agreed with my aunt, and volunteered to arrange the funeral and organize my mother's affairs. Growing up as the middle child, Barbara had been in the position of competing for my mother's attention. That brought a lot of unintended hurt and sadness into her life, but she had worked hard to confront the issues and bring about a more satisfying relationship with our mother. Her career as a drama therapist was not a coincidence. Being aware of how close they were in recent years, I felt better about leaving and turning over the responsibilities for the funeral to Barbara. I also sensed that she wanted to be more in charge. And perhaps she would find her way out of grief this way. I knew that my mother was extremely well organized and everything would be in its proper place for my sister to sort out. So I was able to leave with some peace of mind, and I felt that I was making the right choice under the circumstances.

I was having a costume made in New York and had to pick it up in time to make my London flight. After arriving in Manhattan, it was all I could do to stay focused. I had only a few hours to pick up the costume, pack my bags, and get out of there. By the time I headed to the airport, I was in a walking stupor from fatigue and shock. I arrived early and went immediately to the American Airlines ticket counter. I was afraid that if anyone looked at me too closely or questioned me, I might burst into tears. I made an enormous effort to keep everything on hold until I could be alone again.

Waiting on line, I was in a daze just trying to control myself and get the job done, trying to be in the world of other human beings, trying to be a grown-up. But inside I was a terrified child again. I was booked on coach, and the attendant at the ticket counter kindly offered to put me on an earlier flight. He directed me to a line, where I waited again, clutching my ticket and bags. When my turn came, the flight attendant told me that my passport had expired. With panic setting in, I realized I had been so distracted that I hadn't thought to renew it. Even though my working papers were in order, she said that there was nothing she could do. But there must have been an angel of mercy watching over me because another attendant quickly came over to me, and said, "Wait a minute. Let me call over there. I'll call customs in London and see if they can help you."

It was quite a scare, but she went out of her way and made a call to arrange for me to sort it out in London. When she told me the good news, I was so relieved I almost did burst into tears on the spot. But my angel wasn't finished with me yet.

Boarding the plane, I was struck by how small the cabin was—one of those with only two seats on either side of the aisle. All the passengers appeared to be businessmen, except for one woman in the back with a poodle. There was one seat left in the second row where I took refuge, expecting a long, exhausting flight ahead of me. Still, I was grateful just to have made it onto the plane. I then noticed the rich wood paneling and high-tech computerized panels on the wall in front of me, but it wasn't until after we had taken off that I suddenly nudged the man sitting next to me, who was reading a newspaper. "Is this the Concorde?" I blurted. He lowered his paper slightly, looked at me like I was a crazy lady, and then with raised eyebrow, said, "Yes."

"Oh, look how high we're going. And look how fast!" I exclaimed, like an excited child. Without comment, he continued to read the paper. I thought, *Oh, my God, they've bumped me up from coach to Concorde! How in the world could that have happened?*

I was stunned by this piece of luck. The flight was incredibly smooth and fast, and after we landed, the British officials welcomed me into the country despite my outdated passport. This was unheard of! I was at the airport hours before the scheduled time a car was to pick me up, so I took a taxi to my friend Sue's house in Regents Park where I had arranged to stay. My arrival felt like a miracle. I had no jet lag and even managed to collect my wits for an interview with the London *Times* the next day.

As was my habit in the past, I couldn't wait to tell my mother all about my trip. I would fight that impulse for quite a while. My mother had loved to travel; it may sound like mystical thinking, but I felt like she was very much with me. In fact, it would be very hard for anyone to convince me that the upgraded trip wasn't her doing.

I was to open *Inside the Music* in October at the Jermyn Street Theatre, one block below Piccadilly Circus. It was a jewel box of a theater with only seventy seats. The owner, Penny Horner, along with our company manager, knowing that I was coming from a situation of personal grief, placed a permanent plaque with my mother's name on it on the Royal seats. I thought that was such a kind and generous thing to do, and it confirmed my decision to come to London to open my show. When the programs were printed, I formally dedicated the production to my mother's memory, as "the most beautiful and gracious woman I have ever known."

Preparing the show was a whirlwind juggling act. At the last minute, I lost the conductor who had planned to come over with me. I was distracted as it was, but then had to hunker down in London and find a new conductor. The script for the show was a first draft that Chris Durang had written, utilizing new material as well as some that I had already been using. Michael's ex, Larry Fuller, was an old friend from New York. He had done the choreography on shows like *Evita* and *Sweeney Todd* and had choreographed a number for me in a TV musical called *Aladdin* a couple of years before. Larry happened to be in London "taking meetings" before he had to leave to direct a new musical in Ireland. We had a fortuitous meeting in Joe Allen's restaurant one night, my home away from home when in London. I was telling Larry what I was up against and what a fix I was in and he said, "I'll help you before I leave."

That was another lucky day, because I was so over my head mounting this show on my own, even though I was used to doing things in concert mostly on my own. Larry's hard work and long hours in the theater setting lights and running cues enabled me to focus on my new script and get enough rest to stay healthy and not lose my voice. It was stressful anyway, but I shall never forget his generosity and will be forever grateful for his support. I would never underestimate the importance of a director again, if I ever had.

I brought over a general manager, Mitchell Weiss, to help me because I was also co-producing. Mitch had been the company manager on *State Fair.* The Jermyn Street Theatre's box office didn't take credit cards, and I was working for very little money plus a percentage of the house. I had Mitch handle all the business because it would have been too much for me. I had to rehearse a new band, and rent a house to put up everyone who came over to work on the production. It was a narrow, four-story town house at 21 John Street in Covent Garden behind the Royal Opera House. There were enough rooms for me to put up visiting friends from the States, like my good friend Bill Schelble. Everything was finally in order with no time to spare.

In London, I had a certain recognition after establishing myself with other shows years before and I knew that I could get the most influential critics to review us, which was important. Michael Billington had already written an attractive feature in the London *Times* that carried a lot of weight, but I was starting to worry that we wouldn't have enough time to work out all the remaining rough spots. I was now just trying to get through rehearsals and get the show up without falling apart.

The accommodations backstage were not ideal. I had a small dressing room downstairs with minimal furnishings. The dressing room itself was adequate, but the bathroom was upstairs, and to go down the hallway to the stairs, I had to walk precariously in second position, in order to avoid the gutter with running water in the floor. It was very odd, like finding myself in a street from another century.

Still, even with the minor inconveniences, I knew this London production could be invaluable in the long run. It was to be my out-of-town tryout and might enable me to take the show to the next level back in the States. Larry got me through my dress rehearsal, and we had some adorable people helping us offstage. I called the twenty-year-old fellow who ran the sound and lights "the son I never had." He sometimes fell asleep in rehearsal because he was doing the sound and lights for rock shows until late at night. Even so, he came through for me when I needed him.

I received moral support from quite a few friends. Baayork Lee came over, and Rita Moreno was passing through with her husband, Lenny Gordon. Of course, my dear English friends, for years, Alix and John, were there. Marti Stevens brought Diana Rigg one night, and we went to dinner, which thrilled me because I admire her so much. George Coe happened to be in London to visit his daughters, so we were able to see each other again and wish each other well. I now had a new old friend, David Rawle, whom I had started dating in New York. I hadn't seen him since I was a teenager and we ran into each other again by chance during *State Fair*. I first met David in Massachusetts when he was going to Harvard Business School, and I was a little dancer in Framingham doing summer stock. Meeting him again after so many years was very romantic. Because I was at a place in my life where I was more secure, I was better able to keep intimacy in perspective. However, my heart would skip a beat or two when I thought of his upcoming visit.

There were no rules as to when British critics could come to review a show, but it seemed entirely reasonable to think that they might come opening night, after a week of previews, as advertised. Well, they took me totally by surprise, showing up at my second preview! Critics from all the London newspapers came, as did a writer for *Variety*. When I heard that *Variety* was out in the audience, I wanted to throw up and wondered why I insisted on doing this to myself. I knew the business can be crazy and cruel, but this was too much! I might have felt better about its being judged that night if the first preview had been better, but it was a mess.

But as it turned out that evening, we were warmly received. I actually enjoyed myself in the last number when I danced the final number from *A Chorus Line*. I was turning in a big circle on a small stage, which was on the same level with the first row of patrons. I couldn't help but laugh when I saw all of their legs pull up at the same time to give me more room as I twirled by, as if it had been choreographed by Busby Berkeley.

I couldn't believe how well it went in spite of performing with mind-numbing anxiety. It received unanimously good reviews from eleven critics. Some of them were even raves. While applauding the choice of music and comic sensibility that I was trying to bring to bear on my life, London's *Guardian* suggested I was "bringing out the best of Broadway," and "seeking for a truth hidden inside the performer." The *Herald Tribune* gave me a wonderful kudo, "This is that splendid rarity, a scripted songbook!" The *London Observer* applauded the "Sheer Artistry!" while the *Sunday Telegraph* declared, "It's an authentic blast of Broadway . . . a vintage performance!" Of course, I was delighted with the reception, but mostly relieved, as in "How did I get away with that?" If nothing else, I was gratified to know my serious intent as an artist had been appreciated. The goal all along had been to go beyond the cabaret act and portray the journey of my life as musical theater. I wasn't quite there, but I was getting closer.

As we played over the next three weeks, I felt the show was coming together for me, though it wasn't yet the fully developed piece I envisioned. There were other parts of my story that I wanted to bring into the script eventually. For now, I was grateful to have pulled it off and pleased to be able to add excellent notices to my press kit, with the hope that one day I would have the chance to stage a more ambitious production.

After the show closed in November, I stayed on to perform *A Chorus Line* at the end of the month for the BBC2 radio audience. David Soul, the American actor best known for his role in the TV series *Starsky and Hutch,* performed the part of Zach. He was now living in London and enjoying his career over there. I've always believed that the original cast of *A Chorus Line* could not be equaled. Bob LuPone was the best Zach. That may be my prejudice, but I still feel that way. However, David was really quite marvelous as Zach. He brought a controlled anger and great sex appeal to the role. He understood Zach's personality, and the business of being dismissive to hide feelings. That made it exciting for me to act with him. The rest of the company was terrific as well, with perfectly cast English performers affecting impeccable American accents.

The BBC always employs supremely talented musicians for their radio concert series, which has a large and faithful audience, unlike anything we have in the U.S. The producer for the BBC, John Langridge, hired the show's original musical director, Donald Pippin, to oversee the production. It was absolutely a dream to work with Donald again, revisiting the show together. We planned to make a fun trip to Edinburgh after the recording to celebrate the occasion.

We were scheduled to perform the concert in a suburb north of London called Golders Green. There was to be an audience of about three hundred people, including friends of the cast and others who lined up for free tickets. The balcony of this theater had seats, but the auditorium and orchestra were flattened to serve as a soundstage. There were bleachers on the stage so we in the cast could sit with microphones in front of us. For the radio audience, it was supposed to come off as if the show was actually being performed onstage at that moment, though of course the visual elements had to be left to the imagination.

I suggested to the producer, "Even if it's just for the small audience, I would like to have some space to dance." I explained that the energy of dancing affects the voice, and performing the piece more fully would be exciting for the audience in the theater and could also be appreciated by the listening radio audience. John was enthusiastic about the idea. I thought he might just have them move some of the wires over to make room for me, but he had a special stage built to accommodate my dancing.

Unfortunately, when we went into rehearsals, I discovered that I had forgotten some of the choreography for "The Music and the Mirror" because I was so accustomed to doing a shortened version for my show. Donald Pippin was going to conduct the full orchestration and I was eager to have it all happen as well. Seeing my memory lapse, a young actress, Caroline O'Conner, stepped forward and said very shyly, "Maybe I can help, I know the original dance." She was playing the part of Diana, but she had also performed Cassie the previous year in Manchester. I said, "You do? Oh, please show it to me!" So she proceeded to teach me the dance that I used to perform and had actually helped to choreograph.

She brought all of Michael Bennett's choreography back from memory, and that made the performance into something wondrous. It was such a pleasure to look out at the seventy musicians and Donald Pippin there facing me. After I went through the big dance and turned upstage, I suddenly found myself eye-to-eye with the Cassie who had rescued me. That moment of irony wasn't lost on either of us. It was full of emotion as we shared our knowing grins and private kudos. I thought that was such a rich example of how the spirit of *A Chorus Line* goes on and on, embracing each generation, and then, again, it comes back to me in such a meaningful way.

The radio show was so successful that the BBC invited me to return in February 1997 to perform in a concert of *Follies*. In the interim, I spent the Christmas and New Year holidays making a brief appearance with the San Francisco Opera in a production of Strauss's *Die Fledermaus*, with thanks to Peter Diggins. Dancing as a special guest star in the opera was a novel departure for me and gave me the chance to work with my friend Gary Chryst re-creating a piece to Ravel's *Bolero,* which Peter Gennaro had originally choreographed for Gary and Natalia Makarova. It was a beautiful, balletic ballroom number that was featured in the second-act Masquerade Ball. It was a memorable way to spend the New Year and George came up from Santa Monica to help me celebrate. Without my mother, the holiday season was bittersweet, and I was happy to have work that kept me occupied and gave me little time to brood over my loss.

Returning to London, I stepped into the part of Phyllis in the BBC *Follies* concert. This was the 1971 musical about two unhappy marriages and a fictitious "Weisman (read: Ziegfeld) Follies" reunion, with the older characters coming back to face the ghosts of their younger selves, when they had been *Follies* showgirls. Ahead of its time in 1971, this show had been a fruitful collaboration between James Goldman, Hal Prince, Michael Bennett, and Stephen Sondheim. (Ted Chapin has written the definitive book on the making of *Follies,* entitled *Everything Was Possible.*) I had always loved this musical, and it was another dream come true to have this opportunity, even for one night.

There had been a more recent West End production of *Follies* in which Millicent Martin and also Diana Rigg had played the part of Phyllis, and Julia McKenzie had the role of Sally. John Langridge now wanted me to have the part of Phyllis, so Julia would have the same role she had in the West End. The cast was a spirited ensemble and we were going to perform this concert at the Drury Lane Theatre. Elizabeth Seal played Solange and she was delightful off stage as well as onstage. It was wonderful to be able to share this success with her in the same theater that years before, ironically, wasn't the best chapter in our lives. The event sold out within twenty-four hours.

Stephen Sondheim worked with us the entire time and was helpful with giving performers direction. I thought Stephen was a superb acting coach and felt that he could have been a brilliant director if he ever wanted to do that. I was grateful for his support. We had limited staging, considering this was a concert version. I sang the number "Could I Leave You" to Dennis Quilley, who played Ben. Partnered by two enormously tall and attractive male dancers, I did "The Story of Lucy and Jessie," which was fully staged, sung and danced, with stylish choreography by Steven Mear. It stopped the show.

All the musicians were on bleachers mounted on platforms, and down the center was a long staircase that came to one side of the conductor, Ian Sutherland. Wearing our gowns, we were each to make an entrance from the top of the stairs, trying not to look at our feet as we walked down each step to the main stage floor, as the tenor sang, "Here they come, those beautiful girls."

The show was originally supposed to be done with us holding the book, as in a staged reading. There was little rehearsal time, and at the last minute it was decided that we would not hold the book. Ron Moody, who played Buddy, took exception to this, and I couldn't really blame him. Standing microphones were placed across the stage and the priority was to perform for the mikes. That was especially difficult because there were two thousand people in the audience, and with our theatrical instincts, we wanted to perform for that audience. Ordinarily when you're doing a scene and singing with someone, you tend to look at the person in order to connect, as in real life. But we couldn't really do that, and for the most part we were compelled to remain stationary.

We had to keep our mouths by the mike and then turn our heads only when we weren't singing. So there was never really that sense of fulfillment that comes from realizing an actual performance. I knew then and I still believe it was the hardest and possibly most nerve-racking performance I've ever done because of those conditions. It was live, one time only, and no room for error. I was in a cold sweat the whole time I sang "Leave You," always thinking a little ahead of myself to make sure I could remember the next lyric. This was a really terrible constraint to put on one's emotional life while singing. So, I was happily relieved to have gotten through without slipping up on those lyrics!

But apart from the limitations, the night was a great success. Thommie Walsh, who played Bobby in the original cast of *A Chorus Line,* just happened to be in town, and just happened to get a ticket for that evening. He had no idea that I was also there, performing. He would remind me many years later how thrilling the concert was and how happy it made him to see Sondheim go to me with his congratulations after the concert ended and he was introduced. It is reassuring all these years later to know that I didn't just imagine it.

One of the great things about working in London was that it gave me the opportunity to visit Italy. Alix Kirsta and I had planned a trip to Venice, Florence, and Siena for ten days after the performance at the Drury Lane. Alix had made her mark as a journalist and writer in London, and she loved to travel as I did. Whenever her mate, John Zieger, wasn't able to go with her, she would go with one of her friends.

Over the years, I traveled with Alix to some wonderful places in Italy, France, and Turkey. We saw the *Pietà* weeks before some crazy man attacked it with a hammer. When the story was front-page news in the European papers, it was especially painful to read after being so close to the masterpiece and being so moved by its beauty. We went to the Uffizi museum in Florence to see Michelangelo's statue of David. As we approached the statue from the back of the room, there were six or seven Italian students, teenage boys and girls standing in a group. Instead of looking toward David, they were speaking wildly in Italian, giggling, making a mild disturbance. They kept looking in my direction, and I thought, "Oh, no. They've spotted me. They're going to get the American tourist lady!" I quickened my pace and put on my best "don't mess with me" look that was perfected living in New York all those years. I wasn't about to let them spoil my first encounter with this work of art.

Just as I passed them, one of the girls stepped in front of me. I threw my arms up and said, a little too aggressively, "I don't speak Italian!"

She looked up at me, still smiling, and said, "Holly's mother?"

"What?" I said, as my arms dropped to my side. There were more giggles from the peanut gallery, as she repeated, "You are Holly's mother?"

Another girl stepped up and said, "*Fame? TV?*"

"Oh, I see! You mean *Fame*. The TV show!"

"Sì, sì. TV!"

"Yes, I am Holly's mother," I said laughing. This acknowledgment set them off shrieking and jumping up and down. *Fame* was on Italian television, and they recognized me even though it had been filmed ten years earlier. As I signed autographs for these adorable children, I laughed to myself at the irony of seeing Michelangelo's incomparably beautiful David in the background as this group of students paid homage to a TV actress. I thought, *Oh, the power of television!*

In October 1997, I was cast in the role of Paula McFadden in the musical adaptation of Neil Simon's *The Goodbye Girl,* originally performed by Bernadette Peters on Broadway. In the Oscar-winning 1977 movie version, Paula had been played by Simon's wife, Marsha Mason, who starred with Richard Dreyfuss. The Broadway show had flopped in 1993, and a new production was now being mounted in Philadelphia at the Walnut Street Theatre. While the musical still had structural problems, we had a talented director in Bruce Lumpkin, and I played opposite two talented actors. Tony Freeman had the part of the actor who moves in to share my apartment with me and my daughter, who was played by an adorable ten-year-old, Alyse Wojciechoswki (now a talented actress at New York University).

The Goodbye Girl posed another healthy stretch for me as an actress. Interviewed at the time, I said, "I think it's important to look for roles that will move you forward in your career and in people's perceptions of you. Paula is one of those roles because she emerges so gradually. The challenge is to reveal her good traits in a way that lets the audience see her tougher edges receding." I also lauded Marvin Hamlisch's score, saying, "It's totally singable and danceable, and it gives each of the characters a chance to express him or herself. I love that nothing is static. It gives the audience time to observe. I also think it enhances their appreciation of the woman, Paula, who loses the big chip on her shoulder and learns to listen to her heart."

I had no trouble listening to my own heart early the next year when I heard that Robert Johansen was going to direct a revival of *Follies* at the Paper Mill Playhouse in New Jersey. I had worked there briefly when I was first starting out, and the Paper Mill had a great reputation and following. I figured since I had just performed the role of Phyllis at the Drury Lane, I stood a good chance of being cast in the role. That recent experience in London gave me terrific confidence when I auditioned, which was unusual for me with my dread of auditions. I was walking on air when I went in because I knew the material, and I have to admit I felt I bowled them over with my presentation. The director was obviously excited, and I walked out feeling like the part had to be mine.

Sondheim had final approval of the casting and Robert had to call him to get his blessing for me to play Phyllis. But Stephen said, "No, she's not Phyllis. She's Sally." Go figure! When I first heard that, I figured he had been kind and acquiesced to let me do the role in London, since there was no way Julia McKenzie wasn't going to perform Sally. And then, of course, I also had to wonder if he had been disappointed in my Phyllis.

But my real heart's desire always was to play Sally, ever since I had first seen the show. I wanted to do that role because I related to that character so much. My mother's sadness along with some of my mother's friends, not to mention their suicides, had made a lasting impression on me. I honestly believed it would seem presumptuous of me to ask to audition for Sally, even though I understood so well her distorted perceptions about her past and the men in her life. I was now more able to see how I distorted the perceptions of my relationships and could translate that personal reality artistically. With my next wave of feelings, I thought, *Oh my God, Sondheim really sees me! He's right, and how amazing that he brought it to my attention this way.*

Robert called me back to audition for the role of Sally. I was so excited to work on this new music. I really labored on this audition and enjoyed every minute of it. The music and range fit my voice perfectly and allowed me to use my strength and flexibility easily when acting the songs. When I was offered the role, I felt like I had received the greatest prize in the world, not to mention the distinction of being part of that ensemble. Some of the cast included Broadway veterans like Kaye Ballard, Eddie Bracken, Ann Miller, Liliane Montevecchi, Natalie Mosco, Phyllis Newman, Laura Kenyon, and Donald Saddler. The two pivotal couples were to be played by Dee Hoty and Laurence Guittard and me and Tony Roberts.

We had an unusually creative rehearsal period. James Goldman, who wrote the book, and Stephen Sondheim were reunited on this production after twenty years. Though they had feuded some years back, now they had apparently decided to put the past behind them for the sake of this revival, which was set for its first preview on April 15, 1998. Their reunion would have special poignancy for me in retrospect because of the death of James Goldman soon after *Follies* closed at Paper Mill. I remember saying to Dee Hoty during rehearsals, "Isn't this amazing to be with the creators twenty years after the show opened on Broadway and have them rework this script on us?"

Sondheim stepped in whenever he could to fix or refine a moment, or to give some direction that was better suited for the material or for the performer. Everyone in the cast responded to him. It may be my imagination, but I think he became appreciative of this production, and it was gratifying to see that happen.

Early on, we had to sing our solo numbers privately for Sondheim in order for him to see if we were approaching the music accurately. He was in a rehearsal room with the conductor, Jim Coleman. We were outside in the hall, sitting on fold-up chairs, and it was like waiting to go into the principal's office. I was next to Ann Miller, who had had, of course, quite a wonderful career in film. She was a singing and dancing star of the MGM "Golden Age" musicals. Now in her seventies, she was an indomitable spirit who would describe herself ruefully as "a beat-up old mountain lion."

Awaiting her turn with Sondheim, Ann was beside herself with nerves, and was practically in tears. She was playing Carlotta, and she was afraid she wasn't going to remember all the lyrics in her number, "I'm Still Here," which was the show's anthem of show business survival. The idea of singing for the composer himself was more than daunting. I wasn't thrilled with the idea of being put on the spot and judged either. I certainly didn't want Sondheim to think he made a mistake by suggesting me, so I tried to reassure Ann and myself by saying, "Look, this is rehearsal; we've got two more weeks. We've got time. It's okay."

I was left quaking in my boots, as Ann was called in first. Jim Coleman related this touching scene to me later. Sondheim immediately went to the piano to turn the pages of the score, which was a really sensitive gesture, I believe, intended to put her at ease. And Ann rose to the occasion, singing with such verve, *Good times and bum times, / I've seen them all and, my dear, / I'm still here."* Afterward, Sondheim was so moved by her that he went over, gave her a big hug, and filled with emotion, he said, "Thank you for being here. You're authentic. You're the real thing."

Coaching our numbers in his supportive way instilled confidence in all of us. He gave me one great direction that carried me through the show. This happened during our first-act run-through. Sally makes her entrance after this incredibly beautiful overture, and as she walks down to the edge of the stage, she looks out at what is supposed to be the empty theater. It is the night before the old theater is to be torn down. This theater represented all her youthful dreams and passions. It's where she fell in love, and where she was happy, and for months she could hardly wait for this reunion, for this moment. The audience watches her take it all in, remembering the past as if reclaiming her life. I wasn't allowing the moment to happen to me. Our director had left it to me to find it on my own, and I wasn't there yet. I wasn't walking onstage and letting that experience affect me as deeply as it could.

It was fine in a superficial and technical way. I felt intimidated by such a precise and important moment, so I walked out, looked out, and said the line with perfect inflections. Sondheim could see where I was falling short. He came over and said to me, "When you go out there, take your time. You belong here. Make that recognition, you *belong* here." I felt as if he was talking to me and to Sally, and that simple statement made all the difference between my performance being good or being inspired—being technical or being personal.

I understood from that one piece of direction, not only what that moment meant emotionally to Sally, but how to play the character throughout the whole show. It was like being given a key to unlock a door—for me, it was the door to entitlement. Also, he was giving me permission to give myself permission to be free to feel.

I hadn't really felt that confident and exhilarated on an opening night since *A Chorus Line*. The whole company felt that confidence. We all knew it was one of those rare times in our careers, a time when all the parts come together and inspire each other in their jobs.

The design and costume of my second-act number, "Losing My Mind," were so perfectly informed by the era, they inspired me and took my performance to another place, beyond the rehearsal room. I thought my performance was pretty good in rehearsal. But when I put on the midnight-blue velvet dress with a twenty-foot train, and my long blond wig that was so beautifully styled, and then walked onto the set and stood by the beautiful Greek column, I was transported. Gregg Barnes created the beautiful costume designs, Howard Leonard styled the hair, and Michael Anania was the scenic designer.

During the instrumental section after the first chorus, I was directed to walk across the vast stage, and end stage right. This was my first and only difficult conversation with the director. I had resisted any sort of overstaging of that number in rehearsal. I remembered so clearly the power of the original. Dorothy Collins had stood so simply in front of the curtain as a torch singer. She never moved during the instrumental. The moment was so powerful and she was so moving because she wasn't moving. By the way, it had been staged by Bob Avian, the unsung hero behind Michael Bennett.

At one point our director, Robert, said to me, "It's going to work. You'll see." Having learned in my life to have little trust, the jury was still out on that, but I did what I was told. Then in costume on the set, with lights and hair, I made the move as if choreographed by the music. I instinctively fell into that arch, overdramatized posture as I walked, in the style of a 1930s torch singer. I was terribly worried that the twenty-foot train would be a built-in laugh as I walked across the stage, but I made the leap of faith to go with it. Everything felt like a blessing so far, so why shouldn't I trust? As I reached the proscenium wall, I dramatically reached out and leaned against the portal in overacted grief, the way it might have been staged in the 1930s.

It felt right even though it differed from my ideal. Playing it that way actually made me feel a little insane, the way one feels inside when competing with the performance one is giving on the outside. But it was right for Sally at that moment and seemed to justify the anguish she feels at the end of the number. I had experienced great applause with show-stopping numbers in other shows, but only when I sang and danced. I was now singing a torch song and hearing not just applause but cheers every night. Of course, this response comes about when all the elements work together to lift a moment to such a heightened place. But I felt that I was establishing a new identity as a singer, that another dream was being fulfilled.

Yes, this show was in every way a landmark success for me, and much of it had to do with working with Dee, Larry, and Tony. We had a long and well-paced rehearsal period thanks to our director, Robert. Having that much time to explore the relationships onstage meant everything to me. And the way Larry Guittard sang "The Road You Didn't Take," one of my favorite songs of all time, in his gorgeous baritone made it easy to fall in love with him all over again. Some nights I would sit there onstage, in character, listening to him sing, and I would think, "He was my Frank and I was his Annie, and now I am his Sally and he is my Ben. What a wonderful occupation I have!"

Acting with Tony Roberts was another thrill for me. He is such a superb actor, and his portrayal of Buddy was perfection, with a special kind of bravado and vulnerability. Tony is one of those actors who can go easily from a straight play to a musical, then to a film, and be brilliant in all styles because he is always grounded in reality as an actor. He made it so easy for me to play important moments with him, because all I had to do was to listen and react.

Dee Hoty was a sublime Phyllis, with a cool sophistication, but always a twinkle in her eye. Her knockout body, knockout voice, and knockout number in the second act stopped the show every night. We also became good pals as we were dressing room mates. Dee and I had so much fun onstage and off. Everybody felt so proud and honored to be in that company, and it showed onstage.

After our opening, I sat in the dressing room for a while. I needed some private time to calm down and take it all in before going to the party. I was thinking of Michael and missing him. I hoped that he was somewhere in our midst appreciating our efforts and that he might be aware of the homage I paid him in my performance. I knew how much he loved the show, and that's why I was so deeply touched when the choreographer, Jerry Mitchell, re-created Michael's choreography so precisely in the tap dance in "Who's That Woman?" I thought that was a very right and classy thing to do.

In the midst of my reverie, the stage manager suddenly ran into the room and said, "Donna, aren't you coming to the party? Steve is asking for you!"

"Oh, my God, is he there?" It never occurred to me that he would be there. I was under the impression that he didn't like crowds. Well, I almost broke my neck running to get there before he left. He was standing in the middle of the party, and I said to myself, "Oh, he must hate this!" When I was able to reach him, he gave me the highest compliment an actress could ever receive, coming from the best composer and lyricist of our time. He told me how exciting it was for him to see the actress and the character come together so completely. I just hoped he knew that my "thank you" came from the bottom of my heart. In the *New York Times,* critic Ben Brantley credited me with "the performance of my career," suggesting that I was "born to play Sally." Interviewed during our four-week run, I enthused, "If there's heaven on earth, I'm in it right now!"

We were in a hit, and it might have been in New Jersey, but everyone in New York was coming to see it. The whole experience of that show was such a phenomenal high that I never wanted it to end. Afterward, the letdown caught me off guard, especially after there had been serious conversations with Robert about moving the show to Broadway. We all were told that we had a producer with the money and even a theater!

For a brief time the cast was ecstatic, especially Ann. She suspected that this would be her swan song, and no better way to say good-bye. We then learned that the Broadway rights had already been given to the Roundabout Theatre, before our production even went into rehearsals. That was startling and heartbreaking news.

I have tried over the years to be a realist about show business disappointments. It's a business that is built on daily rejections and insecurity. You have to learn to just let it go, walk away, and look forward to the next opportunity, like walking away from a bad audition. Next! It's much harder for me to say good-bye to the people, all the performers in a show, who have become like a family to me. You've shared so much together, known each other in the most personal, intimate ways, laughed and cried your way through rehearsals, the opening, the closing, and then it seems like everyone disappears. That's what happens when people get other jobs and move on, but irrationally, I started feeling that familiar sense of abandonment again.

I carried that distress with me to London that summer to perform in and choreograph a West End production of *No Way to Treat a Lady*, based on the 1968 movie that starred Lee Remick, Rod Steiger, and George Segal. Douglas Cohen composed the score and wrote the book based on William Goldman's story. The talented cast included Joanna Riding, Tim Flavin, Joan Savage, and Paul Bown. Working on the show and the challenge of choreographing the piece buoyed me temporarily, but by the time I returned to New York, I was down again, slipping back into depression. I was also uprooted, staying with friends and moving around between sublets, which made me feel all the more insecure.

During the downtime that winter, I started getting sick again. I was feeling those twinges in my joints. I couldn't get up in the morning, and all the signs were there that the condition was coming back. Having been through arthritis once, I was determined not to let it happen again. But now I had to take stock and draw on everything that I had learned before. I went back to square one with the diet, suitable exercise, and most importantly, dealing with my emotional life. It's so much a part of human nature that when we start feeling good, it's tempting to revert to our old ways. And in my case, I knew that I was by nature too quick to avoid certain uncomfortable feelings and I realized that I had to deal with what was going on in my life or I could find myself in big trouble.

There had been some warning signs I had ignored. Shortly after my mother died, my hair had started falling out. Not enough to give me bald spots, but enough to get my attention. My unacknowledged feelings were going to have the last word. That's how far I had gone into denial. I spent so much of my life distracting myself in order to survive, fearing that I wouldn't be able to tolerate certain things. That pattern reasserted itself when denial again led to the physical manifestation of my inner conflicts and unresolved grief. My body was saying to me, "Pay attention!"

I couldn't afford going back to analysis and had to deal with it on my own. I dove into myself and played back in my head the mental tapes of sessions that I recalled with Dr. De la Vega and Dr. Saperstein and Dr. Sabbath. I read through my old reference books that educated me about mind-body dynamics. I knew how to fight through the depression, by not fighting and criticizing, but by allowing and accepting. I was more grown up now and knew how to be more interdependent. I had enough confidence and self-love that I could share and reach out to people for their support. It was a measure of my growth for me to realize that we don't live in the world alone.

My sister was my best friend to whom I confided in our adult years, and at a certain point she reminded me that I would always have a depression, a valley, a lull just before the most important changes in my life would occur, coinciding with the most important shows, and that I always bounced back. I told Barbara, "Each time was different." And she said, "No, it's always the same. This has always happened to you. These ups and downs you go through." She was trying to cheer me up, adding, "Don't give up hope. Something will come along. Something good will happen."

I did have hope, but perhaps not enough faith, even though I had come to think of myself as a survivor. I just thought it was so amazing after living through so much, the marriage, divorce, illness, and after all those years of therapy, I was still going into denial about my grief. I was missing my mother so much, and it brought up all the heartache that I associated with my father too, the same issues I had been dealing with for years.

While I managed to recover my health, my equilibrium was still off-kilter because I had no permanent home. Kaye Ballard was a good friend and let me sublet her apartment in the West Village. It was great while it lasted, but one night she called me with good and bad news. Kaye, who is one of the most generous people I have ever known, was *very* upset and apologetic. She told me that she got a play in New York and had to move back right away. I reassured her and started a daily ritual of looking at apartments. I had no luck. I was recording a demo CD at the time and the producer let me stay in the studio on an air mattress at night, while I recorded during the day. I stayed there for two nights on the floor and thought, *Something has to change now. I've been here before.* It was bad enough in my twenties, but now it was verging on pathetic.

My real estate agent was one of the performers in *Follies,* Natalie Mosco. In the show, she had danced the tango with Donald Saddler. Natalie had a thriving career in Australia and while she was struggling in New York she had a backup plan: she recently passed her test to get her real estate license. I needed to move quickly and I needed something inexpensive. My resources were limited because I had no credit after losing my property in Los Angeles. The illegal tenants finally left, but I couldn't come up with thousands of dollars in twelve hours. The bank was unwilling to work things out with me, so it went into foreclosure. I really couldn't afford to fight it legally, so I decided to cut my losses the best way I could. Still, I felt defeated by such a loss. One day Natalie called and said, "Donna, I have a place I think you should see." She described it as a one-bedroom apartment in a great building on Riverside Drive.

I went to see this place even though it was for sale and not for rent. The building had been built in 1906 and still had the original marble and ironwork. It was one of those classically beautiful buildings. I fell in love with it as soon as I walked into the lobby. I said, "I'll take it!"

Natalie laughed and said, "You haven't even seen it yet!"

I said, "I know, but I just want to come home here, to this building every night." We walked through a semiprivate entrance, then up a short staircase and into the apartment. It had two gorgeous European windows that looked out on the river and the park. And there was a fireplace with the figures of two Victorian Greek statues that looked like *Follies* girls in relief on either side. I wondered if that might be an omen. The apartment was relatively inexpensive, given prices in Manhattan, and I didn't have to go before the board. I was Natalie's first client, and she was my angel, because it did seem like divine intervention that I was able to get the loan and buy the apartment that April. Once that fell into place, I knew that I would be fine and that all was possible now, that everything else would follow.

It occurred to me that I had lived in practically every part of this city. I had been traveling like a gypsy for forty years, not just on tours across the country, but also all over this island of Manhattan.

After I moved in, I allowed myself the luxury of catching up with myself. I had time for reflection. It was a home that my mother and father would never see. My mother had always loved to visit me in New York and had seen practically all the others. But a new home is like a new chapter, a new beginning. I thought of myself as the adult now, even though I had been an adult for decades. I felt that I was really growing up at last because I finally was able to come to terms with all the losses in my life.

With my new home, I had a chance to reclaim myself again, which was, after all, what my show was about. That summer I was invited by the Cincinnati Playhouse to do a workshop production of *Inside the Music*. The artistic director, Ed Stern, gave us the rare opportunity to use carte blanche to develop the show in their black box theater. They provided a stage manager, they paid for the musicians, and they gave each of us accommodations and a small weekly stipend.

Chris Durang rewrote the script on the basis of hours of talks that we had. Known for his outrageous humor, I was especially pleased with the eloquence of his writing in the more personal and serious sections. Thommie Walsh was the director, and I had a lot of faith in him. He had come a long way since standing near me on the line at the Shubert. He had two Tony Awards for his association with Tommy Tune as co-director and co-choreographer for *My One and Only* and *A Day in Holly-wood / A Night in the Ukraine.*

Both of my collaborators were artists with style and impeccable taste. I was fortunate to have them there with me. We had everyone in the same room to develop the ideas musically, as well as in the text, which was composed of a series of monologues. I wanted to go deeper into my story, to bring out the darker side, though it had to be consistent with the comic tone of the piece. We needed a new opening and had to rework the rest of the script. I now added anecdotes about Michael, my illness, and what I called "my litany of losses." I also re-created the scene with Dr. De la Vega when he confronted me about my inability to express my anger directly.

At the end of the workshop, we gave three performances for the board of directors of the theater and invited friends. *Inside the Music* was no longer a loosely structured cabaret piece, but a full-blown musical, with text that continued the story between twenty-two songs and six dance numbers. The most important thing to keep me motivated now was not what I thought of our work, but what was being felt and experienced by the audience.

I was impressed by feedback, mostly from women, who related so completely to the plight of repressed anger. They would say things like "I was raised not to express myself in any negative way, so I had trouble expressing myself in any honest way. Act like a lady. Stay as sweet as you are." It excited me to feel our audiences respond to the material in a deeper way. By the time I left Cincinnati, I felt like the show was more polished and at least ready to be tested with audiences on the road.

I spent the next couple of years finding theaters around the country where I might keep the show alive. In between my own productions, I was teaching classes in musical theater at the Herbert Berghof Studio in New York, and I played Desiree in a North Shore revival of Sondheim's *A Little Night Music.* Early in 2001, I had a fabulous time playing Mama Rose in *Gypsy* out in Cleveland in the beautiful old Ohio Theatre, which had been part of the Orpheum circuit that Gypsy Rose Lee traveled, doing her vaudeville act with her sister, June Havoc.

The rest of that year I stayed on the road with *Inside the Music*, playing in Palm Beach, Los Angeles, Philadelphia, Sag Harbor, and Westhampton. The most realized production was at the Colony Theatre in Burbank. It seemed as if I had become a little institution crisscrossing the country. However, it became apparent to me that I could no longer produce the full length theatrical version myself, and I had to let it go for now.

One day, I got a call from Jerry Friedman, who with his business partner, Rich Aronstein, was booking a supper club in New York called Arci's. He asked me if I would be able to pull something together in two weeks. I would be filling in for Margaret Whiting, who was not feeling well and wanted a later date. I knew it was a good opportunity to use some of the set pieces from *Inside the Music* and other material I loved but was unable to use in the theatrical show. I could create an hour-long cabaret show for this and other venues. So I called Chris Durang and asked if I could lift some numbers and scenes from *Inside the Music*. He was sympathetic and generous in giving his permission. The show was billed as *An Evening with Donna McKechnie: My Musical Comedy Life*.

In an interview I later did with the *Washington Post,* I described my approach to the autobiographical character that I was playing in my hybrid theater-cabaret: "I set each song up with a line or two, and then I become the character. Like a falling in love song, I fall in love; and the song right after, I'm in the depths of despair. I go back in time. I take the audience on a little walk through what I call Shubert Alley . . . to my first audition on a Broadway stage . . . and I say these names again that people may not have heard in a long time. Like Frank Loesser, Abe Burrows and George Abbott, and a lot of the director-choreographers, because they were the key to my development. . . . Bob Fosse, Michael Bennett, and Peter Gennaro."

I brought that same sensibility to Arci's. It was a unique club and they actually had decent food. The owner, John, was a charismatic European whom everyone adored. The club, however, did pose certain challenges. The dressing room was like a dirty hole of an office, and I had to walk across a greasy, slippery kitchen floor in my dance shoes to get to the door to make my entrance. I would say hello to all the guys in the kitchen while I was slipping and sliding all the way on my rubber soles. Each night I thought, *Oh, the glamour of show business!*

That engagement made me realize that since I hadn't been seen in New York for a while, there was something newsworthy about my appearance. On my opening night someone told me, "Ben Brantley's out there!" I was shocked to discover that all of the New York critics had come to the show, and I was going to be reviewed by the theater critics rather than the cabaret critics. It hadn't occurred to me that they would come. I had been living in such an insular way, preoccupied with set-tling into my new home and trying to stay focused on the work with Thommie and Chris. I took it as a compliment that I would be reviewed, but at the same time, knowing what I was up against in this club, I felt my nerves giving me a little case of stage fright.

That night, as I prepared to go on, I saw Ben Brantley's profile. The room was carpeted and I had to walk through the audience. It was also darkened and packed with tables. That was a challenge of confidence, as I could only hope that I didn't bump into an elbow or knock over a glass of wine when I walked by. The stage was tiny, eight feet by eight feet, with a big baby grand piano on it, and I was actually going to per-form the shortened dance version of "The Music and the Mirror." I was hitting poses in a style I called "dance illusion." I was singing with a body mike in order to have my arms and hands free. Even if I'm just singing without a dance number, I'm always moving and articulating with my body.

Waiting for my entrance, I gave myself a pep talk, saying, "You know this material works. You've been doing it for so long, when are you going to give yourself a break? You're going to be fine." That was the personal reality with which I always started the show—that and reminding myself to keep breathing. In this case, I was in the kitchen where the audience couldn't see me. They heard the tremolo on the piano, and they heard me singing softly, as if I were in the wings calming my fears. *"You'll be swell, you'll be great, gonna have the whole world on a plate."*

Then, just as I stepped out with the rhythm and came into the room, the strap on my shoe broke. At that point I knew I couldn't do the kick in "The Music and the Mirror," because if I did, the shoe would go into

Ben Brantley's soup. Looking back, the broken strap was a blessing in disguise that helped my performance. Being distracted worrying about my shoe the whole evening, I didn't push at all. When a performer pushes, it can come off as unattractive. The next day Mr. Brantley concluded his notice with words of praise I hoped would always be true: "So scared, so hearty, so happy to be doing what she's doing, she remains the essence of the heroic drive that *A Chorus Line* celebrates."

I had to return to that same club in October, and that was scary because it was just after 9/11, and right then people in New York generally didn't want to go out. I didn't venture into the world for almost two weeks, like a lot of people I knew. No one was in the mood to celebrate anything. It was a very sad time, a time for processing. But Arci's had a booking for me on October 3. If it had been a week earlier, I probably wouldn't have been able to perform. I figured that I would go right back to my little bout of stage fright, and once again walk through the slippery kitchen, saying hello to the guys. But that night, when I heard my chord and started to sing, "You'll be swell," I thought, *Something isn't right, I'm not the same!*

What I realized was that I had no stage fright. Something had changed inside me. I'm sure I'll have stage fright again in my life, and I don't always think it's a bad thing, feeling the excitement and nerves. But that night I was galled by the shift of my psyche with the trauma of that event here in New York and all the shared grief that was still being felt. My little show paled in significance. It was not such a big deal. If anything was a big deal, it was the opportunity to entertain. I wanted to hold on to that fragile spirit and not live in sadness anymore. I was glad that I was able to perform, and it took me just one night to realize that people were ready to laugh and be entertained again, to listen to beautiful music and have a good time. That was all I ever really had to give.

All the New York reviews were flattering, and they gave the show a life of its own that kept me on the road for a couple of years. I had so much fun playing in new theaters and clubs around the country that I decided to put another show together so that I could have return engagements. I developed a show based on my traveling life, with the title, *Gypsy in My Soul.* It was a little more sophisticated than the first show, more mature perhaps because it dealt with a woman of a certain age coming to terms with her choices. It gave me a platform to re-create some of the great leading ladies in musical theater, parts that I had performed on the road: Pistache in Cole Porter's *Can-Can,* Sally in *Follies,* and Mama Rose in *Gypsy.* Before leaving for London, I invited five trusted friends to see a run-through of the show in a rehearsal studio. Pam Shaw, Beau James, Robert Rattigan, Ken Bennett, and Harvey Evans each gave me specific feedback and ideas that helped me tremendously. I opened it in London in 2003 in a supper club. I had a great time with the work, thanks to the musical director, Nathan Martin, still putting numbers in and taking numbers out. And I enjoyed seeing my old friends like Alix and John, Clare and Mark, Sue Kyd and her precious daughter, Nell, Nancy Retchin, Robin Miller, and Ken Oldfield, who brought Jane Summerhays and who was having great success choreographing for film. One night, I had a delightful reunion with Petra Siniawski, the first English Cassie, and Jody Hall, who was one of the dancers in the London production of *Promises, Promises,* when they came to the show.

I shared a beautiful house with Julie Wilson, who was appearing at the same club following my run. I hadn't worked with her since *Company* in Washington, although I never missed seeing her marvelous club performances in New York. She first entered the foyer of the house with a scarf tied under her chin and wearing a long oversize coat, standing a little hunched over, with an enormous suitcase. Julie's allure and stature onstage is legend, but now in her seventies, she looked fragile and vulnerable standing there. I went to help her with the suitcase. She gently pushed me away and said, "No, thank you, I can do it myself." Then the housekeeper rushed over to help and Julie was even more emphatic when she said, "No, please, I've been doing this for sixty years. I think I know what I'm doing!"

It took me a minute to realize that she really did, because that's what kept her going all these years on the road, not letting people lighten her load, not giving in to her age by lifting her own suitcase. That kept her strong, confident, and young. I made a mental note of that. Julie did, however, like it when I cooked for her. She said she loved it when anyone cooked for her, because she loved to eat. It gave me pleasure to do that for her.

A few nights after her arrival, I went to her dress rehearsal just in case she needed me to help her with anything. She came out looking gorgeous in her beaded gown and boa, standing so straight and tall. She didn't need me or anyone at that moment. She was so beautifully happy and at home on that stage.

I eventually went back to New York and more future bookings, thanks to Jerry and Rich. I was beginning to feel proud of what I had accomplished. Even though I would always jump at the chance to do a good musical with a good cast, I had been able to create a whole other niche for myself. It's not always easy to go from "career, to career, to career," to quote Sondheim. Now, after a few years, I had a nice little momentum and was making a living doing what I loved. And I like to think I kept improving. I didn't come to New York originally to do a one-woman cabaret show, but it's been fantastic for me and empowered me in so many ways.

Just to be able to break the "fourth wall" and relate eye-to-eye with the audience in a spontaneous way, and then to take them on your journey, as scripted, in a connected way, has been such a gratifying way to perform. To be able to travel all over the world, having reunions, and meeting new friends, has given me a lot of joy and it has ultimately led me back to myself. It also fueled my desire to write this book, which was something I had hoped to do since 1987. The time felt right to tell my whole story because I had found a physical home and emotional independence, and I wasn't afraid of reliving my life, even the darker episodes that I've related here. And, of course, the higher purpose of the book, to help people, was the *important* thing.

In the spring of 2005, I spent a glorious three weeks in New Orleans doing my *Gypsy in My Soul* show at a sensational supper club called Le Chat Noir. I stayed in the most charming house that had been converted from slave quarters in the French Quarter. It was adjacent to the main house, with French doors opening out onto a lovely pool and garden area. It was quiet, private and divine. Eugene Gwozdz, my incomparable accompanist and musical director, had a great time playing in some of the local jazz clubs after our show came down.

We were wined and dined by some of the most generous and fun-loving people I've ever met. The owner of the club, Barbara Motley, was a wonderful hostess. At our second performance she came to me and asked me if I wouldn't mind singing "Happy Birthday" to a very important woman in the community. It was her eighty-eighth birthday and she brought her sister and friends to the show. "Of course," I told her, "I'd be honored." Ella Brennan and her family were leading citizens in New Orleans. They owned at least five restaurants, including the famous Commander's Palace. Ella was called the "Queen of Creole Cuisine" by *People* magazine. Paul Prudhomme and Emeril Lagasse got their start in her kitchen.

I invited the whole audience to sing "Happy Birthday," which was fun for everyone. After the show, Ella invited me, Eugene, and Barbara to be her guests at the restaurant on our night off. On the night of our arrival, we were met in the foyer with a glass of champagne and a grand tour of the restaurant, dining rooms, and kitchen in this historic, magnificent Southern mansion. Ella's daughter Ti, who now ran the restaurant, joined us, along with Ella's sister, Dotty. We were seven people at a beautifully appointed circular table in the main room, and we had seven waiters serving us, all at the same time, for every course. It reminded me of "The Waiters' Gallop" in *Hello, Dolly!,* as choreographed by Gower Champion.

This was the height of elegance, but hilarious to me at the same time. We were there for almost six hours, tasting everybody's entrée and dessert, and everything was sublime. Ella became my new inspiration that night. Many bottles of wine flowed as we discussed politics with passion and we laughed together as family stories were shared. Mabel Mercer and Bobby Short had been big fans of Ella's and she told me proudly how they would come to dinner and sing to her, and she would sing to them. She loved show tunes!

It's not my forte to sing songs a cappella after drinking a bottle of wine, but I heard my cue, and thought *if Mabel could do it, I can do it.* I then sang a chorus and a half of "Lucky To Be Me," from *On The Town,* which I thought was appropriate. We were making so much noise at one point that I said, "Ella, we are making such a disturbance, that if you didn't own this place, we would be thrown out!" It was another night to remember.

Six months later I watched with fear and forboding for my new friends in New Orleans, as the floodgates broke and toxic water covered the city. My love and appreciation of the city and its citizens made it even more heartbreaking for me to see people losing their homes, their families, and their lives. I was able to track down most of those with whom I had spent time. All survived, but some homes and businesses were lost, and some people temporarily moved to Texas, their lives changed forever. I believe that the city will come back, if there are enough people who care with just half of the energy and passion embodied by Ella Brennan.

Rich Aronstein, having booked me into Joe's Pub in New York for October, called in June to ask me which show I would be doing, since their press department needed a title and description for an immediate release. He also told me that the Public Theater would pitch in because my appearance would be timely to kick off a series of celebrations for the 50th Anniversary of the Shakespeare Festival. I immediately knew I wanted to do a new show, a tribute to Joe Papp and his musicals, because I had done songs from a few of his musicals in other productions and I knew I would have to end with *A Chorus Line.* And what a pleasure I thought, to sing all that wonderful music and how refreshing for once not have it be autobiographical.

I called it *Here's to the Public: The Music of Joe Papp's Public Theater.* When I read the release on the *Playbill* Web site a few days later, I had a scare, because there was no show yet, just a title. But it sounded great as described, with songs from *Hair, Two Gentlemen of Verona, I'm Getting My Act Together and Taking It on the Road, The Mystery of Edwin Drood, The Threepenny Opera, Runaways,* and *A Chorus Line.*

The next thing I knew I was in a lovely house in the Berkshires rooming with three other actresses: Diane Findlay, Diane Houghton, and Natalie Mosco. We were rehearsing a summer production of *Follies,* and

I was playing Carlotta this time, singing "I'm Still Here." At the same time, I was putting the Joe Papp show together and writing this book, and still having experiences you cannot make up.

Julie Boyd, the artistic director of the Great Barrington Stage Company, is a force of nature, who had had a great success developing a show called *The 25th Annual Putnam County Spelling Bee* for Broadway. Many people from New York would drive the three hours to see her productions. With *Follies,* they didn't seem to mind that the theater was in a high school auditorium with faulty air-conditioning during one of the hottest summers ever recorded in Massachusetts.

"What do you mean, Ben Brantley's out there to review us for the *Times*? It's summer stock for God's sake!" I was shrieking. "Stephen Sondheim too!" Sondheim thrilled us all when he came backstage afterward. He leaned toward me after we greeted each other and said, "You've graduated."

As we all stood around Sondheim, he told us that he enjoyed the production, and that it made him feel proud. Then, with such vulnerability that it brought tears to my eyes, he said, "I couldn't help but think of James Goldman and how proud he would feel, if he were here."

I came back to New York in a mild panic and racing against time again. I was gratefully relieved to know that Thommie Walsh would be on board to direct and guide me with his expertise. My concept of the Joe Papp show, with that music from the 1960s, called for a rock and roll band, and two other performers, preferably men. I hired Michael James Scott and Jon Eric Parker without ever meeting them, based on a recommendation from the talented choreographer Ken Roberson, who had a Broadway hit, *Avenue Q.* When they walked into the rehearsal room a few days later, Thommie and I looked at each other like our prayers had been answered. They were very tall, gorgeous, charming and sang and danced like a dream. Sometimes things are just meant to be. The way everything fell into place after that first day of rehearsal gave me that feeling.

My friend Ian Herman conducted and played keyboard, along with other favorite musicians: Ray Grappone on drums, Ray Kilday on bass, and Gregg Utzig on guitar. Putting that show together with my friends was such a joy that it felt illegal. I wasn't really going to make any money for the four performances, having so many salaries to meet. The rehearsal time alone absorbed what money I could make, and I didn't even have a minimum guarantee. But the show started taking on a life of its own and I really needed to do it the right way. As the producer, I would have to make a special effort and try to keep my losses to a minimum.

Just before we opened, I was asked if I would be interviewed for a PBS documentary being made for the 50th Anniversary of the Shakespeare Festival. This was to be filmed in the same building where I was rehearsing, which was the Public Theater building on Lafayette Street. In the 1850s, John Jacob Astor opened the first public library in the city in this building, and called it the Astor Library. I always loved the old Italian architecture and the fact that Joe Papp saved it when he gave the Public Theater a home there. Joe's Pub was located where the old Shakespeare Festival offices used to be.

During *A Chorus Line,* we rehearsed either on the stage of the Newman Theater off the main lobby, or up on the fourth floor in the old Astor Library reading room. Within this enormous space, we had mirrors wheeled in and were able to rehearse and develop many sections of the show. It's also where we had the first orchestra reading. There were so many memories here for me.

For the PBS interview, I walked into the Astor Library, as it was still called, eager to get this over with so I could get back to my rehearsal. I saw that they were still setting up the lights and camera. My interviewer, the young, soft-spoken woman I had talked to on the phone, said, "Please, take a seat. We'll be ready for you in a few minutes."

I took the seat that was being lit, and while I was waiting, I realized that I hadn't been in this room in thirty years. This could be one of the most important rooms I have ever been in during my entire life! I remembered putting the Finale together in this room with the entire cast after Baayork, Bob Avian, and I choreographed it for Michael to stage. The ghosts emerged, and I saw Marvin Hamlisch conducting the orchestra with his Zabar's lunch on the podium, and I saw Michael fall down to motivate us in the accident scene. I saw our crowded opening night party after we all knew we were going to be successful, and I saw myself in my first and only Halston, which Michael bought me for opening night, because he knew that I couldn't afford a new dress. My reverie was broken when I heard, "Okay, we're ready!"

I thought, *How can I possibly tell this well-researched young woman what it was really like here in 1975, before she was even born? Has she ever seen the show on Broadway?* I did the best I could by telling her that the morning after we opened, the line for the box office was over two blocks long. It gave me satisfaction to talk about the vision and humanity of Joe Papp and the determination and talent of Michael Bennett. It was another way to pay homage to them, to thank them, and to keep them alive.

She asked me how I felt about the new production of *A Chorus Line* coming to Broadway in the fall of 2006. I told her quite honestly that I thought it was great. Obviously, I'm still proud of that show. It has played in more than twenty countries and in almost as many languages. Its far-reaching message has changed millions of lives besides just giving people a good and entertaining time.

Having traveled so many full circles, I sensed a new one beginning with this revival of *A Chorus Line*. Thirty years ago it was my whole life. To have a role written for you, from your very words, thoughts, and creative expression, is a rare honor that I never took for granted. There will now be other Cassies, other Zachs, other Bobbys and Sheilas, Vals and Dianas, and Pauls, whom we will applaud.

My reverie was interrupted again, as I heard my interviewer saying, "That was fine, thank you."

"Oh, you're welcome," I answered. "It was my pleasure."

As I left that hallowed space, I was thinking of how far I'd come, having survived all the years of struggle and poor self-esteem, two marriages, two divorces, arthritis, all the personal losses, and yet how grateful I was to have the life I had always wanted.

In finding the way to love myself, I can more easily see the love in other people, and it has renewed my faith. I am more able to reach out for help when I need it and it's always there. So many people have enriched my life with their friendship and generosity. Learning to love and be loved may be the most important achievement in my life.

I thank God for every day I'm here. I have a brother and a sister I love and who have their own individual rich and full lives. Our parents would be proud. I have other family members I love, even if we're separated by distance. I have dear friends I love, and they're my family too. I have a home and I'm living in my favorite city in the world. I have good health and an undying passion for my work.

Now, taking the elevator down to the main floor of the Public Theater, it dawns on me that tonight I have a dress rehearsal. I'm supposed to meet Thommie across the street at the restaurant for notes and a sandwich before the show. I rush through the lobby and out the front door, breathing in the fresh October air. I am exhilarated by its cleansing power. It may be that almost half my book is yet to be written as well as read but, at this moment, I feel as though my heart will burst with happiness.

I feel a catch in my throat as I realize that at this precious instant in time, in the whole wide world, there is no one else I'd rather be.

Acknowledgments

———— ✺ ————

I am grateful to have shared this writing experience with Greg Lawrence. I admired his work long before I met him. His knowledge, skill, easy manner, and nonjudgmental attitude always had a calming effect, even on my most anxious days. He showed me the way by his example, always kind, always encouraging when I got stuck, reminding me to write from the heart. Thank you, Greg.

My gratitude to the Fifi Oscard Agency, and in memory of Fifi Oscard, a great lady who was one of my first agents in New York. Thanks also to our literary agent, Peter Sawyer, who brought us all together with his great instinct. He is so good at his job that he came up with the title of this book, without even knowing that my nickname is Timestep!

My thanks to Jerry Herman for the opportunity to work with him in these last few years. To know him is to love him, and working on *Mack and Mable* was a highlight in my life. Special thanks to Pat Birch for her support, generosity, and wonderful work.

Also in loving memory of Lee Theodore, Rick Mason, and Clive Wilson.

I hold our first editor, Chuck Adams, in high esteem. His acceptance and editing of this book was the important encouragement I needed to set this dream of mine, a story to inspire, in motion. Thank you, Simon & Schuster! Editor Sydny Miner's keen intelligence and responsiveness always made me feel that I was in good hands. And I was. Sarah Hochman was also there to guide with professionalism and sensitivity. Thanks to production editor Ted Landry and his copy editor, Fred Chase. I have never met Fred, but I feel like I know him because of his edits, fixes, and queries in the manuscript. He is very smart (even though he discourages me from using the word "very"). I am grateful to him. My thanks to Victoria Meyer, Tracey Guest, and especially Brianne Halverson, who has made a great effort to get the word out. Thanks also to Elisa Rivlin for her conscientious cuts; Ellen Sasahara, who created the interior design; Joanna Maher, who designed the cover.

My thanks to everyone who shared with me all the pictures and photographs in the book.

I am indebted to my professional friends for their advice and support: Mark Sendroff, Richard J. Alexander, all the agents at Bauman, Redanty and Shaul: Mark, David, Charles, Tim, Naveen, and Amy. Barry Mishon and Raymond Wright. Joan Simmons. Sharon Kline. Hats off to R/J Productions. The Conway-Van Gelder Agency in London, especially Jeremy and Liz. Ralph Wilton, Jim Pierson, Craig Hamrick, Glen Roven, Frank Vlastnik, and Ted Chapin for good help. Thanks to Charlie Siedenburg for his excellent publicity and his happy face. Thank you Harold Breslow at Moss-Adams LLP. Many, many thanks to Julie Boyd. Thanks to Peter Neufeld and everyone at Broadway Cares/Equity Fights AIDS for all the important work they do.

I am forever grateful for the knowledge and training I received from Bikram Choudry. My heartfelt gratitude to the psychologists who helped me: Dr. Gerald Sabath, Dr. De la Vega, Dr. Jerome Saperstein, and Dr. Arnold Wexler. The refrain of their good council and wise words continues to underscore my life.

I must acknowledge Herbert Berghof, who gave me the opportunity to teach at his studio. This enhanced my life beyond measure, along with my students, who taught me how to teach with their passion and desire to learn. I thank each and every one of them. In this company, I must also thank Donna de Matteo for the experience of doing her beautiful and hilarious play, *A Horse Story,* which Herbert directed.

I am blessed with a treasure trove of friends and family. Not all of them emerged in this story, but nevertheless, they are close to my heart and I want them to take a bow: Bob Amaral, Toni Basil, Renee Baughman, Jeremy Bernstein, Sarah Boone, Mary T. Brown, Dennis Buck, Jerry Buckley, Nadia Chigerovich, Wayne Cilento, Darren Cohen, Joanne

Cunningham, Ron Dennis, David Galligan, Diana Gregg, Mitzi Hamilton, Ann Hays, Richard Hillman, Stanley Hura, Michael Karm, Rian Keating, Dr. Barry Kohn, Dale Kubrick, Sharon Kugel, Ron Kuhlman, Nancy Lane, Pricilla Lopez, Mark Mantell, Richard Mawe, Jan McArt, Amanda McBroom, Don Percassi, Patti Ben Peterson, Bill Powell, Paul Rondeau, Carol Skarimbas, Billie Thrash, and Teresa Vuoso.

I wish to express my thanks to all my teachers, including Marge Rivingston, and Judith Farris for voice. Peff Modelski, Luigi, and Paul Liberti for dance.

For their invaluable feedback, a special thanks to Barbara McKechnie, Ron McKechnie, Thommie Walsh, Ken Bennett, Rian Keating, Sarah Boone, Harvey Evans, and Susan Slavin. To my sister's partner, Rob French, with love and appreciation for enhancing her life so completely.

With love to my Aunt Carlie, Aunt Dee, Aunt Betty, Aunt Bev, Aunt Allene, and Uncle Murray.

To my "first" cousins, thank you for all the good times. To Beverly, Jackie, Marge, David, Gail, Jim, Janice, Bill, Patti, Kim, Craig, Arthur, Bob, Chris, Merwin, Gordon, Debbie, Robin, Kevin, Christa, Edie, Danny, Carol, Eileen, Pam and Sharon, and to your children and your children's children, I love you all.

For more information on how I dealt with my arthritis
and a list of resources I find helpful, visit me at
www.donnamckechnie.com

Index